ATS-147   ADMISSION TEST SERIES

This is your
PASSBOOK for...

TASC

Test Assessing Secondary Completion (1 Vol. Condensed)

Test Preparation Study Guide
Questions & Answers

COPYRIGHT NOTICE

This book is SOLELY intended for, is sold ONLY to, and its use is RESTRICTED to individual, bona fide applicants or candidates who qualify by virtue of having seriously filed applications for appropriate license, certificate, professional and/or promotional advancement, higher school matriculation, scholarship, or other legitimate requirements of education and/or governmental authorities.

This book is NOT intended for use, class instruction, tutoring, training, duplication, copying, reprinting, excerption, or adaptation, etc., by:

1) Other publishers
2) Proprietors and/or Instructors of "Coaching" and/or Preparatory Courses
3) Personnel and/or Training Divisions of commercial, industrial, and governmental organizations
4) Schools, colleges, or universities and/or their departments and staffs, including teachers and other personnel
5) Testing Agencies or Bureaus
6) Study groups which seek by the purchase of a single volume to copy and/or duplicate and/or adapt this material for use by the group as a whole without having purchased individual volumes for each of the members of the group
7) Et al.

Such persons would be in violation of appropriate Federal and State statutes.

PROVISION OF LICENSING AGREEMENTS – Recognized educational, commercial, industrial, and governmental institutions and organizations, and others legitimately engaged in educational pursuits, including training, testing, and measurement activities, may address request for a licensing agreement to the copyright owners, who will determine whether, and under what conditions, including fees and charges, the materials in this book may be used them. In other words, a licensing facility exists for the legitimate use of the material in this book on other than an individual basis. However, it is asseverated and affirmed here that the material in this book CANNOT be used without the receipt of the express permission of such a licensing agreement from the Publishers. Inquiries re licensing should be addressed to the company, attention rights and permissions department.

All rights reserved, including the right of reproduction in whole or in part, in any form or by any means, electronic or mechanical, including photocopying, recording, or by any information storage and retrieval system, without permission in writing from the Publisher.

Copyright © 2024 by
National Learning Corporation

212 Michael Drive, Syosset, NY 11791
(516) 921-8888 • www.passbooks.com
E-mail: info@passbooks.com

PASSBOOK® SERIES

THE *PASSBOOK® SERIES* has been created to prepare applicants and candidates for the ultimate academic battlefield – the examination room.

At some time in our lives, each and every one of us may be required to take an examination – for validation, matriculation, admission, qualification, registration, certification, or licensure.

Based on the assumption that every applicant or candidate has met the basic formal educational standards, has taken the required number of courses, and read the necessary texts, the *PASSBOOK® SERIES* furnishes the one special preparation which may assure passing with confidence, instead of failing with insecurity. Examination questions – together with answers – are furnished as the basic vehicle for study so that the mysteries of the examination and its compounding difficulties may be eliminated or diminished by a sure method.

This book is meant to help you pass your examination provided that you qualify and are serious in your objective.

The entire field is reviewed through the huge store of content information which is succinctly presented through a provocative and challenging approach – the question-and-answer method.

A climate of success is established by furnishing the correct answers at the end of each test.

You soon learn to recognize types of questions, forms of questions, and patterns of questioning. You may even begin to anticipate expected outcomes.

You perceive that many questions are repeated or adapted so that you can gain acute insights, which may enable you to score many sure points.

You learn how to confront new questions, or types of questions, and to attack them confidently and work out the correct answers.

You note objectives and emphases, and recognize pitfalls and dangers, so that you may make positive educational adjustments.

Moreover, you are kept fully informed in relation to new concepts, methods, practices, and directions in the field.

You discover that you are actually taking the examination all the time: you are preparing for the examination by "taking" an examination, not by reading extraneous and/or supererogatory textbooks.

In short, this PASSBOOK®, used directedly, should be an important factor in helping you to pass your test.

TEST ASSESSING SECONDARY COMPLETION (TASC)

READY, SET, TEST — THE NEW HIGH SCHOOL EQUIVALENCY EXAM IS HERE

Several states are now using the Test Assessing Secondary Completion (TASC™) as an alternative to, or a replacement of, the GED® for individuals seeking a High School Equivalency diploma. TASC™ is produced by CTB/McGraw-Hill for national use.

THE EXAM
TASC™ includes five sections:
- Language Arts — Reading
- Language Arts — Writing (which includes an essay)
- Mathematics (which includes a calculator section and a non-calculator section)
- Science (calculators are permitted)
- Social Studies

A NEW EXAM BASED ON LEARNING STANDARDS DESIGNED TO HELP EXAMINEES SUCCEED IN THEIR CAREERS AND IN COLLEGE

English language arts and mathematics education in some states is now based on the national Common Core Learning Standards (CCLS). The CCLS are considered more rigorous than the previous learning standards and better at preparing students to succeed in their careers and in college. To ease the transition from the GED® to the new TASC™ exam, the TASC™ will increasingly measure these new learning standards through 2017. The TASC™ is also based on new science and social studies learning standards. Because of these new, more rigorous learning standards in English language arts, mathematics, science and social studies, students may find the TASC™ exam more challenging than the GED® exam.

Examinees should expect and be prepared for a more rigorous test based on these standards. Specifically, many exam questions are more demanding, complex and may require multiple steps to solve. Although examinees may find that the TASC™ questions are more difficult than the questions they may have experienced on the GED®, the score needed to pass the new TASC™ exam accounts for this increased difficulty. Specifically, the number of correct answers required to pass a TASC™ section is lower than the number of correct answers required to pass the corresponding GED® section. As such, examinees should not become discouraged by the difficulty of exam questions while taking the TASC™.

PREPARING for the TASC™ EXAM
The TASC™ takes about nine hours to complete and is usually administered in one or two days. If one or more of the five subject area subtests are not passed, those parts may be retaken after 60 days. First time TASC™ test takers must complete all five subtests.

The following "Test at a Glance" sections provide an outline of the Content and Process Categories for each subject area.

Language Arts – Reading

Test at a Glance

Test Name	Language Arts – Reading
Time	65 minutes
Number of Questions	40
Format	Multiple-choice questions

Content Categories

Application of concepts, analysis, synthesis, and evaluation involving:

I. Literary Texts
II. Informational Texts

Process Categories

A. Comprehension
B. Inference and Interpretation
C. Analysis
D. Synthesis and Generalization

(Pie chart: I. 60%, II. 40%)

About This Test

The Language Arts – Reading test provides evidence of a candidate's ability to understand, comprehend, interpret, and analyze a variety of reading material. The item pool from which the HiSET test forms will be assembled is 60 percent literary content and 40 percent informational content, as defined by CCSS. We note that this is a closer representation of CCSS than the current high school equivalency test. In the ETS HiSET program, candidates will be required to read a broad range of high-quality, increasingly challenging literary and informational texts. The selections are presented in multiple genres on subject matter that varies in purpose and style. The selections may take the form of memoirs, essays, biographical sketches, editorials, or poetry. The texts generally range in length from approximately 400 to 600 words.

Reading Process Categories

In addition to the variety of reading texts, candidates also will answer questions that may involve one or more of the processes described below.

Comprehension

- *Understand restatements of information*
- *Determine the meaning of words and phrases as they are used in the text*

- Analyze the impact of specific word choices on meaning and tone

Inference and Interpretation

- Make inferences from the text
- Draw conclusions or deduce meanings not explicitly present in the text
- Infer the traits, feelings, and motives of characters or individuals
- Apply information
- Interpret nonliteral language

Analysis

- Analyze multiple interpretations of a text
- Determine the main idea, topic, or theme of a text
- Identify the author's or speaker's purpose or viewpoint
- Distinguish among opinions, facts, assumptions, observations, and conclusions
- Recognize aspects of an author's style, structure, mood, or tone
- Recognize literary or argumentative techniques

Synthesis and Generalization

- Draw conclusions and make generalizations
- Make predictions
- Compare and contrast
- Synthesize information across multiple sources

Language Arts – Writing

Test at a Glance

Test Name	Language Arts – Writing
Time	Part 1 – 75 minutes Part 2 – 45 minutes
Number of Questions	51
Format	Multiple-choice questions Essay question

Content Categories – Part 1

   I. Organization of Ideas
   II. Language Facility
   III. Writing Conventions

Content Categories – Part 2

   A. Development of Ideas
   B. Organization of Ideas
   C. Language Facility
   D. Writing Conventions

Pie chart: I – 20%, II – 25%, III – 55%

About This Test

The Language Arts – Writing test provides information about a candidate's skill in recognizing and producing effective standard American written English. Part 1 of the test measures a candidate's ability to edit and revise written text. Part 2 of the test measures a candidate's ability to generate and organize ideas in writing.

Part 1 requires candidates to make revision choices concerning organization, diction and clarity, sentence structure, usage, and mechanics. The test questions are embedded in complete texts in the form of letters, essays, newspaper articles, personal accounts, and reports.

The texts are presented as drafts in which parts have been underlined to indicate a possible need for revision. Questions present alternatives that may correct or improve the underlined portions. Aspects of written language that are tested may include appropriate style, logical transitions, discourse structure and organization, conciseness and clarity, or usage and mechanics.

Part 2 of the test measures proficiency in the generation and organization of ideas through a direct assessment of writing. Candidates are evaluated on development, organization, language facility, and writing conventions.

Content Descriptions

The following are descriptions of the topics covered in the basic content categories of Part 1. Because the assessments were designed to measure the ability to analyze and evaluate writing, answering any question may involve aspects of more than one category.

Organization of Ideas

- *Select logical or effective opening, transitional, and closing sentences*
- *Evaluate relevance of content*
- *Analyze and evaluate paragraph structure*
- *Recognize logical transitions and related words and phrases*

Language Facility

- *Recognize appropriate subordination and coordination, parallelism, and modifier placement*
- *Maintain consistent verb tense*
- *Recognize effective sentence combining*

Writing Conventions

- *Recognize verb, pronoun, and modifier forms*
- *Maintain grammatical agreement*
- *Recognize idiomatic usage*
- *Recognize correct capitalization, punctuation, and spelling*

Part 2 of the Language Arts – Writing test requires that candidates create written responses that are evaluated for development of ideas, organization of ideas, language facility, and conventions.

Development of Ideas

- *Focus on central idea, supporting ideas*
- *Explanation of supporting ideas*

Organization of Ideas

- *Introduction and conclusion*
- *Sequencing of ideas*
- *Paragraphing*
- *Transitions*

Language Facility

- *Word choice*
- *Sentence structure*
- *Expression and voice*

Writing Conventions

- *Grammar*
- *Usage*
- *Mechanics*

Mathematics

Test at a Glance

Test Name: Mathematics

Time: 90 minutes

Number of Questions: 50

Format: Multiple-choice questions

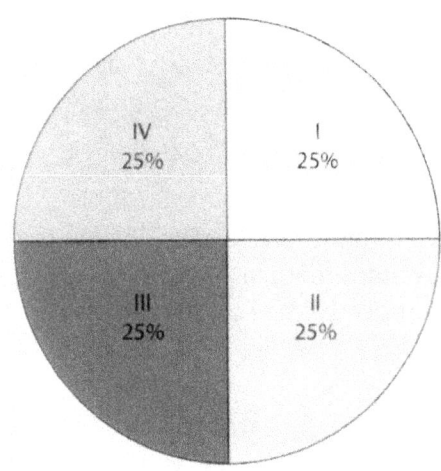

Content Categories

I. Numbers and Operations on Numbers
II. Measurement/Geometry
III. Data Analysis/Probability/Statistics
IV. Algebraic Concepts

Process Categories

A. Understand Mathematical Concepts and Procedures
B. Analyze and Interpret Information
C. Synthesize Data and Solve Problems

About This Test

The Mathematics test assesses mathematical knowledge and competencies. The test measures a candidate's ability to solve quantitative problems using fundamental concepts and reasoning skills. The questions present practical problems that require numerical operations, measurement, estimation, data interpretation, and logical thinking. Problems are based on realistic situations and may test abstract concepts such as algebraic patterns, precision in measurement, and probability. The use of calculators is an option for candidates.

Content Descriptions

The following are descriptions of the topics covered in the basic content categories. Because the assessments were designed to measure the ability to integrate knowledge of mathematics, answering any question may involve content from more than one category.

Numbers and Operations on Numbers may include the following topics: properties of operations, vectors, and matrices; real and complex numbers; absolute values; and computation and estimation with real numbers, exponents, radicals, ratios, proportions, and percents.

Measurement and Geometry may include the following topics: measurable attributes of objects and the appropriate techniques, tools, and formulas to determine measurement and achieve specified degrees of precision. Key ideas in geometry include: properties of geometric figures; theorems of lines and triangles; and the perimeter, surface area, volume, lengths, and angles for geometric shapes.

Data Analysis, Probability, and Statistics may include the basic concepts of probability, linear relationships, and measures of central tendency and variability to solve problems. Concepts and processes may include understanding relations among events, data collection, counting principles, and the aspects of distributions.

Algebraic Concepts may include the concepts of analyzing mathematical situations and structures using algebraic symbols. Candidates should understand patterns, relations, and functions. Topics may include linear functions and inequalities as well as nonlinear functional relations. Candidates may be required to analyze and interpret algebraically, numerically, and graphically; represent, generalize, and solve problem situations; simplify algebraic expressions; analyze and interpret functions of one variable by investigating rates of change and intercepts; and understand the meaning of equivalent forms of expressions, equations, inequalities, and relations.

Mathematics Process Categories

In addition to knowing and understanding the mathematics content explicitly described in the Content Descriptions section, candidates also will answer questions that may involve one or more of the processes described below. Any of the processes may be applied to any of the content areas of the mathematics test.

Understand Mathematical Concepts and Procedures

- Select appropriate procedures
- Identify examples and counterexamples of concepts

Analyze and Interpret Information

- Make inferences or predictions based on data or information
- Interpret data from a variety of sources

Synthesize Data and Solve Problems

- Reason quantitatively
- Evaluate the reasonableness of solutions

Science

Test at a Glance

Test Name: Science

Time: 80 minutes

Number of Questions: 50

Format: Multiple-choice questions

Content Categories

- I. Life Science
- II. Physical Science
- III. Earth Science

Pie chart:
- I. 50%
- II. 25%
- III. 25%

Process Categories

- A. Interpret and Apply
- B. Analyze
- C. Evaluate and Generalize

About This Test

The Science test provides evidence of a candidate's ability to use science content knowledge, apply principles of scientific inquiry, and interpret and evaluate scientific information. Most of the questions in the test are associated with stimulus materials that provide descriptions of scientific investigations and their results. Scientific information is based on reports that might be found in scientific journals. Graphs, tables, and charts are used to present information and results.

The science situations use material from a variety of content areas such as: physics, chemistry, botany, zoology, health, and astronomy. The questions may ask candidates to identify the research question of interest, select the best design for a specific research question, and recognize conclusions that can be drawn from results. Candidates also may be asked to evaluate the adequacy of procedures and distinguish among hypotheses, assumptions, and observations.

Content Descriptions

The following are descriptions of the topics covered in the basic content categories. Because the assessments were designed to measure the ability to analyze and evaluate scientific information, answering any question may involve content from more than one category.

Life Science topics may include fundamental biological concepts, including organisms, their environments, and their life cycles; the interdependence of organisms; and the relationships between structure and function in living systems.

Physical Science topics may include observable properties such as size, weight, shape, color, and temperature; concepts relating to the position and motion of objects; and the principles of light, heat, electricity, and magnetism.

Earth Science topics may include properties of earth materials, geologic structures and time, and Earth's movements in the solar system.

Science Process Categories

In addition to knowing and understanding the science content explicitly described in the Content Descriptions section, candidates also will answer questions on this assessment that may involve one or more of the processes described below. Any of the processes may be applied to any of the content topics.

Interpret and Apply

- *Interpret observed data or information*
- *Apply scientific principles*

Analyze

- *Discern an appropriate research question suggested by the information presented*
- *Identify reasons for a procedure and analyze limitations*
- *Select the best procedure*

Evaluate and Generalize

- *Distinguish among hypotheses, assumptions, data, and conclusions*
- *Judge the basis of information for a given conclusion*
- *Determine relevance for answering a question*
- *Judge the reliability of sources*

Social Studies

Test at a Glance

Test Name	Social Studies
Time	70 minutes
Number of Questions	50
Format	Multiple-choice questions

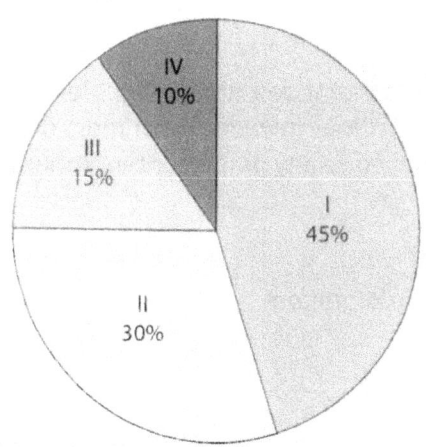

Content Categories

I. History
II. Civics/Government
III. Economics
IV. Geography

Process Categories

A. Interpret and Apply
B. Analyze
C. Evaluate and Generalize

About This Test

The Social Studies test provides evidence of a candidate's ability to analyze and evaluate various kinds of social studies information. The test uses materials from a variety of content areas, including history, political science, psychology, sociology, anthropology, geography, and economics. Primary documents, posters, cartoons, timelines, maps, graphs, tables, charts, and reading passages may be used to present information. The questions may ask candidates to distinguish statements of fact from opinion; recognize the limitations of procedures and methods; and make judgments about the reliability of sources, the validity of inferences and conclusions, and the adequacy of information for drawing conclusions.

Content Descriptions

The following are descriptions of the topics covered in the basic content categories. Because the assessments were designed to measure the ability to analyze and evaluate various kinds of social studies information, answering any question may involve content from more than one category.

History may include historical sources and perspectives; the interconnections among the past, present, and future; and specific eras in U.S. and world history, including the people who have shaped them and the political, economic, and cultural characteristics of those eras.

Civics/Government may include the civic ideals and practices of citizenship in a democratic society; the role of the informed citizen and the meaning of citizenship; the concepts of power and authority; the purposes and characteristics of various governance systems, with particular emphasis on the U.S. government; and the relationship between individual rights and responsibilities, and the concepts of a just society.

Economics may include the principles of supply and demand; the difference between needs and wants; the impact of technology on economics; the interdependent nature of economies; and how the economy can be affected by governments, and how that effect varies over time.

Geography may include concepts and terminology of physical and human geography; geographic concepts to analyze spatial phenomena and discuss economic, political, and social factors; and interpretation of maps and other visual and technological tools, and the analysis of case studies.

Social Studies Process Categories

In addition to knowing and understanding the social studies content described in the Content Descriptions section, candidates also will answer questions that may involve one or more of the processes described below. Any of the processes may be applied to any of the content topics.

Interpret and Apply

- *Make inferences or predictions based on data or other information*
- *Infer unstated relationships*
- *Extend conclusions to related phenomena*

Analyze

- *Distinguish among facts, opinions, and values*
- *Recognize the author's purpose, assumptions, and arguments*

Evaluate and Generalize

- *Determine the adequacy of information for reaching conclusions*
- *Judge the validity of conclusions*
- *Compare and contrast the reliability of sources*

HOW TO TAKE A TEST

You have studied long, hard and conscientiously.

With your official admission card in hand, and your heart pounding, you have been admitted to the examination room.

You note that there are several hundred other applicants in the examination room waiting to take the same test.

They all appear to be equally well prepared.

You know that nothing but your best effort will suffice. The "moment of truth" is at hand: you now have to demonstrate objectively, in writing, your knowledge of content and your understanding of subject matter.

You are fighting the most important battle of your life—to pass and/or score high on an examination which will determine your career and provide the economic basis for your livelihood.

What extra, special things should you know and should you do in taking the examination?

I. YOU MUST PASS AN EXAMINATION

A. WHAT EVERY CANDIDATE SHOULD KNOW
Examination applicants often ask us for help in preparing for the written test. What can I study in advance? What kinds of questions will be asked? How will the test be given? How will the papers be graded?

B. HOW ARE EXAMS DEVELOPED?
Examinations are carefully written by trained technicians who are specialists in the field known as "psychological measurement," in consultation with recognized authorities in the field of work that the test will cover. These experts recommend the subject matter areas or skills to be tested; only those knowledges or skills important to your success on the job are included. The most reliable books and source materials available are used as references. Together, the experts and technicians judge the difficulty level of the questions.
Test technicians know how to phrase questions so that the problem is clearly stated. Their ethics do not permit "trick" or "catch" questions. Questions may have been tried out on sample groups, or subjected to statistical analysis, to determine their usefulness.
Written tests are often used in combination with performance tests, ratings of training and experience, and oral interviews. All of these measures combine to form the best-known means of finding the right person for the right job.

II. HOW TO PASS THE WRITTEN TEST

A. BASIC STEPS

1) Study the announcement

How, then, can you know what subjects to study? Our best answer is: "Learn as much as possible about the class of positions for which you've applied." The exam will test the knowledge, skills and abilities needed to do the work.

Your most valuable source of information about the position you want is the official exam announcement. This announcement lists the training and experience qualifications. Check these standards and apply only if you come reasonably close to meeting them. Many jurisdictions preview the written test in the exam announcement by including a section called "Knowledge and Abilities Required," "Scope of the Examination," or some similar heading. Here you will find out specifically what fields will be tested.

2) Choose appropriate study materials

If the position for which you are applying is technical or advanced, you will read more advanced, specialized material. If you are already familiar with the basic principles of your field, elementary textbooks would waste your time. Concentrate on advanced textbooks and technical periodicals. Think through the concepts and review difficult problems in your field.

These are all general sources. You can get more ideas on your own initiative, following these leads. For example, training manuals and publications of the government agency which employs workers in your field can be useful, particularly for technical and professional positions. A letter or visit to the government department involved may result in more specific study suggestions, and certainly will provide you with a more definite idea of the exact nature of the position you are seeking.

3) Study this book!

III. KINDS OF TESTS

Tests are used for purposes other than measuring knowledge and ability to perform specified duties. For some positions, it is equally important to test ability to make adjustments to new situations or to profit from training. In others, basic mental abilities not dependent on information are essential. Questions which test these things may not appear as pertinent to the duties of the position as those which test for knowledge and information. Yet they are often highly important parts of a fair examination. For very general questions, it is almost impossible to help you direct your study efforts. What we can do is to point out some of the more common of these general abilities needed in public service positions and describe some typical questions.

1) General information

Broad, general information has been found useful for predicting job success in some kinds of work. This is tested in a variety of ways, from vocabulary lists to questions about current events. Basic background in some field of work, such as sociology or economics, may be sampled in a group of questions. Often these are principles which have become familiar to most persons through exposure rather than through formal training. It is difficult to advise you how to study for these questions; being alert to the world around you is our best suggestion.

2) Verbal ability

An example of an ability needed in many positions is verbal or language ability. Verbal ability is, in brief, the ability to use and understand words. Vocabulary and grammar tests are typical measures of this ability. Reading comprehension or paragraph interpretation questions are common in many kinds of civil service tests. You are given a paragraph of written material and asked to find its central meaning.

IV. KINDS OF QUESTIONS

1. Multiple-choice Questions

Most popular of the short-answer questions is the "multiple choice" or "best answer" question. It can be used, for example, to test for factual knowledge, ability to solve problems or judgment in meeting situations found at work.

A multiple-choice question is normally one of three types:
- It can begin with an incomplete statement followed by several possible endings. You are to find the one ending which best completes the statement, although some of the others may not be entirely wrong.
- It can also be a complete statement in the form of a question which is answered by choosing one of the statements listed.
- It can be in the form of a problem – again you select the best answer.

Here is an example of a multiple-choice question with a discussion which should give you some clues as to the method for choosing the right answer:

When an employee has a complaint about his assignment, the action which will best help him overcome his difficulty is to
  A. discuss his difficulty with his coworkers
  B. take the problem to the head of the organization
  C. take the problem to the person who gave him the assignment
  D. say nothing to anyone about his complaint

In answering this question, you should study each of the choices to find which is best. Consider choice "A" – Certainly an employee may discuss his complaint with fellow employees, but no change or improvement can result, and the complaint remains unresolved. Choice "B" is a poor choice since the head of the organization probably does not know what assignment you have been given, and taking your problem to him is known as "going over the head" of the supervisor. The supervisor, or person who made the assignment, is the person who can clarify it or correct any injustice. Choice "C" is, therefore, correct. To say nothing, as in choice "D," is unwise. Supervisors have and interest in knowing the problems employees are facing, and the employee is seeking a solution to his problem.

2. True/False

3. Matching Questions

Matching an answer from a column of choices within another column.

V. RECORDING YOUR ANSWERS

Computer terminals are used more and more today for many different kinds of exams.

For an examination with very few applicants, you may be told to record your answers in the test booklet itself. Separate answer sheets are much more common. If this separate answer sheet is to be scored by machine – and this is often the case – it is highly important that you mark your answers correctly in order to get credit.

VI. BEFORE THE TEST

YOUR PHYSICAL CONDITION IS IMPORTANT

If you are not well, you can't do your best work on tests. If you are half asleep, you can't do your best either. Here are some tips:

1) Get about the same amount of sleep you usually get. Don't stay up all night before the test, either partying or worrying—DON'T DO IT!
2) If you wear glasses, be sure to wear them when you go to take the test. This goes for hearing aids, too.
3) If you have any physical problems that may keep you from doing your best, be sure to tell the person giving the test. If you are sick or in poor health, you relay cannot do your best on any test. You can always come back and take the test some other time.

Common sense will help you find procedures to follow to get ready for an examination. Too many of us, however, overlook these sensible measures. Indeed, nervousness and fatigue have been found to be the most serious reasons why applicants fail to do their best on civil service tests. Here is a list of reminders:

- Begin your preparation early – Don't wait until the last minute to go scurrying around for books and materials or to find out what the position is all about.
- Prepare continuously – An hour a night for a week is better than an all-night cram session. This has been definitely established. What is more, a night a week for a month will return better dividends than crowding your study into a shorter period of time.
- Locate the place of the exam – You have been sent a notice telling you when and where to report for the examination. If the location is in a different town or otherwise unfamiliar to you, it would be well to inquire the best route and learn something about the building.
- Relax the night before the test – Allow your mind to rest. Do not study at all that night. Plan some mild recreation or diversion; then go to bed early and get a good night's sleep.
- Get up early enough to make a leisurely trip to the place for the test – This way unforeseen events, traffic snarls, unfamiliar buildings, etc. will not upset you.
- Dress comfortably – A written test is not a fashion show. You will be known by number and not by name, so wear something comfortable.
- Leave excess paraphernalia at home – Shopping bags and odd bundles will get in your way. You need bring only the items mentioned in the official notice you received; usually everything you need is provided. Do not bring reference books to the exam. They will only confuse those last minutes and be taken away from you when in the test room.

- Arrive somewhat ahead of time – If because of transportation schedules you must get there very early, bring a newspaper or magazine to take your mind off yourself while waiting.
- Locate the examination room – When you have found the proper room, you will be directed to the seat or part of the room where you will sit. Sometimes you are given a sheet of instructions to read while you are waiting. Do not fill out any forms until you are told to do so; just read them and be prepared.
- Relax and prepare to listen to the instructions
- If you have any physical problem that may keep you from doing your best, be sure to tell the test administrator. If you are sick or in poor health, you really cannot do your best on the exam. You can come back and take the test some other time.

VII. AT THE TEST

The day of the test is here and you have the test booklet in your hand. The temptation to get going is very strong. Caution! There is more to success than knowing the right answers. You must know how to identify your papers and understand variations in the type of short-answer question used in this particular examination. Follow these suggestions for maximum results from your efforts:

1) Cooperate with the monitor

The test administrator has a duty to create a situation in which you can be as much at ease as possible. He will give instructions, tell you when to begin, check to see that you are marking your answer sheet correctly, and so on. He is not there to guard you, although he will see that your competitors do not take unfair advantage. He wants to help you do your best.

2) Listen to all instructions

Don't jump the gun! Wait until you understand all directions. In most civil service tests you get more time than you need to answer the questions. So don't be in a hurry. Read each word of instructions until you clearly understand the meaning. Study the examples, listen to all announcements and follow directions. Ask questions if you do not understand what to do.

3) Identify your papers

Civil service exams are usually identified by number only. You will be assigned a number; you must not put your name on your test papers. Be sure to copy your number correctly. Since more than one exam may be given, copy your exact examination title.

4) Plan your time

Unless you are told that a test is a "speed" or "rate of work" test, speed itself is usually not important. Time enough to answer all the questions will be provided, but this does not mean that you have all day. An overall time limit has been set. Divide the total time (in minutes) by the number of questions to determine the approximate time you have for each question.

5) Do not linger over difficult questions

If you come across a difficult question, mark it with a paper clip (useful to have along) and come back to it when you have been through the booklet. One caution if you do this – be sure to skip a number on your answer sheet as well. Check often to be sure that you have not lost your place and that you are marking in the row numbered the same as the question you are answering.

6) Read the questions

Be sure you know what the question asks! Many capable people are unsuccessful because they failed to read the questions correctly.

7) Answer all questions

Unless you have been instructed that a penalty will be deducted for incorrect answers, it is better to guess than to omit a question.

8) Speed tests

It is often better NOT to guess on speed tests. It has been found that on timed tests people are tempted to spend the last few seconds before time is called in marking answers at random – without even reading them – in the hope of picking up a few extra points. To discourage this practice, the instructions may warn you that your score will be "corrected" for guessing. That is, a penalty will be applied. The incorrect answers will be deducted from the correct ones, or some other penalty formula will be used.

9) Review your answers

If you finish before time is called, go back to the questions you guessed or omitted to give them further thought. Review other answers if you have time.

10) Return your test materials

If you are ready to leave before others have finished or time is called, take ALL your materials to the monitor and leave quietly. Never take any test material with you. The monitor can discover whose papers are not complete, and taking a test booklet may be grounds for disqualification.

VIII. EXAMINATION TECHNIQUES

1) Read the general instructions carefully. These are usually printed on the first page of the exam booklet. As a rule, these instructions refer to the timing of the examination; the fact that you should not start work until the signal and must stop work at a signal, etc. If there are any special instructions, such as a choice of questions to be answered, make sure that you note this instruction carefully.

2) When you are ready to start work on the examination, that is as soon as the signal has been given, read the instructions to each question booklet, underline any key words or phrases, such as least, best, outline, describe and the like. In this way you will tend to answer as requested rather than discover on reviewing your paper that you listed without describing, that you selected the worst choice rather than the best choice, etc.

3) If the examination is of the objective or multiple-choice type – that is, each question will also give a series of possible answers: A, B, C or D, and you are called upon to select the best answer and write the letter next to that answer on your answer paper – it is advisable to start answering each question in turn. There may be anywhere from 50 to 100 such questions in the three or four hours allotted and you can see how much time would be taken if you read through all the questions before beginning to answer any. Furthermore, if you

come across a question or group of questions which you know would be difficult to answer, it would undoubtedly affect your handling of all the other questions.

4) If the examination is of the essay type and contains but a few questions, it is a moot point as to whether you should read all the questions before starting to answer any one. Of course, if you are given a choice – say five out of seven and the like – then it is essential to read all the questions so you can eliminate the two that are most difficult. If, however, you are asked to answer all the questions, there may be danger in trying to answer the easiest one first because you may find that you will spend too much time on it. The best technique is to answer the first question, then proceed to the second, etc.

5) Time your answers. Before the exam begins, write down the time it started, then add the time allowed for the examination and write down the time it must be completed, then divide the time available somewhat as follows:
   - If 3-1/2 hours are allowed, that would be 210 minutes. If you have 80 objective-type questions, that would be an average of 2-1/2 minutes per question. Allow yourself no more than 2 minutes per question, or a total of 160 minutes, which will permit about 50 minutes to review.
   - If for the time allotment of 210 minutes there are 7 essay questions to answer, that would average about 30 minutes a question. Give yourself only 25 minutes per question so that you have about 35 minutes to review.

6) The most important instruction is to read each question and make sure you know what is wanted. The second most important instruction is to time yourself properly so that you answer every question. The third most important instruction is to answer every question. Guess if you have to but include something for each question. Remember that you will receive no credit for a blank and will probably receive some credit if you write something in answer to an essay question. If you guess a letter – say "B" for a multiple-choice question – you may have guessed right. If you leave a blank as an answer to a multiple-choice question, the examiners may respect your feelings but it will not add a point to your score. Some exams may penalize you for wrong answers, so in such cases only, you may not want to guess unless you have some basis for your answer.

7) Suggestions
   a. Objective-type questions
      1. Examine the question booklet for proper sequence of pages and questions
      2. Read all instructions carefully
      3. Skip any question which seems too difficult; return to it after all other questions have been answered
      4. Apportion your time properly; do not spend too much time on any single question or group of questions
      5. Note and underline key words – all, most, fewest, least, best, worst, same, opposite, etc.
      6. Pay particular attention to negatives
      7. Note unusual option, e.g., unduly long, short, complex, different or similar in content to the body of the question
      8. Observe the use of "hedging" words – probably, may, most likely, etc.

9. Make sure that your answer is put next to the same number as the question
10. Do not second-guess unless you have good reason to believe the second answer is definitely more correct
11. Cross out original answer if you decide another answer is more accurate; do not erase until you are ready to hand your paper in
12. Answer all questions; guess unless instructed otherwise
13. Leave time for review

   b. Essay questions
1. Read each question carefully
2. Determine exactly what is wanted. Underline key words or phrases.
3. Decide on outline or paragraph answer
4. Include many different points and elements unless asked to develop any one or two points or elements
5. Show impartiality by giving pros and cons unless directed to select one side only
6. Make and write down any assumptions you find necessary to answer the questions
7. Watch your English, grammar, punctuation and choice of words
8. Time your answers; don't crowd material

8) Answering the essay question

Most essay questions can be answered by framing the specific response around several key words or ideas. Here are a few such key words or ideas:

M's: manpower, materials, methods, money, management
P's: purpose, program, policy, plan, procedure, practice, problems, pitfalls, personnel, public relations

  a. Six basic steps in handling problems:
1. Preliminary plan and background development
2. Collect information, data and facts
3. Analyze and interpret information, data and facts
4. Analyze and develop solutions as well as make recommendations
5. Prepare report and sell recommendations
6. Install recommendations and follow up effectiveness

  b. Pitfalls to avoid
1. Taking things for granted – A statement of the situation does not necessarily imply that each of the elements is necessarily true; for example, a complaint may be invalid and biased so that all that can be taken for granted is that a complaint has been registered
2. Considering only one side of a situation – Wherever possible, indicate several alternatives and then point out the reasons you selected the best one
3. Failing to indicate follow up – Whenever your answer indicates action on your part, make certain that you will take proper follow-up action to see how successful your recommendations, procedures or actions turn out to be
4. Taking too long in answering any single question – Remember to time your answers properly

EXAMINATION SECTION

EXAMINATION SECTION

TEST 1

ENGLISH USAGE

DIRECTIONS: This section is based on passages which contain expressions that are inappropriate in standard written English. You are to decide how these expressions can be made appropriate and effective.

The passages are presented in a spread-out format in which various words, phrases, and punctuation have been underlined and numbered. In the right-hand column, opposite each underlined portion, you will find a set of responses numbered to correspond to that of the underlined portion. Each set of responses contains a NO CHANGE option and three alternatives to the underlined version.

Since your judgment about the appropriateness and effectiveness of a response will depend on your perceptions of the passage as a whole, the author's purpose and the type of audience, first read through the entire passage quickly. Then, reread the passage slowly and carefully. As you come to each underlined portion during your second reading, look at the alternatives in the right-hand column and decide which of the four words or phrasings is BEST for the given context. Since your response will often depend on your reading several of the sentences surrounding the underlined portion, make sure you have read ahead far enough to make the best choice.

If you think that the original version (the one in the passage) is best, indicate A in the corresponding space at the right. If you think that an alternative version is best, indicate the letter corresponding to the alternative that you have chosen as best.

In every case, consider ONLY the underlined words, phrases, and punctuation marks; you can assume that the rest of the passage is correct as written.

Thor Heyerdahl became famous for a unique sailing expedition, which he later described in KON-TIKI. Having developed a theory that the original Polynesians had sailed or drifted to the South Sea Islands from South America, <u>it then had to be tested</u>. After careful study, he built a raft
1

1. A. NO CHANGE
   B. he set out to test it
   C. it was decided that it must be tested
   D. the theory was then to be tested

1.____

that was as authentic as possible. Using only primitive equipment, he and five other men sailed into the South Seas from <u>Peru, which he judged to be in the same</u> general
2
area as the land of

2. A. NO CHANGE
   B. Peru, being judged as
   C. Peru, which had been
   D. Peru judged as being

2.____

1

the original Polynesians. As a result, <u>his group and him</u> will long be remembered not
          3
only as thorough scientists but also as courageous men.

    Heyerdahl's courage was first tested in Ecuador. His search for trees <u>that was large enough</u> for the expeditionary raft
          4

sent him to Quito, a city high in the Andes. There, he and his companions were warned about headhunters and bandits on the <u>trail. Feeling undaunted,</u> they
          5

hired a driver and jeep from the U.S. <u>Embassy, going on with</u> their dangerous
          6
task

<u>After the raft was done,</u> Heyerdahl made
      7
final preparations for the expedition. Even before his crew came aboard,

<u>the courage which Heyerdahl possessed</u>
          8
was tested again. As the raft was being towed out of the harbor, it drifted under the stern of a tug. Heyerdahl had to struggle to save it.

<u>Dangers at sea</u> were present, but Heyerdahl
    9
and his men did not show fear. Instead they developed games that were actually tests of courage. Although man-eating fish were nearby, the men swam to relieve

3. A. NO CHANGE
   B. him and his group
   C. his group and himself
   D. he and his group

3.____

4. A. NO CHANGE
   B. which would be of sufficient size
   C. of adequate size
   D. of certainly sufficient size

4.____

5. A. NO CHANGE
   B. trail. Undaunted, they
   C. trail, but they were undaunted, and
   D. trail; undaunted they

5.____

6. A. NO CHANAGE
   B. Embassy; and went on with
   C. Embassy and proceeded with
   D. Embassy, and kept on

6.____

7. A. NO CHANGE
   B. When the raft was ready
   C. The raft was speedily completed and
   D. The raft having been

7.____

8. A. NO CHANGE
   B. Heyerdahls' manly courage
   C. Heyerdahl's courage
   D. the courage of this man

8.____

9. A. NO CHANGE
   B. (Do not begin new paragraph) At sea, dangers
   C. (Begin new paragraph) Dangers, at sea
   D. (Begin new paragraph) At sea, dangers

9.____

their tension, maintaining that the fish were
not dangerous unless a man had already
been cut or scratched. One game consisted
of luring sharks within reach,

catching them, and then they would yank it
onto the raft.

Being on the raft, the sharks thrashed about
and snapped viciously at the men. Another
game was even more dangerous: two men
would paddle away on a rubber dinghy until

they could catch only an occasional glimpse
of the raft, then they would have to paddle
violently to return.

The final portion of the voyage was the most
thrilling. As the raft neared Raoia, it was
carried rapidly toward the reef, where the
waves beat it very bad. Almost miraculously
the

men survived, only to find themselves on a
deserted island. At last their struggle with
the sea had ended. They radioed Rarotonga
and set up camp to await rescue,

Thor Heyerdahl's expedition on the Kon-Tiki
did not necessarily prove his migration theory,
but it did prove that hardy pioneers with
courage, determination, and luck could make
the same trip, even with very primitive
equipment.

10. A. NO CHANGE
    B. tension. Maintaining
    C. tension. He maintained
    D. tension, because it was maintained

11. A. NO CHANGE
    B. then to yank it
    C. and then to yank them up
    D. and yanking them

12. A. NO CHANGE
    B. At that point,
    C. Once there,
    D. A that time,

13. A. NO CHANGE
    B. (Place after *until*)
    C. (Place after *they*)
    D. OMIT

14. A. NO CHANGE
    B. mercilessly
    C. very violent
    D. without any mercy

15. A. NO CHANGE
    B. and only found themselves
    C. only to find themselves
    D. but only found themselves to be

16. A. NO CHANGE
    B. could now do the same trip
    C. could do the same
    D. could have accomplished this the same,

10.____

11.____

12.____

13.____

15.____

KEY (CORRECT ANSWERS)

1.	B	6.	C	11.	D	16.	A
2.	A	7.	B	12.	C		
3.	D	8.	C	13.	A		
4.	C	9.	D	14.	B		
5.	B	10.	A	15.	C		

TEST 2

MATHEMATICS USAGE

DIRECTIONS: Each question or incomplete statement is followed by several suggested answers or completions. Select the one that BEST answers the question or completes the statement. *PRINT THE LETTER OF THE CORRECT ANSWER IN THE SPACE AT THE RIGHT.*

1. Two wells pump oil continuously. One produces 4,000 barrels of oil per day, which is 33 1/3% more than other well produces.
   How many barrels of oil are produced daily by the two wells?
   A. 5333 1/3 B. 6666 2/3 C. 7000
   D. 8333 1/3 E. 9000

   1.____

2. If a car travels a miles in b minutes, how many minutes will it take to travel c miles?
   A. c/a B. c/b C. c/ab D. ab/c E. cb/a

   2.____

3. In the figure at the right, what is the sum of the angles labeled x and y?
   A. 90°
   B. 100°
   C. 130°
   D. 140°
   E. None of the above

   3.____

4. A man purchased 100 shares of stock at $5 a share.
   If each share rose 10 cents the first month, decreased 8 cents the second month, and gained 3 cents the third month, what was the value of the man's investment at the end of the third month?
   A. $505 B. $520 C. $525
   D. $1,545 E. None of the above

   4.____

5. $$\Delta \times \theta = \theta$$
   $$\theta \times \Delta = \theta$$
   $$\Delta \times \Delta = \Delta$$
   The above multiplication scheme uses symbols other than the usual numerals. A corresponds to which base-10 numeral?
   A. 0 B. 1 C. 2 D. 5 E. 10

   5.____

6. What is the length, in inches, of a 144 arc in a circle whose circumference is 60 inches?
   A. 24 B. 12/π C. 12π D. 36 E. 36/π

   6.____

7. What does x equal in the equation $\frac{1}{x} = \frac{1}{5} \cdot \frac{1}{x}$?

   7.____

2 (#2)

8. In the universe of all people, let circle M represent all Mary's friends, circle B all Bill's friends, and circle P all Pete's friends.
What is represented by the shaded portion of the figure?
All the people who are
   A. friends of Mary, Bill, and Pete
   B. friends of Mary and Pete
   C. friends of Mary and Pete, but not of Bill
   D. friends of Pete, but not of Bill
   E. not friends of Bill

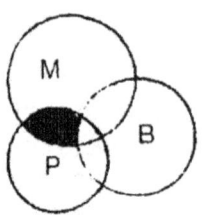

8.____

9. A ship sailing due north past an island travels a course that is 12 miles from the island at its closest point.
If a gun on shore has a firing range of 13 miles, for how many miles will the ship remain within range of the gun?
   A. 1 B. 5 C. 9
   D. 10 E. None of the above

9.____

10. What is the area of the unshaded sector of circle O shown at the right?
   A. $\dfrac{\pi r}{8}$
   B. $\dfrac{\pi r^2}{2}$
   C. $\dfrac{\pi r^2}{4}$
   D. $\dfrac{\pi r^2}{8}$
   E. $\dfrac{\pi r^2}{45}$

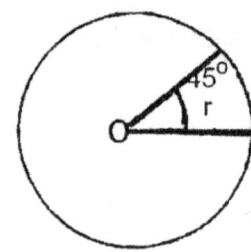

10.____

11. What set of values for x and y(x,y) satisfy the following equations: 3y = x + 4, 6x + 2y = 16?
   A. (-2,2) B. (2,-2) C. (-2,2)
   D. (2,2)   E. None of the above

11.____

12. What is the value of the following expression $\dfrac{A^4 p^{+3} \cdot A^3 p^{+4}}{A^2 p^{+2}}$?

   A. A^{9P+9} B. A^{6P+6} C. A^{3P+3} D. A^{-3P-3} E. A^{5P+5}

12.____

KEY (CORRECT ANSWERS)

1. C
2. E
3. A
4. A
5. B
6. A
7. D
8. C
9. D
10. D
11. D
12. E

TEST 3

SOCIAL STUDIES READING

DIRECTIONS: This test measures your ability to comprehend, analyze, and evaluate reading, materials in such social studies fields as history, political science, economics, sociology, anthropology, and psychology.

To answer these questions, you will have to draw on your background in social studies, as well as on your ability to understand new material.

In addition to the questions based on reading passages, there are some questions that test your general background knowledge in social studies.

Read the passage through once. Then return to it as often as necessary to answer the questions. *PRINT THE LETTER OF THE CORRECT ANSWER IN THE SPACE AT THE RIGHT.*

Questions 1-5.

DIRECTIONS: Questions 1 through 5 are to be answered on the basis of the following passage.

Over the past several decades, the growth of the United States economy has been marked by expansion of metropolitan areas and by "regionalization" of production—that is, a more even geographical distribution of industries over the United States. Such rapid growth causes drastic changes in the geographical structure of metropolitan areas. Manufacturing industries, which were initially attracted to the core of the city by the proximity of the railroads, a steady labor supply, and the economic advantages of mass production, are now moving toward peripheral locations.

No single explanation can be given for this trend toward suburbanization, but as cities have grown, the supply of undeveloped land has decreased. The advantages of the central metropolis continue to attract economic activity, but congestion in the central city and the development of production techniques which demand more space have tended to push industry into the suburbs. The net result has been a pattern of geographical specialization within metropolitan regions. The central city increasingly becomes geared to white-collar and service activities, and the periphery attracts manufacturing, transportation, and other blue-collar job activities.

The development of residential areas has followed industrial movement to some extent, but suburban living (undoubtedly desired for its amenities) is still largely reserved for those who can afford it. Consequently, the central city has been losing middle- and upper-income families to the suburbs. Now people can live in dispersed residential locations; rising incomes and the proliferation of automobiles have made this both economically and technically feasible. However, this "urban sprawl" creates serious financial problems. Since tax-paying industry has fled to the suburbs, the central city has had to bear the cost of public assistance payments and other welfare service for low-income groups.

2 (#3)

When housing developers began building on a large scale, many suburbs rapidly doubled and tripled in size. This new population required more schools and teachers, more fire and police protection, and sizable expenditures for water and sewer lines and roads. Frequently, these towns were entirely dependent on property taxes for their revenues.

To meet ever-increasing expenses and broaden their tax base, some communities have tried to attract new industry. However, when town officials found themselves competing intensely for these industries, they often conceded partial exemption from property taxes to new industry in order to bargain more favorably. As a result, an area often found its tax base weakened rather than strengthened by winning new industry. As a consequence of all these changes, both the suburbs and the central city are entangled in thorny financial problems.

1. According to the author, a rise in wages earned by employees of service industries will PRINCIPALLY tend to
   A. *increase* the physical separation between zones of residence and zones of work
   B. *decrease* the tax revenues of the suburbs
   C. *decrease* the tax revenues of the metropolitan areas
   D. *increase* the work force in the periphery

   1.____

2. The MOST efficient way to solve the financial problems of a metropolitan area would be to
   A. *cut* personal taxes in central cities
   B. *cut* personal taxes in the suburbs
   C. *decrease* public expenditures in central cities
   D. *place* the entire area under one fiscal authority

   2.____

3. Which of the following problems should be given FIRST consideration on the basis of the changing urban structure outlined in the passage?
   A. Commuter traffic between areas of residence and areas of work
   B. Highway passenger traffic between two metropolitan areas
   C. Congestion due to heavy truck traffic in downtown areas
   D. The centralization of railroad freight stations in downtown areas

   3.____

4. The author would consider the giant modern city *essentially* a by-product of the
   A. invention of the internal combustion engine
   B. development of monopolistic industries
   C. Industrial Revolution
   D. capitalist system

   4.____

5. If the trend outlined in paragraph three continues, the centers of large American cities are more likely than the suburbs to have a HIGH percentage of
   A. small-scale manufacturing firms   B. large-scale factories
   C. railroad stations   D. banks and insurance companies

   5.____

9

Questions 6-9.

DIRECTIONS: Questions 6 through 9 are to be answered on the basis of the following passage.

(In 1845, congressional leaders debated the annexation of Texas. The issues considered were many and complex, as the following excerpts from the debate illustrate.)

Speaker 1:
In annexing Texas, we do not adopt its war with Mexico, if any such exists. In annexation, we will not abide by Texas law; Texas will abide by ours. The United States are not to be merged in Texas, but Texas in them. When we purchased Louisiana from France, France was at war; we did not assume the French war. Mexico, however, may regard annexation as an act of extreme unfriendliness and make it the pretext for declaring war on the United States.

Speaker 2:
Since the landing of the Pilgrims, our people have moved forward, acquiring territory, unfurling the banner of liberty and equality, creating a power (more potent than that of armies), before which the nations of this continent will continue to give way. No nation can withstand the impact of this principle of enlightened liberty. Under this principle—though I regret to say, sometimes backed by the sword—we have been a progressive, but peaceful, people.

Speaker 3:
The Anglo-Saxon race, like a mighty flood, has swept over the continent. Some say the flood ought to stop at the Del Norte. I can tell them that it will not. In fifty years it will cover Mexico; in a hundred, Argentina.

Speaker 4:
The question of admitting Texas seems to make many apprehensive about the balance of political power. Let them look at the complexion of the House. Let them look also at the map and see the broad expanse of land in the north and northwest which is yet to be made into states where slavery can never exist. In addition, by rejecting Texas, we ensure the spread of slavery. Admit Texas, and the Rio Bravo constitutes the limits of this institution. Reject her, and slavery will not stop until its standard waves in triumph over Mexico.

Speaker 5:
Those who advocate annexation contend that the federal government is one of limited powers. Yet they ask that Congress assume the important power of adding a foreign nation to our own. We are referred to the provision in the Constitution that authorizes Congress to admit new states. History shows that this clause was intended only to confer on Congress the power of admitting new states created from territory already belonging to the United States.

Speaker 6:
This is the true cause of most of the opposition: fear that an influence opposed to the interests of the manufacturers would be added to the national councils. —

6. Which speaker's argument seems to stem DIRECTLY from a belief in the inevitability of historical events?
   A. 5   B. 4   C. 3   D. 1

1.____

7. Which of the following is TRUE of Speaker 2's description of the United States' method of acquiring new territory as *peaceful*?
   It
   A. is contradicted by other parts of his statement
   B. is supported by U.S. success in acquiring territories
   C. supports a Marxist interpretation of history
   D. is an accurate but unsupported statement

8. What EARLIER action of Congress was based on the principle of *balance of power* to which Speaker 4 refers?
   The
   A. Northwest Ordinance   B. Judiciary Act
   C. Missouri Compromise   D. Great Compromise

9. The argument of which speaker implies that United States territory should be limited to that acquired by an agreement?
   A. 5   B. 3   C. 2   D. 1

Questions 10-15.

DIRECTIONS: Questions 10 through 15 are NOT based on a reading passage. You are to answer these questions on the basis of your background in social studies.

10. Andrew Jackson's term as President is noteworthy LARGELY because during that period
    A. peaceful relations were established with the Plains Indians
    B. the common man came too have more of a say in government
    C. a national bank was established, resulting in this country's first stable currency
    D. women received the right to vote for the first time

11. The 80-day injunction provision of the Taft-Hartley Act was included for what purpose?
    To
    A. provide a cooling-off period allowing labor and management additional time to resolve disputes
    B. permit the unions to arrange for a survey of membership opinion regarding a strike
    C. permit management to update the profit-loss picture for the forthcoming quarter
    D. give government negotiators the time to make a decision about whether a strike would be advisable

12. Which of the following might anthropologists find SIMILAR in purpose to the rain dance of the Pueblo Indians?
    A. The playing of the national anthem before sporting events
    B. Traditional country folk dancing
    C. Studies carried out by a college of agriculture to improve the yield of wheat
    D. A prayer meeting in an American church

13. The MOST significant advance of the Charter of the United Nations over the Covenant of the League of Nations is the
    A. article providing for an international police force to prevent aggression
    B. provision granting veto power to the five permanent members of the Security Council
    C. belief in the maintenance of world peace by international cooperation
    D. establishment of a council with authority to formulate plans for the reduction of armaments

14. The MAIN purpose of the Bill of Rights is to
    A. prevent presidents from telling states what to do
    B. enlarge the scope of the powers of the federal government
    C. reduce the power of the Supreme Court to declare acts of Congress unconstitutional
    D. limit the power of the federal government to abuse individual freedom

15. When Western Europe was cut off from some of its Middle Eastern oil by the Suez crisis in 1956, MOST of the petroleum deficit was made up by the United States and
    A. Canada
    B. Eastern Europe
    C. Indonesia
    D. Venezuela

KEY (CORRECT ANSWERS)

1.	A	6.	C	11.	A
2.	D	7.	A	12.	D
3.	A	8.	C	13.	A
4.	C	9.	A	14.	D
5.	D	10.	B	15.	D

TEST 4

NATURAL SCIENCES READING

DIRECTIONS: This test measures your ability to understand, analyze, and evaluate passages on scientific topics and descriptions of experiments in such fields as biology, chemistry, physics, and physical science.

To answer these questions, you will have to draw on your scientific background as well as on your ability to understand new material.

In addition to the questions based on reading passages, there are some questions that test your general background knowledge in the sciences.

Read the passage through once. Then return to it as often as necessary to answer the questions. *PRINT THE LETTER OF THE CORRECT ANSWER IN THE SPACE AT THE RIGHT.*

Questions 1-5.

DIRECTIONS: Questions 1 through 5 are to be answered on the basis of the following passage.

As the cells that make up different tissues and organs differ in structure and function, so also do they differ in their response to radiation. The law of Bergonie and Tribondeau states that the radiosensitivity of a tissue is directly proportional to its reproductive capacity and inversely proportional to its degree of specialization. In other words, immature, rapidly-dividing cells will be most harmed by radiation. In addition, three other factors are important: undernourished cells are less sensitive than normal ones, the higher the metabolic rate in a cell the lower its resistance to radiation and cells are more sensitive to radiation at specific stages of division.

Radiation alters the electrical charges of the atoms in the irradiated material, breaking the valence bonds holding the molecules together. For example, radiation passing through a cell is most likely to strike water molecules. The breakdown products from these molecules may combine with oxygen to form bleaches, which in turn can break down protein molecules in the cell. One class of these proteins comprises the enzymes that not only play a role in nearly all biochemical reactions but also control cell division. Such inhibition of cell division may permit cells to grow to an abnormal size; when such a cell dies, there is no replacement to fill the void in the tissue. If the cell has been altered so that its daughter cells are genetically different from the parent cell, the daughter cells may die before they reproduce themselves; they may continue to grow without dividing or they may divide at a higher or lower rate than the parent cell.

Because of these possible effects, doctors and scientists have been concerned about the exposure of humans to radiation. A study of the effects of radiation on the human body indicates that the following organ and tissue groups are most affected by radioactivity: (1) blood and bone marrow, (2) lymphatic system, (3) skin and hair follicles, (4) alimentary canal, (5) adrenal glands, (6) thyroid gland, (7.) lungs, (8) urinary tract, (9) liver and gallbladder, (10) bone,

(11) eyes, and (12) reproductive organs. Although no permissible level for exposure of humans to radiation has been established, data reported in 1957 indicate that 25 roentgens cause no observable reaction, 50 roentgens produce nausea and vomiting, 400 to 500 roentgens give the individual a fifty-fifty chance of survival without medical care, and 650 roentgens are lethal.

1. In the first paragraph, the metabolic rate of a cell refers to the cell's
   A. chemical activities
   B. degree of specialization
   C. stage of division
   D. maturity

   1._____

2. Why is muscle tissue relatively unaffected by radiation?
   It(s)
   A. cells contain no water
   B. is highly specialized
   C. is protected by the bony skeleton
   D. cells have a unique method of reproduction

   2._____

3. If radiation can cause cancer as implied in the second paragraph, then which of the following BEST justifies the use of radiation in treating cancer?
   A. Cancer tissue is highly specialized, hence very sensitive to radiation.
   B. Only the cancer cells receive the radiation.
   C. Cancer cells divide relatively rapidly.
   D. The patient may die anyway, and desperate measures are appropriate in such instances.

   3._____

4. Which of the following would the author probably consider the MOST serious long-range effect of exposure to radiation on human populations?
   A. Possible destruction of natural resources essential to survival
   B. Hereditary changes that might occur in the population
   C. The world's population increasing at a higher rate than the world's food supply
   D. The daughters of people exposed to radiation dying before they can have children

   4._____

5. Why would a man in outer space be in GREATER danger from radiation than a man on earth?
   A. He would not be shielded from cosmic rays by the earth's atmosphere.
   B. The reduced pressure in a space vehicle inhibits cell division.
   C. Biochemical reactions essential to life cannot occur in outer space.
   D. In a weightless condition, cells are more vulnerable to radiation.

   5._____

Questions 6-9.

DIRECTIONS: Questions 6 through 9 are to be answered on the basis of the following passage.

A series of experiments was designed to determine how bats are able to fly at night without colliding with obstacles. Bats were released in a closed room across which were strung fine wires adapted to register every time they were touched by one of the bats. The bats were released in the room under the following conditions:

Experiment 1:
   The room was well illuminated.

Experiment 2:
   The room was completely darkened.

Experiment 3:
   The room was darkened, and the bats' eyes were sealed with soft black wax.

Experiment 4:
   The room was darkened, the bats' eyes were waxed closed, and numerous small radar transmitters were set in operation throughout the room.

Experiment 5:
   The radar transmitters were replaced with loudspeakers which emitted high-frequency sound waves. The room was dark, and the bats' eyes were waxed closed.

Experiment 6:
   The lights were turned on, and the bats, without wax on their eyes, were released while the loudspeakers were still producing high-frequency sounds.

   On the basis of these experiments, the following observations were made:

   In Experiments 1 through 4, the bats did not collide with the wires.

   In Experiment 5, the bats seemed confused and frequently collided with the wires.

   In Experiment 6, the bats were initially confused and collided with the wires; however, the number of collisions soon decreased.

6. Which conclusion, if any, can be drawn from Experiment 1?
   A. Bats need light to see where they are going.
   B. Bats need sound waves in order to avoid obstacles.
   C. Bats can see in the dark,
   D. None of the above

7. Which conclusion, if any, can be drawn from Experiment 4?
   A. Bats evidently use some sort of radar to guide themselves.
   B. The presence of radar waves has no apparent effect on the bats.
   C. The presence of radar waves confuses the bats by obstructing their natural means of locating obstacles.
   D. None of the above

8. Which experiment or group of experiments listed below shows that bats can ordinarily fly safely without using their eyes?
   A. 3 only   B. 1 and 2   C. 1 and 3   D. 1, 2, 3

9. Which of the following is TRUE about the statement: *Bats are nocturnal animals because daylight interferes with their ability to avoid obstacles.*
The statement
   A. agrees with the data
   B. is contradicted by the data
   C. cannot be judged without more data
   D. is an experimental assumption

Questions 10-13.

DIRECTIONS: Questions 10 through 13 are NOT based on a reading passage. You are to answer these questions on the basis of your background in the natural sciences.

10. The emergence of new strains of houseflies capable of withstanding the poisonous effects of the chemical DDT is an example of
   A. adaptation
   B. the Mendelian law
   C. implementation
   D. regeneration

11. What is the MAIN difference between a gas and a liquid?
   A. Molecular weight
   B. Shape of the particles
   C. Geometric arrangement of the molecules
   D. Average distance between the molecules

12. How were the coral reefs of tropical seas formed? By
   A. the accumulation of the remains of small marine animals
   B. the erosion of islands by wind and sea
   C. the accumulation of salts and minerals precipitated by the sea
   D. undersea earthquakes

13. A warm breeze may seem cool to a bather who has just come out of the water because
   A. water is a good conductor of heat
   B. moisture from the air condenses on the skin and cools it
   C. the evaporation of water from the wet skin absorbs heat
   D. water is denser than air

KEY (CORRECT ANSWERS)

1.	A	6.	D	11.	D
2.	B	7.	B	12.	A
3.	C	8.	A	13.	C
4.	B	9.	B		
5.	A	10.	A		

EXAMINATION SECTION

TEST 1

DIRECTIONS: Read each sentence. Then print in the blank a word or phrase that means the same thing as the underlined word.

For example, suppose you were given this sentence:
    John walked down the street rapidly.
This is how you might have answered:
    Rapidly means quickly.
Or, you might have answered this way:
    Rapidly means in a hurry.

1. The leader found a great deal of opposition among his men.
   Opposition means _____.

2. The boy's behavior was inexcusable.
   Inexcusable means _____.

3. The school was very progressive.
   Progressive means _____.

4. She talked continuously.
   Continuously means _____.

5. Tom's new jacket was inexpensive.
   Inexpensive means _____.

6. It was a poor assumption.
   Assumption means _____.

7. His act was unconstitutional.
   Unconstitutional means _____.

8. His unawareness was surprising.
   Unawareness means _____.

9. The name was unfamiliar.
   Unfamiliar means _____.

10. There are many groups today working to equalize opportunities for women.
    Equalize means _____.

11. The term plastics covers a wide range of materials, but plastic is not a natural material. All plastics are synthetic.
    Synthetic means _____.

12. The judge tried to figure out what the thief's motive might have been, but there seemed to be no logical explanation for the crime. The man had no need for the money he took; he had no reason for wanting to hurt the man he stole from.
    Motive means _____.

13. The town's water supply was rapidly diminishing. In fact, it was being used up so quickly that there was real danger of the supply running out altogether.
    Diminishing means _____.

14. A person must set up an ultimate goal, even though he needs temporary short-term aims along the way.
    Ultimate means _____.

15. Tom was worried about his low grade, so his teacher assured him that the quiz was of no real consequence, that it hardly mattered at all.
    Consequence means _____.

16. Even though the mechanic didn't agree with his boss, he believed he should acquiesce. He knew that he was likely to lose his job if he went against the wishes of the employer.
    Acquiesce means _____.

17. The boy didn't do his homework, so when the teacher asked him a question, his answer was very vague and uncertain.
    Vague means _____.

18. Many southern plantation owners wanted to keep their slaves, but Abraham Lincoln was in favor of liberating them.
    Liberating means _____.

19. Insects which do not live in groups, or colonies, are said to be solitary.
    Solitary means _____.

20. When you say that all people will take advantage of you if they're given the chance, you stereotype them. You're saying that all people are the same.
    Stereotype means _____.

3 (#1)

KEY (CORRECT ANSWERS)

1. Opposition
   Correct response should present idea of <u>going against</u>.
       disagreement; argument

2. Inexcusable
   Correct response should present idea of <u>not following acceptable behavior pattern</u>.
       unforgivable; not to be excused

3. Progressive
   Correct response should present idea of <u>being ahead of the average</u>.
       advanced; modern; forward-looking

4. Continuously
   Correct response should present idea of <u>continuing action</u>.
       all the time; without stopping

5. Inexpensive
   Correct response should present idea of <u>not costing very much money</u>.
       cheap; not expensive; doesn't cost very much; at a low price

6. Assumption
   Correct response should present idea of <u>being something that was figured out through the use of logic</u>.
       something figured out; a guess; something assumed

7. Unconstitutional
   Correct response should present idea of <u>not being in accord with the law</u>.
       illegal; against the law

8. Unawareness
   Correct response should present idea of <u>not being aware</u>.
       not knowing; ignorance

9. Unfamiliar
   Correct response should present idea of <u>lack of acquaintance with</u>.
       strange; not known

10. Equalize
    Correct response should present idea of <u>making two things equal</u>.
        to make the same; to make equal

11. Synthetic
    Correct response should present idea of <u>not being found in nature</u>.
        man-made; manufactured

4 (#1)

12. Motive
Correct response should present idea of <u>intention</u>.
purpose; aim; reason; goal

13. Diminishing
Correct response should present idea of <u>becoming smaller in amount</u>.
decreasing; getting smaller; being used up

14. Ultimate
Correct response should present idea of <u>long-range and permanent</u>.
final; long-term

15. Consequence
Correct response should present idea of <u>having importance or influence</u>.
importance; significance; mattering

16. Acquiesce
Correct response should present idea of <u>giving in</u>.
go along with; give in

17. Vague
Correct response should present idea of <u>being unclear</u>.
uncertain; unclear; not clear; not sure

18. Liberating
Correct response should present idea of <u>granting freedom</u>.
freeing; letting go

19. Solitary
Correct response should present idea of <u>being alone</u>.
alone; not in groups

20. Stereotype
Correct response should present idea of <u>classing together</u>.
label; call them the same

TEST 2

DIRECTIONS: Each question or incomplete statement is followed by several suggested answers or completions. Select the one that BEST answers the question or completes the statement. *PRINT THE LETTER OF THE CORRECT ANSWER IN THE SPACE AT THE RIGHT.*

Questions 1-7.

DIRECTIONS: Questions 1 through 7 are to be answered on the basis of the following map.

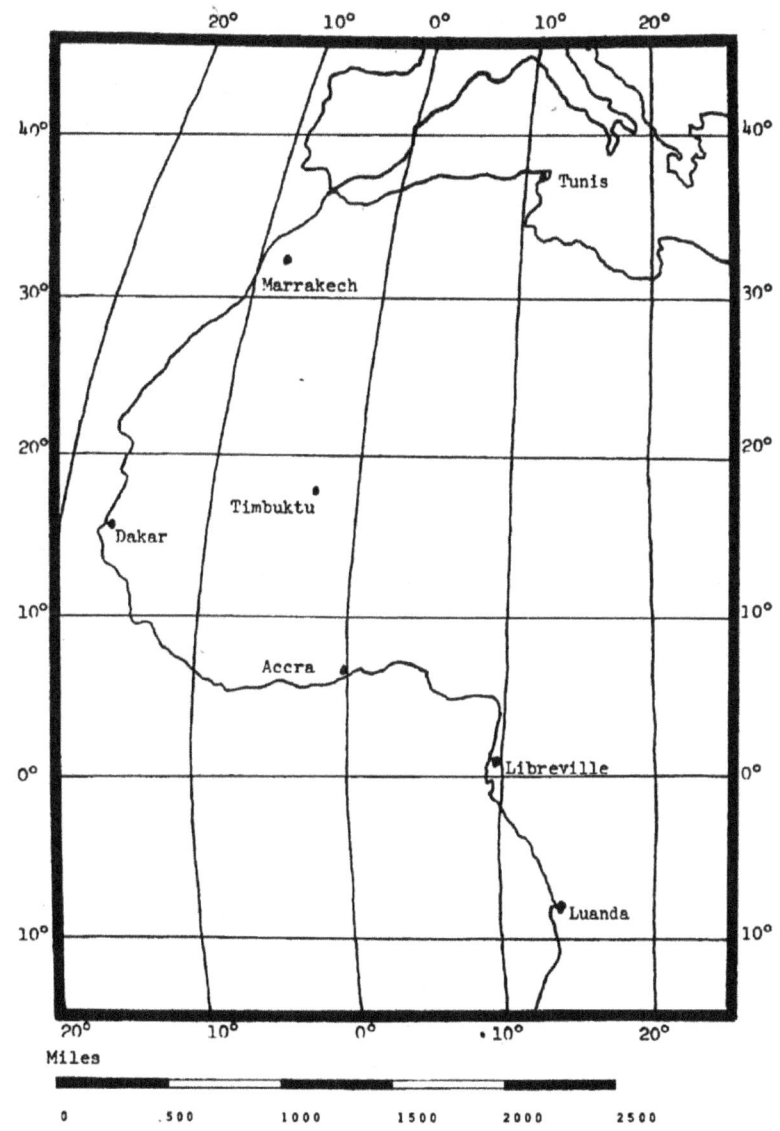

1. Which of the cities on the map; above is located at 8W longitude and 32N latitude?
   A. Luanda
   B. Accra
   C. Timbuktu
   D. Marrakech
   E. Dakar

1.____

21

2. In which two hemispheres is Tunis located? 2._____
   A. eastern and northern
   B. western and northern
   C. eastern and southern
   D. western and southern

3. If you traveled from Luanda to Accra, in which direction would you be going? 3._____
   A. northwest B. southwest C. northeast D. southwest

4. The distance from Timbuktu to Accra is APPROXIMATELY _____ miles. 4._____
   A. 300 B. 450 C. 600 D. 750 E. 900

5. Mapmakers draw lines on maps to help locate points. Lines running east and west are called _____ lines. 5._____

6. Which city is closest to the prime meridian? 6._____

7. Which of these cities is located furthest inland? 7._____
   A. Tunis B. Marrakech C. Timbuktu
   D. Dakar E. Accra

Questions 8-11.

DIRECTIONS: Questions 8 through 12 are either TRUE (T) or FALSE (F). Print the letter of the CORRECT answer in the space at the right.

8. Coastal regions have milder temperatures than inland regions. 8._____

9. The elevation of a mountain is the number of feet from its base to its highest peak. 9._____

10. The Southern Hemisphere is warmer than the Northern Hemisphere. 10._____

11. When air is forced to rise, it loses its moisture. 11._____

12. The term "temperature range" refers to the 12._____
    A. hottest and coldest temperatures recorded in a location
    B. average temperature of a location
    C. usual temperature of a day in the spring or fall
    D. sum of the temperatures divided by the number of days measurements were made

Questions 13-14.

DIRECTIONS: Questions 13 and 14 are to be answered on the basis of the following information.

Region A: 5 inches of annual rainfall
Region B: 9 inches of annual rainfall
Region C: 14 inches of annual rainfall
Region D: 34 inches of annual rainfall
Region E: 47 inches of annual rainfall
Region F: 98 inches of annual rainfall

13. Which of the regions listed above are desert regions?
    A. Only Region A
    B. Regions A, B, and C
    C. Regions A and B
    E. All of the above except Regions E and F

14. Which of the above would be MOST suitable for growing crops without irrigation?
    A. Regions F and E
    B. Regions D and C
    C. Regions E and D
    D. Regions C and B

15. The word "moderate" means
    A. up-to-date
    B. in the middle
    C. extreme
    D. acceptable

16. The climatic zone around the equator is called the ____ zone.
    A. polar
    B. tropic
    C. temperate

17. In the Southern Hemisphere, January comes during the
    A. winter
    B. summer
    C. spring
    D. fall
    E. month of June

18. To what does the environment refer?
    A. Artificial
    B. Improvement
    C. Climate
    D. Surroundings

Questions 19-23.

DIRECTIONS: In answering Questions 19 through 23, print the letter of the items in Column II with the subject in Column I under which they would MOST likely be studied.

COLUMN I	COLUMN II	
19. Anthropology	A. The study of plants and animals	19._____
20. Biology	B. The study of the behavior of men and animals	20._____
21. Economics	C. The study of the ways groups of people live	21._____
22. Psychology	D. The study of the ways man makes a living	22._____
23. Sociology	E. The study of man's development	23._____

Questions 24-28.

DIRECTIONS: In answering Questions 24 through 28, print the letter of the subject in Column II with the definition in Column I under which they would MOST likely be studied.

COLUMN I	COLUMN II	
24. The location of the Ohio River	A. Economic geography	24._____
25. The boundary between the United states and Mexico	B. Physical geography	25._____
	C. Political geography	
26. The coal mining regions of the world		26._____
27. The location of New England fruit farms		27._____
28. The location of state capitals in the United States		28._____

Questions 29-32.

DIRECTIONS: Questions 29 through 32 are either TRUE (T) or FALSE (F). Print the letter of the CORRECT answer in the space at the right.

29. All societies have the same culture.   29._____

30. Human beings are the only animals that have culture.   30._____

31. Language, beliefs, and ways of doing things are part of any culture.   31._____

32. Man transmits culture through language.

33. Prehistoric man's environment is mostly 33.____
    A. artificial because he has a great deal of culture
    B. artificial because he has no culture
    C. natural because he has little culture

34. Primitive means 34.____
    A. living close to the natural environment
    B. not being able to read or write
    C. not having good manners
    D. not knowing how to solve problems

Questions 35-40.

DIRECTIONS: In answering Questions 35 through 40, print the letter A in the space at the right if they are <u>acquired</u> or an I if they are <u>instinctive</u>.

35. Culture 35.____

36. Learned behavior 36.____

37. Natural desires 37.____

38. The ability to speak a language 38.____

39. The desire to read books 39.____

40. The need to eat and sleep 40.____

Questions 41-42.

DIRECTIONS: Questions 41 and 42 are to be answered on the basis of the following passage.

In 1954, the United States Supreme Court ruled that racial segregation* in public schools was illegal. Before 1954, many southern states legally segregated the schools. Therefore, these states had to take steps toward integrating** their schools. There were no state laws segregating schools in the North. However, after 1954, people began to notice what was happening in the North. It was seen that students were supposed to go to the school nearest their homes; and housing conditions forced black people to live in separate areas.

*The word "segregation" in this context means "separating people of different races."
**The word "integrating" in this context means "uniting people."

41. What is the implication of this passage? 41.____
    A. Northern cities and towns had poor housing conditions.
    B. Northern states might try to pass laws to segregate schools.
    C. Segregation did, in fact, exist in the North.
    D. The Supreme Court was going to have to pass new laws about the North.

42. You can infer from this passage that, in the North,
    A. the Supreme Court made a ruling about integrating housing
    B. there was complete integration because there were no state laws requiring segregation
    C. there was segregation in housing because there was segregation in schools
    D. there was segregation in the schools because there was segregation in housing

Questions 43-44.

DIRECTIONS: Questions 43 and 44 are to be answered on the basis of the following passage.

It is easy to see that without free public education, the great intangible which we call "freedom" would not mean very much. Of what value is freedom of the press, for example, to a man who cannot read or write? What is the good of freedom of thought if a person does not have enough education to be able to think intelligently about the problems of the day? And how can there be such a thing as freedom to choose a career if only a lucky few have the chance to gain enough education to enter the more desirable fields of work?

43. The author of the above passage implies that
    A. people will not know how to vote intelligently unless they are educated
    B. people would value their education more if they had to pay for it
    C. political freedom is not related to education
    D. private education should be made illegal

44. Which of the following BEST summarizes the above passage?
    A. A free public school system cannot work in a democracy.
    B. "Freedom" causes many problems for the uneducated.
    C. "Freedom" would be nearly meaningless in a country that didn't have free schools.
    D. Only educated people deserve freedom.

45. To interpret means to
    A. choose between two alternatives
    B. figure out something from what is given
    C. figure out the main idea
    D. think clearly

KEY (CORRECT ANSWERS)

1.	D	11.	T	21.	D	31.	T	41.	C
2.	A	12.	A	22.	B	32.	T	42.	D
3.	A	13.	B	23.	C	33.	C	43.	A
4.	D	14.	B	24.	B	34.	A	44.	C
5.	latitude	15.	C	25.	C	35.	A	45.	B
6.	Accra	16.	B	26.	A	36.	A		
7.	C	17.	B	27.	A	37.	I		
8.	T	18.	D	28.	C	38.	A		
9.	F	19.	E	29.	F	39.	A		
10.	F	20.	A	30.	T	40.	I		

TEST 3

DIRECTIONS: Each question or incomplete statement is followed by several suggested answers or completions. Select the one that BEST answers the question or completes the statement. *PRINT THE LETTER OF THE CORRECT ANSWER IN THE SPACE AT THE RIGHT.*

Questions 1-3

DIRECTIONS: In answering Questions 1 through 3, print the letter of the term from Column II that BEST matches the definition in Column I. (Select only one response for each question.)

	COLUMN I	COLUMN II	
1.	The making of goods or products	A. Barter	1._____
2.	The using of goods or products	B. Consumption C. Division of labor	2._____
3.	The exchange of one product for	D. Labor E. Product F. Production G. Raw materials H. Surplus	3._____

4. Division of labor can lead to 4._____
   A. few occupations
   B. les consumption
   C. less production
   D. a surplus of products
   E. a surplus of raw materials

5. To discriminate between two things means to 5._____
   A. disagree with them
   B. figure out the ways they resemble each other or are alike
   C. tell them apart, to tell the difference between them
   D. tell which one is a fact and which one is an opinion

Questions 6-9.

DIRECTIONS: In answering Questions 6 through 9, print the letter of the definitions in Column II with the terms in Column I.

COLUMN I   COLUMN II

6. Anarchy   A. A country in which a tax expert is   6._____
                                           elected each year to decide what
7. Direct democracy   that year's taxes will be   7._____
                                        B. A country in which the people vote
8. Representative democracy   on how much taxes to collect each   8._____
                                           year
9. Totalitarianism   C. A town in which the mayor can have   9._____
                                           anyone put into jail whenever he
                                           wants to
                                        D. a village which has almost no laws
                                           or rules

10. Which of the following could be found in a totalitarian state? (Choose one   10._____
    or more answers.)
    A. Despot   B. Dictator
    C. Elected president   D. Representative
    E. Tyrant

Questions 11-13.

DIRECTIONS: In answering Questions 11 through 13, print the letter of the term in Column II with its definition in Column I.

COLUMN I   COLUMN II

11. A family in which each person does A. Extreme anarchy   11._____
    what he wants   B. Extreme democracy
                                        C, Moderate anarchy
12. A large country where only men over D. Moderate democracy   12._____
    the age of 25 are allowed to vote

13. A small town that has very few laws   13._____
    and a mayor who is almost powerless

Questions 14-18.

DIRECTIONS: In answering Questions 14 through 18, mark each with an F if it is a fact, I if it is an issue, or O if it is an opinion.

14. Causes of juvenile delinquency   14._____

15. It's going to rain tomorrow.   15._____

16. No one should ever be given a death sentence for a crime. 16._____

17. Some girls wear dresses 10 inches above their knees. 17._____

18. The influence of French designers on women's dress fashions in the United States is harmful. 18._____

19. The Empire State Building is one of New York's most frequently visited sights. It is located on Fifth Avenue between 34th and 33rd Streets. It was once the tallest building in the world. No one will ever create a structure more impressive than the Empire State Building. It is the most beautiful building ever constructed. 19._____
    Which of the following statements come before statements of opinion? (Choose one or more answers.)
    A. It is the most beautiful building every constructed.
    B. It is located on Fifth Avenue between 34th and 33rd Streets.
    C. It was once the tallest building in the world.
    D. No one will ever create a structure more impressive than the Empire State Building.
    E. The Empire State Building is one of New York's most frequently visited sights.

Questions 20-23.

DIRECTIONS: Questions 20 through 23 are to be answered on the basis of the following paragraph.

It is not at all obvious that reading comic books and viewing crime dramas cause delinquency. Many young people are exposed to so-called harmful dramas and do not become delinquents. Mass entertainment provides may people with jobs and pumps millions of dollars into our economy. If crime dramas produce delinquency, no one has yet shown how. Many people feel that mass entertainment should not be subject to censorship*, but there are no conclusive studies to justify limiting our freedom of speech and freedom of the press.

*Censorship in this context means controlling the subjects allowed in comic books and on television. It means limiting the subjects.

20. The issue being discussed in this passage is 20._____
    A. censorship
    B. mass entertainment
    C. crime
    D. the increase in juvenile delinquency
    E. philosophies of life

21. The author's opinion could BEST be summarized by saying: 21.____
    A. comic books and TV dramas are valuable
    B. comic books and TV dramas cause delinquency
    C. mass entertainment has been shown to be harmful
    D. mass entertainment should not be censored
    E. newspapers should not be censored

22. Which facts support the author's opinion? (Choose one or more answers.)   22.____
    A. Many young people who read comic books and watch harmful dramas do not become delinquent.
    B. Many young people who read comic books and watch harmful dramas become delinquent.
    C. Reading comic books and watching harmful dramas cause delinquency.

23. Which statement is NOT relevant to the author's opinion?   23.____
    A. It is not obvious that harmful dramas cause delinquency.
    B. If mass entertainment is harmful, this has not been conclusively shown.
    C. Many young people are exposed to harmful dramas and do not become delinquents.
    D. Mass entertainment provides many people with jobs and pumps millions of dollars into our economy.
    E. There are no conclusive studies to show that we should have censorship.

24. A topic about which people have differing opinions is called a(n) _____.   24.____

KEY (CORRECT ANSWERS)

1.	F		11.	A
2.	B		12.	D
3.	A		13.	C
4.	D		14.	I
5.	C		15.	O
6.	D		16.	O
7.	B		17.	F
8.	A		18.	O
9.	C		19.	A, D
10.	A, B, E		20.	A

21. D
22. A
23. D
24. issue

TEST 4

DIRECTIONS: Each question or incomplete statement is followed by several suggested answers or completions. Select the one that BEST answers the question or completes the statement. *PRINT THE LETTER OF THE CORRECT ANSWER IN THE SPACE AT THE RIGHT.*

Questions 1-2.

DIRECTIONS: In answering Questions 1 and 2, print the letter of the definition in Column II which describes the term in Column II.

COLUMN I	COLUMN II	
1. Capital	A. Any product of past labor that is used to make more products	1.____
2. Profit	B. Money left over after cost of producing and trading goods has been paid	2.____

Questions 3-8.

DIRECTIONS: In answering Questions 3 through 8, print the letter P if the item is making products or an S if the item is performing services.

3. Building brick walls   3.____

4. Coining money   4.____

5. Mending clothes   5.____

6. Producing cloth   6.____

7. Sharpening knives   7.____

8. Transporting goods   8.____

9. When a country brings in products or raw materials from another country, it is _____ products and materials.   9.____
   A. exporting   B. importing

Questions 10-14.

DIRECTIONS: In answering Questions 10 through 14, print the letter T if the item would lead to a trading economy or S if the item tends to keep an economy on a subsistence level.

10. Abundant (many) raw materials   10.____

11. A location favorable for traveling   11._____

12. A location that is surrounded by mountains   12._____

13. Polar climate   13._____

14. Surplus products   14._____

15. In a representative democracy, there should   15._____
    A. be a one-party system
    B. be several parties of equal power in the government
    C. not be a one-party system

Questions 16-21.

DIRECTIONS: Questions 16 through 21 are either TRUE (T) or FALSE (F). Print the letter of the CORRECT answer in the space at the right.

16. Anarchy can result when each representative in a government sticks to his   16._____
    own opinion and refuses to compromise.

17. A local government cannot have direct democracy if the federal government   17._____
    is an indirect democracy.

18. A minority party cannot pass laws.   18._____

19. Representative democracies have political parties so that people can vote   19._____
    directly on issues and laws.

20. An independent voter is someone who votes only for candidates who do   20._____
    not belong to political parties.

21. A political system containing many different parties tends to create an   21._____
    unstable government.

22. Representatives of a political party   22._____
    A. agree on all the issues
    B. cannot belong to a party unless they agree with and support every
       opinion the party favors
    C. may vote differently than other members of the same party

23. The MAJOR issue about which United States political parties differ is: 23._____
    A. how much power the federal government should have and how it should
       be used
    B. when the majority vote and when the minority vote is important
    C. the number of candidates allowed to run in a presidential election
    D. whether or not the federal government should be based on direct or
       indirect democracy

Questions 24-25.

DIRECTIONS: Questions 24 and 25 are to be answered on the basis of the following passage.

Art should express the thoughts and feelings of the artist. Universal feelings should be expressed so that anyone who looks at the work of art can understand what the artist is trying to say. Modern paintings that are just splashes of color do not express any such thoughts or feelings.

24. Which of the following statements would the author of the above passage endorse?
Modern art
   A. does not deserve to be called art.
   B. is a clear expression of modern man's thoughts and feelings.
   C. expresses the artist's thoughts and feelings.

25. Would the author of this passage probably agree to a plan to give government aid to painters of modern art?
   A. Yes
   B. No

26. Assumption comes closest in meaning to
   A. attitude
   B. inference
   C. obligation
   D. relevance

Questions 27-29.

DIRECTIONS: Questions 27 through 29 are to be answered on the basis of the following passage.

Speaker A: It is never a wise thing for two people of different races to marry. It causes nothing but pain for the couple and for the children. Other people in the community do not accept them, and call their children mongrels.* Take my advice; don't marry a person of another race.

Speaker B: During World War II, many American soldiers married Japanese women. These marriages have been successful, and the couples have certainly been accepted in our society. As for the "mongrel" issued, that is ridiculous. We are all human beings with the same cells, tissues, and organs. Men and women have been intermarrying for thousands of years. There is no such thing as a pure race of people. People are not dogs bred for specific characteristics.

*Mongrel is the term given to a dog that is not a purebred. For example, the puppy of a German Shepherd and a Boxer would be a mongrel.

27. What assumption(s) does Speaker A make?
   A. That human races are pure in the same sense that different breeds of dogs are
   B. That intermarrying is all right for some races but not for others
   C. That marriage does not have to be based on racial characteristics

4 (#4)

28. Which speaker would <u>endorse</u> a law that forbids marriage between people of different races? 28.____
    A. Speaker A   B. Speaker B

29. Which speaker would be LESS likely to agree that it is unwise for people of different religions to marry? 29.____
    A. Speaker A   B. Speaker B

KEY (CORRECT ANSWERS)

1.	A	11.	T	21.	T
2.	B	12.	S	22.	C
3.	P	13.	S	23.	A
4.	P	14.	T	24.	A
5.	S	15.	C	25.	B
6.	P	16.	T	26.	B
7.	S	17.	F	27.	A
8.	S	18.	F	28.	A
9.	B	19.	F	29.	B
10.	T	20.	F		

TEST 5

DIRECTIONS: Each question or incomplete statement is followed by several suggested answers or completions. Select the one that BEST answers the question or completes the statement. *PRINT THE LETTER OF THE CORRECT ANSWER IN THE SPACE AT THE RIGHT.*

Questions 1-6.

DIRECTIONS: In answering Questions 1 through 6, print the B for before if the item took place before the Industrial Revolution or A for after if the item took place after the Industrial Revolution.

1. Goods are made by hand with tools and simple machines.   1.____

2. Production is large-scale, for a widely spread market.   2.____

3. Most workers live in small villages where they do a little farming in addition to producing goods.   3.____

4. Workers are employed in large factories.   4.____

5. Most workers are skilled craftsmen who make complete products.   5.____

6. In a short period of time, technology drastically changed man's environment.   6.____

Questions 7-10.

DIRECTIONS: Questions 7 through 10 are either TRUE (T) or FALSE (F). Print the letter of the CORRECT answer in the space at the right.

7. Mass production leads to the development of big businesses.   7.____

8. On an assembly line, every worker is responsible for completing a certain number of finished products.   8.____

9. In times before the Industrial Revolution, skilled craftsmen were able to produce standardized goods.   9.____

10. Standardized goods are mass produced on assembly lines.   10.____

11. What is technology?   11.____
    A. The study of teaching methods and techniques
    B. The techniques of painting and other fine arts
    C. Using knowledge of natural laws to solve man's practical problems

12. Which of these is NOT an example of craftsmanship? 12.____
    A. A skilled cabinetmaker who makes an entire cabinet and installs it
    B. A skilled mechanic making one part of an automobile engine
    C. A skilled shoemaker making a complete pair of shoes

13. The President is head of the _____ branch of our government. 13.____

14. Congress belongs to the _____ branch of our government. 14.____

15. Which of the following systems was developed to prevent any single 15.____
    branch of our government from becoming too powerful?
    A. Checks and balances   B. Division of labor
    C. Representative democracy   D. Taxation system

16. The power to declare a law unconstitutional lies with the 16.____
    A. citizens of the United States   B. Congress
    C. President of the United States   D. Supreme Court

17. To veto a law means to 17.____
    A. break it   B. make its meaning clear
    C. pass it   D. refuse to approve it

Questions 18-27.

DIRECTIONS: Questions 18 through 27 are either TRUE (T) or FALSE (F). Print the letter of the CORRECT answer in the space at the right.

18. An unripe orange is an orange that is past ripe. 18.____

19. An insensitive person is a person who is very sensitive. 19.____

20. A nonviolent protest is a protest which is not violent. 20.____

21. A bimetal cup is a cup made of three kinds of metal. 21.____

22. A postwar recession is a recession that comes after a war. 22.____

23. Subfreezing temperatures are temperatures above freezing. 23.____

24. An interschool competition is a competition within a school. 24.____

25. A misapplied rule is a rule that is not applied. 25.____

26. A transcontinental pipeline is a pipeline that goes between two continents. 26.____

27. An animal that has been declawed is an animal whose claws have been removed. 27.____

KEY (CORRECT ANSWERS)

1.	B	11.	C	21.	F
2.	A	12.	B	22.	T
3.	B	13.	Executive	23.	F
4.	A	14.	Legislative	24.	F
5.	B	15.	A	25.	F
6.	A	16.	D	26.	F
7.	T	17.	D	27.	T
8.	F	18.	F		
9.	F	19.	F		
10.	T	20.	T		

TEST 6

DIRECTIONS: Each question or incomplete statement is followed by several suggested answers or completions. Select the one that BEST answers the question or completes the statement. *PRINT THE LETTER OF THE CORRECT ANSWER IN THE SPACE AT THE RIGHT.*

1. The molecules of which item listed below are held together most closely and move the least? 1.____
    A. A glass of water
    B. A melted chocolate bar
    C. A piece of iron
    D. Steam from boiling water

2. What do we call matter? 2.____
   Everything that
    A. has weight and occupies space
    B. we can hear or see
    C. can be measured

3. What are the three states of matter? 3.____

4. Molecules will move faster and farther apart if _____ is applied. 4.____

Questions 5-7.

DIRECTIONS: In answering Questions 5 through 7, print the letter S if the example describes solubility, V if it describes viscosity, and F if it describes fluidity.

5. Hot bacon grease poured from a skillet 5.____

6. Hot tar poured on a roof 6.____

7. Sugar stirred into hot tea 7.____

8. Choose from the list below three properties which CANNOT be used to tell one kind of matter from another. 8.____
    A. Solubility   B. Color   C. Fluidity
    D. Hardness   E. Mass   F. Taste
    G. Odor   H. Shape   I. Boiling point
    J. Melting point K. Volume   L. Weight

9. The properties which you selected in Question 8 are called _____. 9.____

39

Questions 10-16.

DIRECTIONS: In answering Questions 10 through 16, match the units of measurement in Column I with the items they are used to measure in Column II.

COLUMN I	COLUMN II	
10. Centimeters	A. Area	10._____
11. Cubic meters	L. Length	11._____
12. Grams	V. Volume	12._____
13. Kilometers	W. Weight	13._____
14. Liters		14._____
15. Square centimeters		15._____
16. Square meters		16._____

Questions 17-22.

DIRECTIONS: Can the items listed below be classified as matter or energy? Are there some items listed that cannot be classified as either matter or energy. In answering Questions 17 through 22, print the letter M for matter, E for energy, and N if the item describes neither matter nor energy.

17. A container 17._____

18. An inch 18._____

19. Invisible ink 19._____

20. The sound of music 20._____

21. Sunlight 21._____

22. An idea 22._____

Questions 23-27.

DIRECTIONS: In answering Questions 23 through 27, print the letters CC if they represent a chemical change, and PC if they represent a physical change.

23. A burnt marshmallow 23._____

24. The manufacture of bread crumbs from bread 24._____

25. The manufacture of sawdust from wood   25.____

26. The melting of butter   26.____

27. A tree set on fire by lightning   27.____

28. Which of the following statements are scientific laws?   28.____
    A. Matter can be converted into energy.
    B. One kind of matter can never be changed into another kind of matter.
    C. Sometimes all of the properties of a substance are altered in a physical
       change.

Questions 29-32.

DIRECTIONS: In answering Questions 29 through 32, print the letter of the charge
             in Column II that is carried by the items in Column I.

    COLUMN I   COLUMN II

29. The atom as a whole   A. No charge   29.____
                                      B. Negative charge
30. An electron   C. Positive charge   30.____

31. A neutron   31.____

32. A proton   32.____

33. The atomic mass of an atom is equal to the number of its   33.____
        A. electrons and protons   B. protons
        C. protons and neutrons

34. The atomic number of an atom is equal to the number of its   34.____
        A. electrons and protons   B. protons
        C. protons and neutrons

35. A compound is a result of a _____ change.   35.____
        A. chemical   B. physical

KEY (CORRECT ANSWERS)

1.	C	11.	V	21.	E	31.	A
2.	A	12.	W	22.	N	32.	C
3.	Solid, liquid, gas	13.	L	23.	CC	33.	C
4.	Heat	14.	V	24.	PC	34.	B
5.	F	15.	A	25.	PC	35.	A
6.	V	16.	A	26.	PC		
7.	S	17.	M	27.	CC		
8.	E, K, L	18.	N	28.	A		
9.	General	19.	M	29.	A		
10.	L	20.	E	30.	B		

TEST 7

DIRECTIONS: Each question or incomplete statement is followed by several suggested answers or completions. Select the one that BEST answers the question or completes the statement. *PRINT THE LETTER OF THE CORRECT ANSWER IN THE SPACE AT THE RIGHT.*

1. Some atoms do not react chemically. This is related to 1.____
    A. the distribution of their electrons
    B. the number of their neutrons
    C. the size of their nucleus
    D. some unknown characteristic feature of these atoms

2. If a atom has two or more orbits, the MAXIMUM number of electrons that it can have in its outermost orbit is 2.____
    A. 2   B. 6   C. 8   D. 10   E. 12

3. Atoms which have less than the maximum number of electrons in their outermost orbits are said to be 3.____
    A. inactive   B. inert   C. active
    D. stable   E. deficient

4. The readiness with which one element will combine with another is a 4.____
    A. physical property   B. chemical property
    C. general property   D. both A and C

5. Which of the following does NOT describe a chemical reaction? 5.____
    A. Atom W loses 2 neutrons
    B. Atom X gains 1 electron
    C. Atom Y loses 2 electrons
    D. Atom Z and atom W share a pair of electrons

6. An ion 6.____
    A. usually has no electrical charge
    B. always has a positive charge
    C. always has a negative charge
    D. may have either a positive or a negative charge
    E. may have both a positive and a negative charge

7. A molecule always has 7.____
    A. a negative charge
    B. a positive charge
    C. either a positive or a negative charge
    D. no charge

Questions: 8-10.

DIRECTIONS: Questions 8 through 10 are either TRUE (T) or FALSE (F). Print the letter of the CORRECT answer in the space at the right.

8. Two atoms which are sharing a pair of electrons have formed an iconic bond.   8.____

9. The word "synthesis" describes a chemical reaction in which a molecule is broken into smaller molecules or elements.   9.____

10. Energy is always released or absorbed in a chemical reaction.   10.____

11. The symbol Cl_2 represents   11.____
    A. a molecule composed of two elements
    B. two atoms of the same element chemically bonded
    C. two atoms of the same element not chemically bonded
    D. a formula for synthesis
    E. a formula for analysis

12. Which of the following forms of energy cannot be transferred directly by means of waves?   12.____
    A. Electricity   B. Heat   C. Light   D. Sound

Questions: 13-18.

DIRECTIONS: Questions 13 through 18 are either TRUE (T) or FALSE (F). Print the letter of the CORRECT answer in the space at the right.

13. The random movement of molecules is called mechanical energy.   13.____

14. Convection is the transfer of heat energy from molecule to molecule.   14.____

15. Radiation is the transfer of heat energy by the movement of waves.   15.____

16. Energy released in the process of synthesis is called chemical energy.   16.____

17. Electricity flowing through a power line is an example of a static charge.   17.____

18. Fusion is one of the forms of nuclear energy.   18.____

KEY (CORRECT ANSWERS)

1. A
2. C
3. C
4. B
5. A

6. D
7. D
8. F
9. F
10. T

11. B
12. A
13. F
14. F
15. T

16. T
17. F
18. T

TEST 8

DIRECTIONS: Each question or incomplete statement is followed by several suggested answers or completions. Select the one that BEST answers the question or completes the statement. *PRINT THE LETTER OF THE CORRECT ANSWER IN THE SPACE AT THE RIGHT.*

1. A pilot was forced to land 525 miles from his destination after flying 3 hours. There was a 1½ hour delay. If the pilot is to arrive on schedule 6¾ hours after his original take-off, how fast must he fly?   1.____

2. What is the inside diameter of a tank when the outside diameter is 15 $1/16$ feet and the walls are 1 $3/8$ feet thick?   2.____

3. How many pipes 7 ¾ inches long can be cut from a pipe 3 feet long?   3.____

4. A storage room measures 15.6 feet by 10.2 feet, and another storage room measures 20.9 feet by 14.4 feet. Find the total storage area to the nearest tenth of a square foot.   4.____

5. Truck No. 1 is able to travel thirteen and eight-tenths miles on a gallon of gasoline, and its tank can hold eighteen and four-tenths gallons. Truck No. 2 is able to travel fourteen and three-tenths miles on a gallon of gasoline, and its tank can hold sixteen and nine-tenths gallons. Which truck is able to travel farther on a tank of gasoline? How much farther?   5.____

6. Floor tiles cost seventeen and three-tenths cents each. How much will 250 of them cost?   6.____

7. If the sale price of a television set after a 25% reduction is $187.50, what was the original price of the set?   7.____

8. John earns $280 per week. Several deductions are taken from his paycheck: 14% withholding tax, 3 $5/8$% Social Security, and 3% state tax. What is his take-home pay?   8.____

9. One rainy morning last month, 35% of the 460 employees of Zap Electronics were late for work. How many employees were on time?   9.____

2 (#8)

KEY (CORRECT ANSWERS)

1. 233 $\frac{1}{3}$ MPH

2. 12 $\frac{5}{16}$ feet inside diameter

3. 4 pieces of pipe

4. 460.1 sq.ft.

5. Truck No. 1
    12.25 miles farther

6. $43.25

7. $250.00

8. $222.25

9. 299 employees

CORRECTNESS AND EFFECTIVENESS OF EXPRESSION

This test consists of two parts, for which the total time is two hours. Part I is a test in spelling consisting of 20 items of the multiple-choice type. Each item contains four words, only one of which may or may not be misspelled. This is much the easier part of this test. The spelling question is presented as follows:

Four words are listed in each question. These are lettered A to D. The fifth option always reads *none misspelled.* The examinee is to select one of the five choices: one of the words if one of the words is misspelled, or item E, none misspelled, if all four words are correctly spelled in the question.

Following is the plan of this book to ensure maximum learning in the spelling area:

Ten (10) tests, closely following this format, appear in order of difficulty, each consisting of twenty (20) questions as will appear on the examination itself. These words have been carefully selected and constitute a representative sampling of what may be expected on the examination. Tests 9 and 10, while following the format, introduce novel elements of presentation and comprehension in the spelling area, as will be readily noted. If you can successfully answer Tests 9 and 10, you may consider yourself well prepared in this area, for these tests furnish an unusual degree of enrichment and extension in the spelling part.

Then follow a programmed text in the spelling area, including *spelling demons,* words presenting special difficulties, and, finally, twenty (20) more tests in spelling, consisting of ten questions each, each question consisting of five (5) items, the fifth choice being a fifth word, not the easier fifth option, *none misspelled.*

The directions for this part of the test are approximately as follows:

DIRECTIONS: Mark the space corresponding to the one MISSPELLED word in each of the following groups of words. If no word is misspelled, mark the last space.

The five (5) spelling choices are presented in columnar form, making it easy for the candidate to scan the lines and note each word. Two examples are presented for illustration:

Sample 1
A. length
B. strength
C. eighth
D. museum
E. none misspelled

Since none of the words is misspelled, E would be marked on the answer sheet.

Sample 2
A. tailor
B. magnitude
C. sergent
D. effectual
E. none misspelled

Since *sergeant* is misspelled, C would be marked on the answer sheet.

The directions listed above will, in general, govern or underlie the tests that follow.

Part II constitutes the heart of this test and consists of eighty (90) of the one hundred (100) questions in this area. This test is intended to measure the candidate's ability to write correctly and effectively. Several passages or *themes* are presented such as might have been written by a high school student. These compositions have been systematically corrupted to include many of the most common errors or faults to be found in writing of high school students. The candidate is to indicate, in accordance with the special directions, what corrections should be made in the selections. These corrections entail thought and decision as to the choice of words, uniformity, coherence, emphasis, sequences of tenses, redundancy, parallelism, capitalization, agreement of subject and verb, and sentence structure — the major phases of expressional writing.

The questions below illustrate some of the types of questions that are included in this test.

SAMPLE QUESTIONS AND ANSWERS

DIRECTIONS: In each of the sentences below, four portions are underlined and lettered. Read each sentence and decide whether any of the UNDERLINED parts contains an error in spelling, punctuation, or capitalization, or employs grammatical usage which would be inappropriate for carefully written English. If so, note the letter printed under the unacceptable form and blacken the space beneath the corresponding letter on your answer sheet. If all four of the underlined portions are acceptable as they stand, blacken the space labeled E. No sentence contains more than one unacceptable form.

Questions

1. <u>Like</u> it <u>says</u> in the editorial, war is <u>neither</u> inevitable nor <u>irrepressible</u>.
     A   B   C   D

2. In my <u>opinion</u>, the State Department is <u>more</u> important <u>than</u> <u>any</u> division of government.
          A   B   C   D

3. He <u>is</u> in Washington only two weeks and has <u>already</u> <u>seen</u> <u>nearly</u> all the sights.
       A   B   C   D

4. <u>Whom</u> do you believe <u>to be</u> the <u>best</u> tennis player now at the <u>College</u>?
     A   B   C   D

5. It <u>would be</u> very difficult to <u>ascertain</u> what it really is that makes the food <u>taste</u> so <u>peculiar</u>.
       A   B   C
      D

6. "It is <u>I,"</u> he sai<u>d</u>. <u>Where</u> did you come <u>from?"</u> I replied.
          A   B   C   D

50

7. By virtue of his office, he $\underset{A}{\underline{\text{supersedes}}}$ even those $\underset{B}{\underline{\text{courtiers}}}$ whose $\underset{C}{\underline{\text{geneology}}}$ and $\underset{D}{\underline{\text{lineage}}}$ are far more glittering than his.

8. $\underset{A}{\underline{\text{Let's}}}$ $\underset{B}{\underline{\text{you}}}$ and $\underset{C}{\underline{\text{I}}}$ $\underset{D}{\underline{\text{plan}}}$ next summer's vacation.

9. The $\underset{A}{\underline{\text{owner of the market}}}$ $\underset{B}{\underline{\text{with his assistant}}}$ $\underset{C}{\underline{\text{is}}}$ applying the most modern $\underset{D}{\underline{\text{principals}}}$ of merchandise display. D

10. The $\underset{A}{\underline{\text{freshman}}}$ who had transferred from $\underset{B}{\underline{\text{Duke}}}$ was the $\underset{C}{\underline{\text{heaviest}}}$ of all the $\underset{D}{\underline{\text{other}}}$ candidates for the football team.

Answers
1. A   (As)
2. D   (any other)
3. A   (has been)
4. D   (college)
5. E
6. C   ("Where)
7. C   (genealogy)
8. C   (me)
9. D   (principles)
10. D   (omit)

Following is the plan of this book to ensure maximum learning in the expressional area:

Twenty (20) tests are presented hereafter, paralleling and reflecting format, structure, contents, and quality of these questions actually appearing on the examination itself. In fact, inasmuch as the tests are presented in an order of difficulty and in a variety of forms fully transcending the levels and frames appearing on the examination, provision has been thus assured for enrichment and for self-instruction beyond average needs or requirements.

Tests 1 to 9 reflect closely the material to be encountered on the examination as these systematically follow the content, the format, and the style. Tests 10 and 11 go beyond the requirements of the examination itself and point up the power element of error recognition. Tests 12 to 16 carry the student one step

forward in the direction of error attribution. Tests 17 to 20 develop further the candidate's power to discern and evaluate whole sentences as correct or incorrect from the standpoint of correctness and effectiveness of expression through the use of a novel question form presented here for the first time.

Then follow a programmed text in correct usage, including common errors and additional tests in usage presented in varying formats; and an exhaustive guide to correct usage and effective expression.

The directions for this part of the test are approximately as follows:

DIRECTIONS: In the left-hand column below, certain portions of a story are numbered. In the right-hand column, several ways of writing each underlined portion are suggested. Mark the answer space corresponding to the way which you consider the best. Sometimes all are grammatically correct, but one way is more effective than the others. (No correct answer contains an error in grammar, diction, or punctuation, even if the character who is speaking might have made such an error.)

Concretely, the test presents each theme on the left-hand side of the page with certain words, phrases, and sentences underlined and lettered consecutively. On the right-hand side of the page appear several ways of revising each lettered portion. Now, in each exercise, the examinee is to select the one best or correct way of revising the defective theme, and thus restore it to its original form.

The directions listed above will, in general, govern or underlie the tests that follow.

EXAMINATION SECTION
TEST 1

DIRECTIONS: Each question or incomplete statement is followed by several suggested answers or completions. Select the one that BEST answers the question or completes the statement. *PRINT THE LETTER OF THE CORRECT ANSWER IN THE SPACE AT THE RIGHT.*

1. Which one of the following groups contains the names of people famous for their achievements in unrelated field of endeavor?

    A. Benjamin Lovejoy and Wendell Phillips
    B. Frances Wright and the Grimke Sisters
    C. George Goethals and Ferdinand DeLesseps
    D. Maxwell Anderson and Edward MacDowell
    E. Walter Reed and William Gorgas

2. Which one of the following problems did NOT accompany the *end* of the frontier in the United States?

    A. Growing sense of job insecurity among factory workers
    B. Need for a changed viewpoint in our economic thinking
    C. Rapid decline of interest in imperialistic enterprises
    D. Rapid rise of disease in large cities
    E. Recognition of the need for conservation of natural resources

3. Which one of the following economic policies is NOT consistent with the other four?

    A. Decrease of the rediscount rates by the Federal Reserve Banks
    B. Government appropriations under the European Recovery Program
    C. Increase in individual income taxes
    D. Increase in open-market buying operations by the Federal Reserve Banks
    E. Increase in time permitted for paying installment buying obligations

4. The principle of *unanimous consent* is illustrated in the

    A. decisions of the United States Supreme Court
    B. method of admitting new states to our Union
    C. procedures in the General Assembly of the United Nations
    D. provision for amending the Articles of Confederation
    E. vote of the House of Representatives in impeachment proceedings

5. In which one of the following groups are the terms NOT arranged in correct chronological order?

    A. Alien and Sedition Acts, Kentucky and Virginia Resolutions, Personal Liberty Laws
    B. Bland-Allison Act, Sherman Silver Purchase Act, Gold Standard Act
    C. Granger Laws, Wabash Railroad Case, Interstate Commerce Act
    D. Hawley-Smooth Tariff, Underwood Tariff, Payne-Aldrich Tariff
    E. Maximilian Affair, Venezuela Boundary Dispute, Venezuela Debt Dispute

6. Which one of the following was NOT true of both the League of Nations and the United States under the Articles of Confederation?

    A. Members might have several representatives, but only one vote.
    B. Membership was declined by some who were eligible.
    C. Membership was held by states, not by individuals.
    D. The power to collect taxes was lacking.
    E. The sovereignty of the states was retained.

7. A MAJOR cause for the decrease in farm exports from the United States immediately after World War I was that

    A. production in the United States declined
    B. competition with other agricultural nations increased
    C. domestic demands increased
    D. Europe quickly regained her economic self-sufficiency
    E. exports shifted to factory goods

8. Which one of the following statements regarding the periods after both World War I and World War II is TRUE?

    A. American investment bankers loaned huge sums to European countries to aid in recovery.
    B. Germany was forced to sign a peace treaty which weakened her whole economy.
    C. Heavy cash reparations were exacted from Germany.
    D. The Union of Soviet Socialist Republics took an active part in the postwar conferences.
    E. The exchange reserves in Europe were low.

9. Since 1900, which one of the following has been the MOST consistent trend in the United States?
A(n)

    A. *decline* in mortality rates
    B. *decline* in population
    C. *decrease* in emigration
    D. *increase* in mortality rates
    E. *increase* in the birth rate

10. An IMPORTANT argument for the United States Presidential Succession Act in 1947 was that

    A. conditions which caused the passage of the original act no longer applied
    B. the president of the Senate should succeed to the Presidency
    C. only an elected official should be the nation's chief executive
    D. there was no law providing for succession to the Presidency in case of the death of the Vice President
    E. it would make it possible for a President to resign by delivering his resignation to the office of the Secretary of State

11. An example of the use of an implied power by the Congress of the United States is the

    A. declaration of war in 1941
    B. adoption of the Gold Standard Act, 1900
    C. imposition of the present federal income tax
    D. repeal of the national prohibition amendment
    E. enactment of the Securities and Exchange Act, 1934

12. The Marshall proposal offered United States aid in the economic recovery of Europe if the European countries FIRST

    A. abolished discriminatory trade practices
    B. outlined a reconstruction program for Europe as a whole
    C. drew up a plan for a United States of Europe
    D. outlawed communism in their countries
    E. signed a pact guaranteeing civil liberties in each nation

13. A large deficit in a national budget is MOST likely to result in

    A. inflation
    B. deflation
    C. high interest rates
    D. low profits
    E. an unfavorable balance of trade

14. In the first half of the twentieth century, the BEST evidence of social mobility in the United States as a whole is found in the increase in the

    A. number of new millionaires from decade to decade
    B. average per capita income from decade to decade
    C. percentage of white collar workers whose fathers worked at blue collar industrial jobs
    D. percentage of agricultural workers who migrated to the cities

15. English colonization differed from Spanish and French colonization in that the English

    A. were the first to understand and act upon the economic potential of New World colonies
    B. came to the New World mainly as settlers rather than soldiers, missonaries, and trappers
    C. controlled vaster lands and large populations
    D. established better relations with the Indians and Blacks

16. Which of the following contributed MOST to the development of religious toleration in the British colonies? The

    A. stand of Roger Williams in defense of liberty of conscience
    B. Puritan guarantee of religious freedom to settlers in the Massachusetts Bay Colony
    C. common interest of each of the numerous sects in preventing domination by any of the others
    D. attitude of religious indifference that permeated the colonial aristocracy

17. The Preamble of the Declaration of Independence appeals to which of the following principles?   17.____

    A. Governments founded in popular consent
    B. Strict majoritarian rule
    C. The right of all men to protection of their property
    D. The right of all citizens to vote

18. The Federal Constitution EXPLICITLY authorized the   18.____

    A. creation of presidential nominating conventions
    B. power of federal courts to declare acts of Congress unconstitutional
    C. creation of the Cabinet
    D. power of Congress to regulate interstate commerce

19. The Bill of Rights explicitly provides for all of the following EXCEPT   19.____

    A. freedom of speech and of the press
    B. freedom of enterprise
    C. freedom of assembly and of petition
    D. the right of trial by jury

20. The aim of the Monroe Doctrine, as it was proclaimed in 1823, was to   20.____

    A. prevent the outbreak of democratic revolutions in Latin America
    B. guarantee preferential trading rights to the United States in Latin America
    C. secure a territorial outlet for American slavery in Latin America
    D. ensure that the United States, rather than Europe, would be the dominant power in the Western Hemisphere

21. All of the following characterized the Jacksonian Democrats EXCEPT   21.____

    A. hostility toward the institution of slavery
    B. support for freedom of economic opportunity
    C. opposition to special privilege and large business corporations
    D. opposition to internal improvements at federal expense

22. In the politics of the decade after the Civil War, the issue of slavery focused on whether   22.____

    A. racial equality should be the foremost national priority
    B. slavery should be permitted to exist in the territories
    C. slavery should be eliminated where it already existed in the states
    D. the foreign slave trade should be reopened

23. Republican policies toward the South during the post-Civil War Reconstruction Era can be described MOST accurately as   23.____

    A. aiming consistently to protect the interests of postwar big business at the expense of the newly freed slaves
    B. leading to unparalleled corruption among the entrenched carpetbagger governors and their allies in the Black dominated legislatures of the defeated states
    C. leading to significant but only partially implemented constitutional changes on the state level in the South and also on the national level
    D. leading to an effective program of land redistribution that gave to large numbers of newly freed slaves *forty acres and a mule*

Questions 24-25.

DIRECTIONS: Questions 24 through 25 are to be answered on the basis of the following business leaders:
  I. John D. Rockefeller
  II. Andrew Carnegie
  III. J. Pierpont Morgan
  IV. Henry Ford

24. Which business leader adapted the trust as a device for large-scale industrial organization?

 A. I B. II C. III D. IV

25. Which business leader mobilized the power of the banks to curb industrial competition and to facilitate corporate mergers and reorganizations?

 A. I B. II C. III D. IV

KEY (CORRECT ANSWERS)

1.	D	11.	E
2.	C	12.	B
3.	C	13.	A
4.	D	14.	C
5.	D	15.	B
6.	B	16.	C
7.	B	17.	A
8.	E	18.	D
9.	A	19.	B
10.	C	20.	D

21. A
22. B
23. C
24. A
25. C

TEST 2

DIRECTIONS: Each question or incomplete statement is followed by several suggested answers or completions. Select the one that BEST answers the question or completes the statement. *PRINT THE LETTER OF THE CORRECT ANSWER IN THE SPACE AT THE RIGHT.*

Question 1.

DIRECTIONS: Question 1 is to be answered on the basis of the following business leaders:

   I. John D. Rockefeller
   II. Andrew Carnegie
   III. J. Pierpont Morgan
   IV. Henry Ford

1. Which business leader pioneered in the mass production assembly line?   1.____
   A. I   B. II   C. III   D. IV

Questions 2-5.

DIRECTIONS: Questions 2 through 5 are to be answered on the basis of the following groups:

   I. Northern and Western Europeans (e.g., Germans and Irish)
   II. Southern and Eastern Europeans (e.g., Italians and Russians)
   III. African slaves
   IV. Mexicans

2. For which group were the peak years of entry into the United States 1700-1800?   2.____
   A. I   B. II   C. III   D. IV

3. For which group were the peak years of entry into the United States 1840-1880?   3.____
   A. I   B. II   C. III   D. IV

4. For which group were the peak years of entry into the United States 1885-1915?   4.____
   A. I   B. II   C. III   D. IV

5. For which group were the peak years of entry into the United States 1910-1930?   5.____
   A. I   B. II   C. III   D. IV

6. The defeat of the Versailles Treaty in the Senate after the First World War was due to the   6.____

   A. growing conviction in the United States that the Kellogg-Briand Pact outlawing war posed a better alternative for the future conduct of foreign affairs
   B. widespread view in the United States that proposed neutrality legislation to prohibit citizens from traveling on belligerent ships except at their own risk would suffice to keep the United States out of future European wars
   C. inability of President Wilson and his political opponents to reach a compromise on the issue of United States participation in the collective security arrangements of the League of Nations
   D. widespread view in the United States that the League of Nations had been tainted by its admission of the Soviet Union to membership

7. Which of the following BEST describes the domestic changes brought about by the New Deal?

   A. The enactment of a number of new economic regulations, joined with new relief and welfare measures
   B. A vast increase in governmental ownership of business
   C. A major redistribution of income and wealth in favor of the poorest segment of the population
   D. The restoration of a free market as a result of effective antitrust action

8. In the years immediately after the Second World War, the United States assumed

   A. the dominant role in an alliance of Western nations for the purpose of containing Soviet power
   B. its traditional policy of non-involvement in world affairs
   C. the burden of arming friendly democratic nations with atomic weapons
   D. the leadership of Third World countries seeking independence from their colonial rulers

9. Before the Supreme Court's decision in 1954 that racial segregation in the public schools was unconstitutional, the Court had

   A. refused to consider cases about racial segregation
   B. justified racial segregation in public facilities by the *separate-but-equal* doctrine
   C. been prevented from considering cases about racial segregation by Southern filibusters in Congress
   D. required desegregation of public facilities *with all deliberate speed,* but stopped short of ordering the President to enforce the decision

10. Even in areas where the right to vote was widespread, voters in the British colonies consistently returned a relatively small number of wealthy and prominent men to office. This indicates that

    A. the British government suppressed the idea of democracy in the colonies until just before the American Revolution
    B. the colonists generally did not regard deference to one's *betters* as being incompatible with political liberty
    C. the wealthy and prominent controlled the colonial electorate
    D. apathy was the prevailing characteristic of colonial politics

11. From 1763 to 1776, the CHIEF aim of colonial resistance to British policies was to

    A. bring about a long-suppressed social revolution against the colonial aristocracy
    B. achieve in America the ideals proclaimed in the French Revolution
    C. ensure that the colonists were represented in Parliament
    D. restore what the colonists perceived to be the rights of Englishmen

12. All of the following contributed to Great Britain's defeat in the American Revolution EXCEPT

    A. an initial tendency to underestimate the scope and intensity of the rebellion
    B. the rapid defection of loyalists to the patriot cause after the battle of Bunker Hill
    C. the indecisiveness of General Howe in exploiting colonial military weaknesses
    D. the French decisions to provide money, supplies, and military and diplomatic support to the colonists

13. The Articles of Confederation were MOST severely criticized in the 1780s for their lack of

    A. a plan for the admission of new states
    B. equal representation of the states in Congress
    C. a bill of rights
    D. a national taxing power

14. In the decade after the ratification of the Constitution, the American political party system developed from all of the following EXCEPT

    A. the belief of the founding fathers that a two-party system was crucial to the maintenance of a stable political order
    B. the conflict engendered by Secretary of the Treasury Alexander Hamilton's proposed economic policies
    C. the conflict engendered by the foreign policies of George Washington's administration in relation to Great Britain and France
    D. ideological differences between Hamilton and Thomas Jefferson over the nature of republican government

15. The feminist movement, which originated in the second quarter of the nineteenth century, succeeded in accomplishing all of the following before the Civil War EXCEPT

    A. broadening the right of married women to hold property in their own names
    B. gaining the right of women to vote in national elections
    C. expanding the opportunity for women to receive a college education
    D. improving the job opportunities for women in the teaching profession at the elementary level

16. The strategy of the Confederacy at the start of the Civil War was based on all of the following assumptions EXCEPT:

    A. Cutting the North in two by seizing Washington and thrusting northward into Maryland and Pennsylvania would force the North to sue for peace
    B. The dependence of Great Britain and France on Southern cotton would lead them to grant diplomatic recognition and give military aid to the Confederacy
    C. Arming the slaves would help the South to offset superior Northern manpower
    D. Southern control of the port of New Orleans would induce the states in the upper Mississippi Valley to join the Confederacy

17. Federal policy toward Indians between the 1880s and the 1930s was based MAINLY on the assumption that

    A. the Indians should be assimilated into white society
    B. Indian culture and tribal organization should be nurtured
    C. interference with Indian culture and tribal organization should not be permitted
    D. the Indians should be removed from their homeland areas and relocated in Indian Territory

18. The aim of the Open Door policy of 1900 was to

    A. guarantee American industry a supply of cheap labor from China
    B. protect American commercial interests against discrimination in China

C. establish China as a buffer against Russian and Japanese expansion
D. encourage the forces of liberalism in China to throw off the yoke of European domination

19. In the first decade of the twentieth century, Black leaders debated the issues of direct political action to obtain civil rights and the type of training or education Blacks should seek.
The CHIEF figures in these debates were

   A. Benjamin Banneker and Frederick Douglass
   B. Booker T. Washington and W.E.B. DuBois
   C. Marcus Garvey and Father Divine
   D. A. Philip Randolph and the Rev. Martin Luther King, Jr.

19.____

20. A MAJOR issue debated among progressives during the first two decades of the twentieth century was whether

   A. labor unions should be organized by craft or by industry
   B. the federal government should establish a social security system
   C. the federal government should permit the free coinage of silver
   D. the federal government should abolish economic monopolies or permit them to exist under regulation

20.____

21. Collective bargaining between labor and management became widespread in American industry AFTER

   A. the voluntary acquiescence of large industries that had suffered major strikes in the late nineteenth century
   B. a Supreme Court decision written by Justice Holmes in the early twentieth century
   C. legislation enacted during the administration of President Wilson before the First World War
   D. legislation enacted during the administration of President Franklin D. Roosevelt in the 1930s

21.____

22. President Harry S. Truman's decision to have the atomic bomb dropped on Japan was influenced by all of the following considerations EXCEPT the

   A. desire to counter Republican charges that the Democrats were the party of appeasement and defeat
   B. desire to avoid the large number of casualties that would occur in a United States invasion of Japan
   C. desire to prod the Soviet Union to be more cooperative as it began to formulate its postwar plans
   D. difficulty of devising a test demonstration of the atomic bomb that would unfailingly impress the Japanese government

22.____

23. The Korean and Vietnam Wars were similar in all of the following respects EXCEPT:

   A. Warnings were voiced by some respected military leaders against the United States becoming bogged down in a land war in Asia
   B. Domestic support of the war declined as the possibility of a quick and decisive United States military victory grew remote

23.____

C. United States troops were engaged against an essentially guerilla enemy force
D. The war remained limited rather than leading to war directly between, or among, the major powers

Question 24.
DIRECTIONS: Question 49 is to be answered on the basis of the following statement.

...3 saddlers, 3 hatters, 4 blacksmiths, 4 weavers, 6 boot and shoemakers, 8 carpenters, 3 tailors, 3 cabinet makers, 1 baker, 1 apothecary, and 2 wagon makers' shops–2 tanneries, 1 shop for making wool carding machines, 1 with a machine for spinning wool, 1 manufactory for spinning thread from flax, 1 nail factory, 2 wood carding machines. Within the distance of six miles from the town were–9 merchant mills, 2 grist mills, 12 saw mills, 1 paper mill with 2 vats, 1 wooden factory with 4 looms and 2 fulling mills.

24. The diversity of local manufacturing shown in the census above for a small town in Ohio in the early nineteenth century was characteristic of an area that had yet to

   A. adopt the system of rectangular land surveys and establish credit facilities for persons buying land at public auction
   B. make the transition from a barter to a cash economy
   C. accumulate as adequate supply of skilled labor to facilitate industrial growth
   D. be made accessible as a market for Eastern manufactures by the construction of canals and railroads through the Appalachian barrier

25. Presidential elections in the United States that had to be settled by the House of Representatives were those of

   A. 1876 and 1916   B. 1800 and 1900
   C. 1800 and 1916   D. 1800 and 1824

KEY (CORRECT ANSWERS)

1. D
2. C
3. A
4. B
5. D

6. C
7. A
8. A
9. B
10. B

11. D
12. B
13. D
14. A
15. B

16. C
17. A
18. B
19. B
20. D

21. D
22. A
23. C
24. D
25. D

EXAMINATION SECTION
TEST 1

DIRECTIONS: Each question or incomplete statement is followed by several suggested answers or completions. Select the one that BEST answers the question or completes the statement. *PRINT THE LETTER OF THE CORRECT ANSWER IN THE SPACE AT THE RIGHT.*

1. Which of the following statements is *true* of the Federal Constitution? It

    A. describes the powers of the states and leaves all other powers to the federal government
    B. outlines specifically the duties of both federal and state governments
    C. lists the broad powers of the federal government and leaves all other powers to the states or to the people
    D. describes in detail the powers of the federal government and says nothing about the states

    1.____

2. All of the following powers of the President are specifically enumerated in the Federal Constitution EXCEPT the power to

    A. command the military and naval forces
    B. make treaties with the approval of the Senate
    C. recognize new foreign governments
    D. convene special sessions of Congress

    2.____

3. The right to vote for federal officials is

    A. granted by Congress subject to constitutional restrictions
    B. assured by the Bill of Rights
    C. limited to persons who pay the poll tax
    D. determined by the states subject to the restrictions imposed by the Federal Constitution

    3.____

4. The principle of direct democracy is illustrated by all of the following EXCEPT the

    A. New England town meeting
    B. recall of judges
    C. initiative
    D. election of the President of the United States

    4.____

5. Which of these statements are TRUE of the system of checks and balances in our federal government?

    I. The Congress may override a Presidential veto by a two-thirds vote of both houses
    II. Appointments made by the President must be approved by both houses of Congress.
    III. The President chooses justices of the federal courts with the approval of the Supreme Court.
    IV. A two-thirds vote of the Supreme Court is required to declare a law *unconstitutional.*

    The CORRECT combination is:

    A. I *only*   B. I, II, IV   C. I, III   D. II, III

    5.____

6. Which of these statements are TRUE of the governments of both Great Britain and the United States?
    I. Members of the lower house of the legislative body are elected by universal suffrage.
    II. The recognized procedure for removing the chief executive from office is impeachment.
    III. The chief executive and members of the cabinet may introduce bills in the legislature.
    IV. Constitutionality of any law passed by the national legislature may be tested in court.
    The CORRECT combination is:

    A. I only	B. I, II	C. I, II, IV	D. I, III

7. For which of the following does the Constitution of the United States provide by name?
    I. Supreme Court
    II. District Courts
    III. Customs Court
    IV. A Court of Claims
    V. Circuit Courts of Appeals
    The CORRECT combination is:

    A. None of these	B. I
    C. I, II, V	D. I, III, IV

8. For which of the following has the original method of selection been changed by constitutional amendment?
    I. Members of the House of Representatives
    II. United States Senators
    III. Federal judges
    IV. Cabinet members
    V. Vice-President of the United States
    The CORRECT combination is:

    A. I, III, IV	B. II only	C. II, III, V	D. II, V

9. Which of the following statements are TRUE regarding American political parties?
    I. The Democrats consider George Washington the founder of their party.
    II. The Republican party of 1860 opposed a strong central government.
    III. The Populist party of the late 19th century represented business and financial interests
    IV. A split in the Republican party contributed to the election of Wilson in 1912.
    V. Third parties seldom win elections but exert considerable influence on major parties.
    The CORRECT combination is:

    A. I, III	B. I, V	C. II, IV	D. IV, V

10. Which of the following is a fundamental requirement for the realization of a workable system of world government?

A. Agreement on a method of atomic control
B. Reduction of armaments
C. Limitation of national sovereignty in certain fields
D. International control of waterways

11. The government of Canada resembles that of the United States in which of the following respects?

    A. The head of the government is elected directly by the people.
    B. It has the federal form of government.
    C. It is a republic.
    D. Elections are held at specified intervals.

12. Which of these quotations are from the Declaration of Independence?
    I. All men are created equal
    II. Congress shall make no law respecting an establishment of religion
    III. A government of the people, by the people, for the people
    IV. Governments are instituted among men, deriving their just powers from the consent of the governed

    The CORRECT combination is:

    A. I, II, III   B. I, III   C. I, III, IV   D. I, IV

13. By which of the following may powers granted by the Constitution be extended?
    I. Federal legislation
    II. Custom
    III. Court interpretations
    IV. Formal amendment

    The CORRECT combination is:

    A. I, II, IV   B. I, III   C. I, IV   D. All of these

14. Within its borders a state controls all of the following EXCEPT

    A. qualifications for voting
    B. chartering of corporations
    C. naturalization of aliens
    D. the insruance business

15. The Federal Government was empowered to regulate interstate and foreign commerce by a(n)

    A. law passed by Congress
    B. provision in the Federal Constitution
    C. compromise between Hamilton and Jefferson
    D. amendment to the Federal Constitution

16. Which of the following has had the effect of strengthening the system of checks and balances in the national government?

    A. National political parties
    B. The power of judicial review
    C. The popular election of United States senators
    D. Federal grants-in-aid

17. The MOST effective power of the United States Congress in influencing executive action in foreign policy making is its

   A. role in the treaty-making process
   B. exclusive authority to declare war
   C. control over the appropriations process
   D. role in confirming presidential appointments

18. Which of the following statements concerning executives in the Federal Government of the United States is correct?

   A. Political executives, appointed by the President or by heads of agencies, tend to have common backgrounds and work experiences.
   B. While the President has had little success in coordinating and directing the work of the executive branch, the department heads have successfully overcome the preference of their bureaus and divisions for operating autonomy.
   C. Normally, Congress has clearly defined the objectives of various administrative programs and so has reduced the range and degree of discretion exercised by executives.
   D. Heads of agencies and their political assistants rarely have complete control over their programs partly because other agencies with related and perhaps conflicting interests must be consulted.

19. Which of the following expressions BEST applies to the Federal Constitution as it was first adopted? A(n)

   A. almost unanimously accepted plan
   B. slight revision of the Articles of Confederation
   C. series of compromises that satisfied no one of its signers completely
   D. well defined idea of one man which, after a hard fight, was adopted as originally outlined

20. Some of the BEST arguments for the ratification of the Federal Constitution are found in

   A. THE FEDERALIST by Alexander Hamilton, James Madison and John Jay
   B. COMMON SENSE by Thomas Paine
   C. LETTERS OF A FARMER IN PENNSYLVANIA by John Dickinson
   D. George Washington's Farewell Address

KEY (CORRECT ANSWERS)

1. C	6. A	11. B	16. B
2. C	7. B	12. D	17. C
3. D	8. D	13. D	18. D
4. D	9. D	14. C	19. C
5. A	10. C	15. B	20. A

TEST 2

DIRECTIONS: Each question or incomplete statement is followed by several suggested answers or completions. Select the one that BEST answers the question or completes the statement. PRINT THE LETTER OF THE CORRECT ANSWER IN THE SPACE AT THE RIGHT.

1. The modern Republican Party was formed from an alliance of 1.____

    A. Northern Whigs, Free Soilers, and Democratic opponents of the Kansas-Nebraska Act
    B. Southern Whigs, members of the Liberty Party, and Free Soilers
    C. Know-Nothings, Free Soilers, and Populists
    D. Democratic opponents of the Kansas-Nebraska Act, members of the Constitutional Union Party, and Free Soilers

2. Of the following, which one advocated a course of action by the federal government regarding secession which was different from that advocated by the other three? 2.____

    A. Wendell Phillips   B. Abraham Lincoln
    C. Horace Greeley   D. Jefferson Davis

3. Which one of the following is TRUE of federal regulatory commissions? 3.____

    A. Presidential appointment may be made without the consent of the Senate.
    B. Decisions of regulatory agencies are subject to review by the courts.
    C. The president may remove a commissioner from office at any time.
    D. The president has a free choice to appoint members of his own party whenever a vacancy occurs.

4. The American and British systems of government are similar in that they 4.____

    A. provide for separation of powers between executive and legislative branches
    B. provide for nonpartisan Speakers of the House in the lower house of their legislatures
    C. provide for the separation of church and state
    D. require that tax bills originate in the lower house of the legislature

5. Power within the organizational structure of the Democratic and Republican parties rests PRIMARILY with 5.____

    A. the national chairmen   B. the national committee
    C. local political bosses   D. local party units

6. The importance of the principle of *police powers* lies in the fact that it 6.____

    A. weakens the powers of the States
    B. applies solely to the federal government
    C. recognizes public welfare, health and morals as areas of state legislative activity
    D. increases the powers of the executive branch of the government at the expense of the legislative

7. The Speaker of the House of Representatives exercises great influence over legislation as a result of his 7.____

A. authority to name the personnel of all standing committees
B. membership on the Rules Committee
C. right to refuse to recognize a member seeking the floor
D. control of the legislative schedule

8. In which one of the following ways can the United States constitution be amended? A proposal by

   A. a majority of Congress and ratification by a majority of the state legislatures
   B. 2/3 of Congress and ratification by 3/4 of the states in convention
   C. a majority of the state legislatures and ratification by 3/4 of the state legislatures
   D. a convention called at the request of the majority of the state legislatures and ratification by 3/4 of the state legislatures

9. A student report on the Camp David Summit Conference on Egyptian-Israeli relations should refer to all of the following EXCEPT an agreement to

   A. set up a Palestinian State
   B. sign an Egyptian-Israeli Peace Treaty in the near future
   C. return the Sinai Desert region to Egypt
   D. decide within 5 years the fate of Palestinians living in the West Bank

10. To which section of the United States Constitution would a segregationist turn for support?

    A. Full faith and credit clause
    B. Due process clause
    C. Reserved powers clause
    D. Delegated powers clause

11. The purpose of the Committee of the Whole in Congress is to

    A. obtain a full House to consider a bill
    B. expedite debate and legislative action
    C. provide a roll call
    D. bind the House to House-Senate conference decisions

12. The Speaker of the House of Representatives was stripped of the power to appoint the Rules Committee during the incumbency of

    A. John Nance Garner
    B. Thomas B. Reed
    C. Joseph G. Cannon
    D. Champ Clark

13. The control of the activities of the Central Intelligence Agency is the responsibility of

    A. a permanent congressional watchdog committee
    B. the executive branch of government
    C. the joint chiefs of staff
    D. the Senate Foreign Affairs Committee

14. Which one of the following can be regarded as a protagonist of a government based on checks and balances, designed for the protection of liberty?

    A. James Harrington
    B. Gaetano Mosca
    C. Thomas Hobbes
    D. Vilfredo Pareto

15. The Speaker of the New York State Assembly has the

    A. power to appoint all employees and committees of the Assembly
    B. right to serve as ex-officio member of the Rules Committee
    C. right to serve as the subordinate of the Majority Leader
    D. power to serve only as moderator of the Assembly

16. Which one of the following correctly describes the power common to the President of the United States and to the Governor?

    A. Each has the right to deliver an inaugural message on the condition of the Union and of the State respectively.
    B. Neither has the power to veto single items of appropriation bills.
    C. Each has the power to appoint all department heads.
    D. Each has the power to appoint judges to the highest court of their respective jurisdictions.

17. Congress may check the President in his appointive powers through the

    A. use of the filibuster
    B. practice of senatorial courtesy
    C. caucus
    D. seniority rule

18. The Boxer Protocol of 1901, the Atlantic Charter, and the *destroyer-bases* agreement are examples of

    A. treaties of the United States
    B. joint resolutions
    C. reciprocal agreements
    D. executive agreements

19. In which one of the following parts of the Constitution of the United States are express limitations on the powers of Congress found?

    A. Article I, section 10
    B. the 1st Amendment
    C. the 10th Amendment
    D. Article I, section 8

20. On which of the following postulates is the doctrine of nullification based?
    A. The people of the United States created the Constitution.
    B. Nullification is implied in the reserved powers.
    C. The sovereignty of the states is indestructible.
    D. The sovereignty of the states is unimpaired by the adoption of the Constitution
    The *CORRECT* combination is:

    A. abd   B. bcd   C. cd   D. bc

21. A reading of the 15th, 19th, and 24th amendments would lead one to the conclusion that

    A. all citizens have the right to vote under state law.
    B. Congress may not impose voting procedures on the states.
    C. the states may regulate voting qualifications, subject to certain limitations
    D. Congress and the states jointly determine voting procedures

22. The 25th amendment to the Federal Constitution provides

    A. that the President be limited to two full terms
    B. for the filling of a vacancy in the office of Vice President

C. for the reform of the Electoral College
D. that Congress initiate action in case of possible Presidential disability

23. Which one of the following would be required in order that the President have the power of vetoing specific items in Congressional legislation? The

   A. passing of a bill granting him this authority in perpetuity
   B. proposal of a constitutional amendment to this effect
   C. adoption of a concurrent resolution granting its approval
   D. repealing of existing legislation denying him this right

23.____

24. Which of the following statements are TRUE with respect to the amending process of the Constitution?
   A. States may ratify an amendment even after prior refusal to do so.
   B. The President may veto a constitutional amendment.
   C. The Supreme Court may declare an amendment unconstitutional.
   D. Congress may fix a time limit within which an amendement may be ratified.
   E. Congress may select one of two methods of ratification stipulated in the Constitution.

   The CORRECT combination is.

   A. acd   B. ade   C. bde   D. abc

24.____

25. The MAJOR factor in changing the character of the electoral college from a deliberative body to its present status of a *rubber stamp* was

   A. public opinion following the Hayes-Tilden election results
   B. the transfer from the state legislatures to the voters of the right to select the electors
   C. the rise of political parties on the American scene
   D. the change in electoral college procedures as a result of the 12th Amendment

25.____

KEY (CORRECT ANSWERS)

1.	A	11.	B
2.	B	12.	C
3.	B	13.	B
4.	D	14.	A
5.	D	15.	A
6.	C	16.	A
7.	C	17.	B
8.	B	18.	D
9.	A	19.	B
10.	C	20.	C

21. C
22. B
23. B
24. B
25. C

TEST 3

DIRECTIONS: Each question or incomplete statement is followed by several suggested answers or completions. Select the one that *BEST* answers the question or completes the statement. *PRINT THE LETTER OF THE CORRECT ANSWER IN THE SPACE AT THE RIGHT.*

1. The New York State Court of Appeals differs from the United States Supreme Court in that the New York Court

   A. does not have appellate jurisdiction
   B. cannot rule on constitutional issues
   C. does not have original jurisdiction
   D. may retry cases to permit introduction of new evidence

   1.____

2. Which one of the following is true of the House of Representatives and the President of the United States Senate?

   A. Both are selected by party caucuses.
   B. Both may appoint members of standing committees.
   C. Unlike the Speaker of the House, the President of the Senate need not be a member of the majority party.
   D. Unlike the President of the Senate, the Speaker of the House is not permitted to vote on propositions before the House except in the case of a tie.

   2.____

3. Which of the following are some of the powers of a Congressional standing committee chairman?
   A. He may call meetings at his pleasure.
   B. He may override the vote of the committee on any measure.
   C. He always directs floor debate on any measure reported out of his committee.
   D. He has great freedom in the preparation of the committee's agenda.
   The *CORRECT* combination is:

   A. acd   B. ade   C. bde   D. abc

   3.____

4. The Disability Amendment (25th) to the U.S. Constitution provides that

   A. the Speaker of the House becomes Acting President in the event of Presidential disability
   B. the Vice President becomes Acting President on a finding of Presidential disability by the Surgeon General and the Supreme Court
   C. a special Presidential election be held if the Vice President and a majority of the cabinet declare the President disabled
   D. the Vice President becomes Acting President if the President declares his disability in writing

   4.____

5. The term that BEST characterizes the foreign policy of the United States since World War II is

   A. appeasement   B. isolationism
   C. containment   D. non-intervention

   5.____

6. Which one of the following references to the members of the House of Representatives appears in the Constitution?

   6.____

A. Representatives are to be chosen by those persons of the respective states who are qualified to vote for the members of the most numerous branch of their state legislatures.
B. Representatives must be residents of the Congressional district that they represent.
C. The Governor of the state may appoint representatives to fill vacancies until the next regular election occurs, or until a special election is held.
D. Representatives must have resided in their respective states for at least seven years to be eligible to run for Congress.

7. A restriction on the right of unlimited debate in the United States Senate is the requirement that

   A. discussion be germane to the motion before the Senate
   B. the presiding officer assign one hour maximum time for each speaker
   C. a vote of two-thirds of the Senators present is needed to approve a cloture petition
   D. a simple majority of the Senators present must approve a cloture petition

8. By establishing a system of checks and balances, the framers of the federal Constitution sought to

   A. prevent the usurpation of power by any branch of the government
   B. prevent the federal government from infringing on the power and authority of the States
   C. strengthen the power of the executive branch
   D. limit the powers of the States

9. The clause . . . *the House of Representatives shall choose immediately, by ballot, the President* was the constitutional basis for the election to the Presidency of

   A. John Qunicy Adams   B. Andrew Jackson
   C. James K.Polk   D. Martin Van Buren

10. In the House of Representatives, the majority party whip functions as

    A. a liaison officer to the Senate
    B. an aide to the majority floor leader
    C. chairman of the House Rules Committee
    D. the chief formulator of party policy

11. As a result of the twenty-third amendment to the United States Constitution,

    A. Hawaii and Alaska were permitted to vote in the 1964 Presidential election
    B. the District of Columbia casts three electoral votes for the Presidency
    C. a guarantee for equal free broadcast time for Presidential candidates was provided
    D. the number of representatives in the House of Representatives was increased

12. Delegates to national presidential nominating conventions are selected by

    A. direct primary in each state
    B. the party committees of each state
    C. members of the state legislatures
    D. a variety of methods in different states

13. Under the United States Constitution, the decision to permit eighteen-year-olds to vote can be made by

    A. constitutional amendment only
    B. act of Congress
    C. Presidential executive order
    D. each state individually

14. Which is common to both the federal government and any state government?

    A. Right to an item-veto over appropriations bill by the Chief Executive
    B. A bicameral legislature
    C. An elected Attorney General
    D. An appointed Supreme Court

15. The historical origin for the provision requiring the House of Representatives to initiate money bills stems from the colonial practice in which the

    A. governor usurped the tax power
    B. assembly made annual appropriations of money
    C. upper house imposed taxes and made fiscal appropriations
    D. assembly passed permanent revenue laws

16. According to Amendment XXV to the United States Constitution,

    A. the Speaker of the House of Representatives assumes the office of President upon the death or resignation of the President and Vice-President
    B. the Secretary of State assumes the office of President upon the death or resignation of the President and Vice-President
    C. the office of the Vice-President remains vacant until the next election if the Vice-President should die or resign
    D. the President nominates a Vice-President, whenever there is a vacancy, who then takes office if confirmed by a majority of both houses of Congress

17. The local City Council differs from the U.S. Congress in that

    A. the Council does not use the committee system
    B. the Council requires a two-thirds vote when overriding an executive veto
    C. the Council may not increase budget items whereas Congress may
    D. Council members may hold other government offices while serving as legislators

18. The legislative power of Illinois State's Governor differs from the legislative powers of the United States' President in the following way:

    A. Illinois State executive departments have the right to submit bills to the legislature.
    B. The Governor's annual message to the legislature lacks the specific recommendations of the President's State of the Union message.
    C. Only the Governor has a *pocket veto*.
    D. The Governor may veto specific items of a budget bill.

19. All of the following are Congressional checks on administrative departments and boards EXCEPT the 19.____

    A. supervision of the General Accounting Office headed by the Comptroller General
    B. questioning of department heads on the floor of Congress
    C. investigations by Congressional committees
    D. approval or disapproval of items in the President's budget

20. Which one of the following is TRUE of the President's appointive power? 20.____

    A. All Presidential appointments require the approval of the Senate.
    B. The President has the power to remove appointed officials whose duties are purely executive.
    C. The President is expected to consult the senators of the opposition party of the state in which the position is to be filled.
    D. The Constitution clearly draws the line between *superior officers* which require Senate approval and *inferior officers* which do not.

KEY (CORRECT ANSWERS)

1. C	6. A	11. B	16. D
2. C	7. C	12. D	17. C
3. D	8. A	13. D	18. D
4. D	9. A	14. B	19. B
5. C	10. B	15. B	20. B

TEST 4

DIRECTIONS: Each question or incomplete statement is followed by several suggested answers or completions. Select the one that *BEST* answers the question or completes the statement. *PRINT THE LETTER OF THE CORRECT ANSWER IN THE SPACE AT THE RIGHT.*

1. The rejection of Robert Bork's nomination to the Supreme Court resulted in the nomination and confirmation of

   A. Antonin Scalia
   B. Anthony M. Kennedy
   C. Learned Hand
   D. William Rehnquist

   1.____

2. Which one of the following is a power that Congress can exercise in its relations with the federal judiciary?

   A. Determine the original jurisdiction of the Supreme Court
   B. Obtain advisory opinions from the Supreme Court regarding the constitutionality of laws
   C. Reduce the salaries of incumbent judges during their term of office
   D. Determine the size of the Supreme Court

   2.____

3. The number and types of cases which the Supreme Court decides on appeal from the lower courts are, in general,

   A. all cases in which murder is involved
   B. limited by the discretion of the Supreme Court itself
   C. those in which the lower courts have given majority and minority decisions
   D. all cases in which an appeal is made from a lower court decision

   3.____

4. Under which of the following circumstances would a writ of mandamus be applicable?

   A. To require the presence of a witness in court
   B. To require the presence of a prisoner in court
   C. To require the Board of Elections to include a name on the ballot
   D. To require a homeowner to correct a dangerous building violation

   4.____

5. The term obiter dictum, as applied to a judicial decision, refers to

   A. statements tangential to the main issue, but binding on the parties to the suit
   B. a dissenting opinion
   C. statements of a general principle to be followed in future decisions
   D. observations by the judge but not a part of the decision proper

   5.____

6. Which one of the following is TRUE about a Congressional investigatory committee?

   A. It cannot investigate administrative agencies.
   B. Its powers are derived from the *necessary and proper clause* in order to enact more effective laws.
   C. It is created by executive order of the president.
   D. Its power to subpoena private persons to appear before it has been declared unconstitutional.

   6.____

7. An important power of the president that is *implied* rather than specifically granted in the Constitution is the power to

    A. receive foreign ambassadors and ministers
    B. head the military forces as commander-in-chief
    C. make executive agreements
    D. initiate and negotiate treaties

8. An illustration of the use of an *implied* power by Congress is the

    A. passage of the Landrum-Griffin Act (Labor-Management Reporting and Disclosure Act), 1959
    B. granting of statehood to Alaska, 1958
    C. lowering of the excise taxes on liquor, etc.
    D. enactment of the Patent Reform Act of 1967

9. Which one of the following committees in the House of Representatives is empowered to determine the order in which bills will be voted on by the House?

    A. Ways and Means
    B. House Administration
    C. Government Operations
    D. Rules

10. A power exercised solely by the House of Representatives and not by the Senate is the

    A. proposing of amendments to the Constitution
    B. impeaching of civil officers of the United States government
    C. admission of new states into the union
    D. approval of judicial appointments of the president

11. An example of the *unwritten constitution* as it relates to the Congress of the United States is that

    A. appropriation bills must originate in the House of Representatives
    B. senatorial courtesy can be invoked in cases of presidential appointments
    C. the Senate shall have the sole power to ratify a treaty
    D. the Vice President shall be the presiding officer of the Senate

12. All of the following items are enumerated in the original Constitution of the United States EXCEPT

    A. treason, naturalization, bills of attainder
    B. creation of inferior courts, admission of new states, report on the State of the Union
    C. political parties, senatorial courtesy, congressional committees
    D. appointment of public officials, convening Congress, calling out the militia

13. Cases involving patent and copyright laws are tried in

    A. federal courts only
    B. state courts only
    C. either federal or state courts
    D. the Court of Claims only

14. *Pork barrel* legislation has traditionally been MOST closely related to

A. appropriations for rivers and improvements of harbors
B. enactment of agricultural relief measures
C. appropriations for welfare and relief to individual states
D. unrestricted funds allotted to the executive departments

15. The right of members of Congress to be privileged from arrest for anything said orally or in writing before Congressional committees or on the floor of Congress is derived from

    A. the full-faith-and-credit clause of Article IV
    B. the right of each house to judge the conduct of its membership, Article I, Section 5
    C. the immunity clause of Article I, Section 6
    D. the right of each house to determine the rules of its proceedings, Article I, Section 5

16. A MAJOR purpose of a *rider* in legislative action by the House of Representatives or Senate is to

    A. force a bill out of committee
    B. obtain the passage of a bill likely to be vetoed if submitted alone
    C. get a roll call vote of the membership on the measure
    D. set limitation of debate by the membership on the bill

17. The grant-in-aid given by Congress to states is based on all of the following EXCEPT the

    A. assumption that some state activities are matters of *general welfare*
    B. response to public pressures in providing Federal funds to aid in financing state functions
    C. fact that the Federal government's revenue resources are enormous compared with those of the states
    D. general welfare provison of the Constitution which provides for sharing of Federal revenues

18. Which one of the following would be required in order to construct a road through the State forest preserve?

    A. Approval of the Governor
    B. Approval of the Commissioner of Conservation
    C. A law passed by the State Legislature
    D. An amendment to the State Constitution

19. Which one of the following is NOT correct about the Electoral College?

    A. Each state has as many electors as it has senators and representatives.
    B. In a state in which the Republican votes for President are in the majority, all the electors will be of that party.
    C. Electors in each state are chosen by the people.
    D. Electors in all states are legally bound to vote for the candidate who carried their state.

20. While committee assignments in both houses of Congress are confirmed by the members of these bodies, the actual committee assignments are drawn up by the

   A. presiding officer in each House
   B. party committee in each House
   C. senior members of each House
   D. majority and minority leaders in each House

21. The Supreme Court of the United States has by precedent refused to

   A. hear a case where a state is sued by an individual
   B. try cases started in the highest state courts
   C. render declaratory judgements unless asked by a regulatory agency
   D. give to the President or to Congress advisory opinions

22. The following power is specifically granted to the Federal government by the Constitution of the United States:

   A. Issuance of franchises to public utilities
   B. Regulation of bankruptcy
   C. Regulation of internal waterways
   D. Chartering of banks

23. Which one of the following cases must go directly to the Supreme Court?

   A. An alleged kidnapper takes his victim from New York to Florida.
   B. A corporation challenges the constitutionality of a federal regulatory law.
   C. Arizona brings suit against Nevada regarding the use of the waters of the Colorado River.
   D. A citizen of New Jersey sues the State of Alabama because of the violation of his civil rights under the 14th Amendment.

24. Which one of the following is NOT a function of the Treasury Department?

   A. The collection of national revenue
   B. The control of narcotics
   C. The preparation of the budget
   D. The operation of the Coast Guard in peace time

25. Which one of the following may NOT be removed from office by impeachment?

   A. The Chief Justice of the United States Supreme Court
   B. The Secretary of State of the United States
   C. The Vice President of the United States
   D. A member of the United States Senate

KEY (CORRECT ANSWERS)

1.	B	11.	B
2.	D	12.	C
3.	B	13.	A
4.	C	14.	A
5.	D	15.	C
6.	B	16.	B
7.	C	17.	D
8.	A	18.	D
9.	D	19.	D
10.	B	20.	B

21. D
22. B
23. C
24. C
25. D

EXAMINATION SECTION
TEST 1

DIRECTIONS: Each question or incomplete statement is followed by several suggested answers or completions. Select the one that BEST answers the question or completes the statement. *PRINT THE LETTER OF THE CORRECT ANSWER IN THE SPACE AT THE RIGHT.*

Questions 1-8.

DIRECTIONS: Questions 1-8 refer to the passage that follows. Base your choice on the info mation given in the selection and on your own understanding of science.

Whenever micro-organisms have successfully invaded the body and are growing at the expense of the tissues, the process is called an infection. The term *infection* should always imply the existence of an abnormal state or unnatural condition resulting from the harmful action of micro-organisms. In other words, the simple presence of an organism is not sufficient to cause disease. .

Infection may arise from the admission of microorganisms to the tissues through the gastrointestinal tract, through the upper air passages, through wounds made by contaminated teeth or claws of animals or by contaminated weapons, and by the bite of suctorial insects. Another type of infection sometimes occurs when for some reason the body has become vulnerable to the pathogenic action of bacteria whose normal habitat is the body.

The reaction of the body to the attack of an invading organism results in the formation of substances of a specific nature. Those reaction bodies which circulate mainly in the blood serum are known as antibodies and are classified according to their activity. Some known as antitoxins, neutralize poisonous substances produced by the infecting organism. Others, called bacteriolysins, destroy bacteria by dissolving them. Opsonins or bacteriotropins prepare the bacteria for destruction by phagocytes, while precipitins and agglutinins have the property of grouping the invading agents into small clumps or precipitates. The formation of defensive substances is specific for each organism.

1. The passage states "the formation of defensive substances is specific for each organism." This implies that

    A. organisms inherit the ability to produce antibodies
    B. only specific organisms can produce antibodies
    C. the same organism cannot cause the production of two kinds of antibodies
    D. diphtheria antitoxin will not neutralize tetanus toxin
    E. only specific microorganisms can cause the production of antibodies in the human body

1.____

2. The passage you have read defines the term *infection*. In the light of what it says, which of the following conditions would illustrate an infection?

    A. A guinea pig is injected with diphtheria toxin. It becomes very ill and dies.
    B. A nurse taking care of a tubercular patient inhales some tuberculosis bacilli.
    C. A man cuts his finger with a dirty knife. He uses no antiseptic.

2.____

D. A student examines his saliva with a microscope. Under high power he observes some streptococci.
E. An anopheles mosquito bites a healthy soldier. Some time thereafter, the soldier experiences alternate periods of chin and fever.

3. Phagocytes are mentioned in the last paragraph of the passage. Of the following, the statement that is TRUE of phagocytes is:

   A. All white corpuscles are phagocytes.
   B. Some white corpuscles are phagocytes.
   C. Phagocytes are always red corpuscles.
   D. Phagocytes are usually platelets.
   E. Parasitic amebas are phagocytes.

3.____

4. In their control of infection the phagocytes are aided by

   A. enzymes   B. insulin   C. fibrinogen   D. lipids
   E. lymph glands

4.____

5. The passage mentions several ways in which germs may enter the body. One of those mentioned is by way of the gastrointestinal tract. A disease that enters in this way is

   A. beriberi   B. typhoid   C. typhus
   D. yellow fever   E. cancer of the stomach

5.____

6. With which of the following statements would the author of the passage agree?

   A. The white blood corpuscles help ward off infection by distributing antibodies to all parts of the body.
   B. A disease organism may live in the body of a person without having any bad effect on the person.
   C. Antibodies are classified according to the type of organism they attack.
   D. Infection is usually accompanied by swelling and the formation of pus.
   E. Antitoxins are formed against every organism which enters the body.

6.____

7. A child comes down with diphtheria. His brother, who has never had diphtheria and has never been immunized against it, should receive

   A. the Shick test
   B. injections of diphtheria toxin
   C. injections of diphtheria antitoxin
   D. injections of diphtheria toxoid
   E. nothing, as any treatment would be ineffective

7.____

8. Not long ago a child in a large city died of diphtheria. The following opinions were expressed by different people when they read about this. Which opinion is in best keeping with modern medical knowledge and practice?

   A. In the struggle for existence the weak die off. Therefore, the death of this child is of advantage to society because the child was probably a weakling.
   B. Diphtheria is a disease of childhood and some children must die of it.
   C. In a large city some deaths from diphtheria must be expected despite all precautions.

8.____

D. This death was unnecessary. The child could have been saved if the proper medical care had been provided while the child was ill.
E. No child should sicken with diphtheria, much less die of it. Where children still die of diphtheria, either the parents are ignorant of the fact that it is preventable or they are negligent of the welfare of their children.

9. Accidents in the home occur MOST frequently from

   A. burns B. falls C. firearms D. poisons
   E. suffocation

10. When a motor car is going 20 miles per hour, its brakes can stop it in 40 feet. When the same car is going 40 miles per hour, its brakes ought to stop it in about

    A. 40 ft. B. 80 ft. C. 160 ft. D. 200 ft.
    E. 240 ft.

11. Emotional stability is a characteristic of mental health that is MOST important to

    A. clearness of complexion
    B. digestion
    C. muscle tone
    D. resistance to infectious disease
    E. respiration

12. Anne and Margaret went to a restaurant for lunch. Anne had a cup of consomm?, four saltines, a square of butter, a serving of plain jello and a gingersnap. Margaret had a cup of tomato soup, two slices of buttered toast, a glass of milk and a baked apple. Comparison of their lunches indicated that

    A. Margaret's lunch was a poorer source of calcium than Anne's
    B. Margaret's lunch was a poorer source of vitamin C
    C. Anne's lunch was higher in caloric value than Margaret's
    D. Anne's lunch was a better source of iron than Margaret's
    E. Anne's lunch was a poorer source of vitamin A

13. A family consists of father, mother and three children aged fifteen, thirteen and five. The MINIMUM amount of milk the family should buy per week is

    A. 7 quarts B. 14 quarts C. 21 quarts
    D. 28 quarts E. 35 quarts

14. In buying citrus fruit for juice it is MOST economical to select the fruit

    A. with thick skins B. heavy for their size
    C. extra large in size D. small in size
    E. with most highly colored skins

15. In selecting eggs for the family, it is BEST to buy those that

    A. are fertile B. are whitest in color
    C. seem light in the hand D. have smooth, shiny shells
    E. have rough, dull shells

16. In caring for plastics (such as bakelite), it is important to know that

    A. an abrasive is a good cleanser for them
    B. they can be subjected to high temperatures
    C. they are resistant to water and most chemicals
    D. they are molded
    E. their colors are apt to fade

17. Which of the following circuits could you wire from this diagram?

    A. code oscillator   B. doorbell system
    C. electric chime   D. radio receiving set
    E. electric train signal

18. Which process does the illustration represent?

    A. heading a rivet   B. flattening a bolt
    C. setting a nail   D. clinching a nail
    E. forming the head of a screw

19. Which drawing illustrates a wired edge in sheet metal work?

    A.   B.   C.   D.   E.

20. Which symbol represents an electrical ground connection?

    A.   B.   C.   D.   E.

21. With what kind of saw should the type of curve illustrated below be cut?

    A. back saw   B. coping saw   C. dovetail saw
    D. key-hole saw   E. rip saw

22. In squaring up a piece of rough lumber, which of the surfaces indicated would you plane first?   22._____

23. Which diagram illustrates the CORRECT method of determining the position of a circle?   23._____

   A.   B.   C.   D.   E.

24. All of the following are drawing instruments EXCEPT   24._____

   A. T-square   B. compass   C. triangle
   D. scale rule   E. plumb bob

25. The instrument used to regulate the temperature of a refrigerator is a   25._____

   A. thermocouple   B. thermograph
   C. thermometer   D. thermoscope
   E. thermostat

26. The source from which MOST electromagnetic waves radiate is   26._____

   A. electromagnets   B. power plants   C. the spectrum
   D. the sun   E. uranium 235

27. If the bulb of a glass thermometer is plunged into hot water, the mercury first falls before rising because the   27._____

   A. air above the mercury expands
   B. mercury contracts from the shock
   C. glass expands faster than the mercury
   D. mercury has a negative coefficient of expansion
   E. expanding glass absorbs heat from the mercury

28. A Diesel engine operates without   28._____

   A. a crankshaft   B. a cooling system
   C. an ignition coil   D. a flywheel
   E. pistons

29. Electric clocks commonly used in homes rarely need setting because they   29._____

   A. are well regulated at the factory
   B. keep in step with carefully regulated generators
   C. are manufactured with such fine tolerances
   D. contain ingenious governors
   E. are kept wound by small motors

30. The fuse in a household wiring circuit is a metal with a high

   A. capacity
   B. combustion point
   C. coefficient of expansion
   D. melting point.
   E. resistance

31. The area of a regular-size postage stamp is about

   A. 8 square millimeters
   B. 1 square centimeter
   C. 5 square centimeters
   D. 50 square centimeters
   E. 2.4 square decimeters

32. The spectroscope is used to

   A. calibrate periscopes
   B. study the interior of the lungs
   C. magnify small objects enormously
   D. analyze the composition of hot materials
   E. discover the defects in large castings

33. The Beaufort scale is used in the measurement of

   A. wind velocity
   B. very low temperatures
   C. earthquake intensities
   D. light intensity
   E. small changes in gravitational forces

34. Electrons are

   A. neutral particles
   B. the nuclei of atoms
   C. negative particles
   D. neutralized protons
   E. positive particles

35. The differential in an automobile is a device that allows

   A. a continuous change of gear ratio
   B. the rear wheels to turn independently of each other
   C. a variable battery-charging voltage
   D. traction for one rear wheel when the other is on a slippery surface
   E. compensation for gasolines of various octane ratings

36. A railroad locomotive stopped with a crankshaft on dead center is started forward by

   A. an auxiliary engine
   B. the stored inertia from previous motion
   C. the opposite piston
   D. cranking the crankshaft off center
   E. first backing up

37. The exhaust gas of an automobile is mainly carbon, carbon dioxide, carbon monoxide, nitrogen, and

   A. hydrogen
   B. oxygen
   C. steam
   D. gasoline vapor
   E. silicon carbide

38. A woman bought a navy blue dress with white polka dots in a store illuminated with a pure yellow light. The colors of the dress as they appeared in the store were

    A. blue with yellow polka dots
    B. black with white polka dots
    C. black with yellow polka dots
    D. green with white polka dots
    E. green with yellow polka dots

38.____

39. Of the following, the one that weighs MOST is

    A. 50 grams of feathers
    B. 1 pound of cotton
    C. 12 ounces of lead
    D. 1 cubic centimeter of mercury
    E. 600,000 milligrams of sulfur

39.____

40. Water is obtained from an artesian well

    A. with a shallow lift pump
    B. with a shallow force pump
    C. with a deep lift pump
    D. with a deep force pump
    E. without a pump

40.____

41. Which one of the following items would NOT have to be seriously considered by a group of scientists exploring on the moon?

    A. Effects of insolation
    B. Effects of gravity
    C. Temperature changes after nightfall
    D. Changing weather conditions
    E. Communication with the earth

41.____

42. Each day between March 21 and June 21, the sun appears to set a tiny bit farther north of west than it rose north of east because the

    A. days are getting longer
    B. earth has moved on its orbit during the day
    C. earth's axis tilts a little more each day
    D. earth rotates on its axis
    E. earth is coming closer to the sun

42.____

43. The twinkling of a star is caused by

    A. the star itself
    B. interplanetary dust
    C. defects in the structure of the human eye
    D. objects passing between the star and our eyes
    E. turbulence within the atmosphere

43.____

44. The Aurora borealis and the Aurora australis are indications that

    A. the earth's atmosphere is more than 200 miles in depth
    B. large ice sheets reflect considerable light
    C. the earth's orbit and its axis are not mutually perpendicular
    D. moonlight is reflected from cirrus clouds
    E. moonlight is reflected from nimbus clouds

44.____

45. A point on the earth's surface diametrically opposite latitude 40° N, longitude 70° W is

   A. 40° N 70° E   B. 40° S 70° E   C. 50° S 110° E
   D. 40° S 110° E   E. 50° S 70° E

46. The BEST estimate of the age of the earth comes from studies of

   A. the total thickness of sedimentary rocks
   B. certain changes in radioactive minerals
   C. the amount of salt in the ocean
   D. the amount of erosion
   E. the mineralization of the lowest fossil-bearing rock

47. Which of the following elements related to the process of nuclear fission does NOT occur in nature?

   A. barium   B. curium   C. radium   D. thorium
   E. uranium

48. The nucleus of an atom of uranium 235 contains

   A. 235 protons
   B. 235 neutrons
   C. 92 protons and 143 neutrons
   D. 90 protons and 146 neutrons
   E. 146 protons and 89 neutrons

49. A mineral mined in large quantities in the East is

   A. aluminum   B. coal   C. magnesium   D. salt
   E. sulfur

50. Certain metals are added to increase the hardness and toughness of steel. A group of such metals is

   A. magnesium, cadmium, antimony
   B. manganese, chromium, nickel
   C. carbon, tin, copper
   D. zinc, lead, aluminum
   E. nickel, tin, zinc

KEY (CORRECT ANSWERS)

1. D	11. B	21. B	31. C	41. D
2. E	12. E	22. E	32. D	42. B
3. B	13. D	23. A	33. A	43. E
4. E	14. B	24. E	34. C	44. A
5. B	15. E	25. E	35. B	45. D
6. B	16. C	26. D	36. C	46. B
7. C	17. D	27. C	37. C	47. B
8. E	18. A	28. C	38. C	48. C
9. B	19. C	29. B	39. E	49. D
10. C	20. C	30. E	40. E	50. B

TEST 2

DIRECTIONS: Each question or incomplete statement is followed by several suggested answers or completions. Select the one that BEST answers the question or completes the statement. PRINT THE LETTER OF THE CORRECT ANSWER IN THE SPACE AT THE RIGHT.

1. A relatively inert gas, such as argon, is included in many incandescent electric lamps because the gas

   A. excludes oxygen, which would corrode the filament
   B. glows when electrically excited
   C. reacts with the filament to cause the glow
   D. permits rapid vaporization around the filament
   E. prevents rapid vaporization around the filament

   1.____

2. Wet wood will usually burn but does NOT make good tinder because

   A. water does not burn
   B. so much heat is needed to evaporate the water
   C. wet wood has a higher kindling temperature than dry wood
   D. the water vapor produced smothers the fire
   E. wet wood has a lower kindling temperature than dry wood

   2.____

3. When coal burns in a furnace, the weight of all the substances derived from the burning will be equal to the weight of

   A. the coal
   B. the ashes taken from the furnace
   C. all the air entering the furnace
   D. the air entering the furnace plus the weight of the ashes
   E. the oxygen entering the furnace plus the weight of the coal

   3.____

4. Hard coal burns with less smoke than soft coal because hard coal

   A. is more nearly pure carbon
   B. contains more volatile materials
   C. has a lower kindling temperature
   D. undergoes chemical change more readily
   E. contains more smoke-reducing compounds

   4.____

5. A metal much used in the construction of permanent magnets is

   A. brass   B. copper   C. nickel
   D. tin   E. zinc

   5.____

6. The frequency of visible light falls between that of

   A. infrared rays and radio waves
   B. X rays and cosmic rays
   C. ultraviolet rays and X rays
   D. short radio waves and long radio waves
   E. ultraviolet rays and infrared waves

   6.____

7. In the visible spectrum, yellow is between

   A. red and orange
   B. orange and green
   C. green and blue
   D. green and blue
   E. blue and violet

8. The centripetal force that holds the earth in a nearly circular orbit is

   A. the momentum of the earth
   B. the inertia of the earth
   C. the gravitational attraction of the earth and sun for each other
   D. the atomic energy of the sun
   E. the electromagnetic attraction of the sun for the iron core of the earth

9. A light year is a measure of

   A. acceleration
   B. distance
   C. intensity
   D. time
   E. velocity

10. The atmosphere contains about 1%

    A. argon
    B. carbon dioxide
    C. helium
    D. hydrogen
    E. krypton

11. Air that has a relative humidity of 50%

    A. has half as much water vapor as it can hold
    B. is half water vapor and half air
    C. has half its water vapor condensed
    D. has its water vapor half way condensed
    E. has half its water content condensed and half evaporated

12. As a mass of air rises

    A. its temperature increases and its pressure increases
    B. its temperature decreases and its pressure increases
    C. its temperature decreases and its pressure decreases
    D. its temperature increases and its pressure decreases
    E. its temperature stays the same and its pressure increases

13. The meridian at which the time is 5 hours earlier than the time at Greenwich is

    A. 105° E
    B. 105° W
    C. 75° E
    D. 75° W
    E. none of these answers

14. Which of the following will absorb MOST water per given volume?

    A. gravel
    B. humus
    C. quartz
    D. sand
    E. sandy loam

15. Coal consists of organic matter which, during geologic ages, was 15.____

   A. thoroughly decayed
   B. unable to oxidize
   C. thoroughly oxidized
   D. preserved unchanged
   E. incompletely calcified

16. The plants of which of the following groups act as hosts to nitrogen-fixing bacteria? 16.____

   A. Wheat, oats, rye
   B. Corn, rye, barley
   C. Pumpkins, squash, cucumbers
   D. Beets, carrots, turnips
   E. Clover, alfalfa, soybeans

17. Of the following deciduous trees, the one that loses its leaves *LAST* after a summer's growing season is the 17.____

   A. box elder
   B. elm
   C. oak
   D. poplar
   E. sumac

18. Seedless orange trees are produced by 18.____

   A. planting oranges that contain no seeds
   B. cross-pollination
   C. careful breeding
   D. budding or grafting
   E. planting an orange segment that has no seeds

19. The oxygen absorbed from water by aquatic animals is 19.____

   A. dissolved in the water
   B. produced by the respiration of plants
   C. produced by the respiration of animals
   D. derived by breaking down water into hydrogen and oxygen
   E. produced by oxidation of decaying materials

20. Which of the following is the *BEST* definition of photosynthesis? The 20.____

   A. action of sunlight on chlorophyl
   B. process by which plants give off oxygen
   C. building of protoplasm by a plant
   D. manufacture of carbohydrate by a green plant
   E. process by which plants use carbon dioxide

21. Muskrats share with beavers the habit of 21.____

   A. cutting down trees
   B. building dams
   C. building lodges
   D. slapping the water with their tails when alarmed
   E. digging canals

22. The primary source of fish food in a pond is   22.____

    A. one-celled animals   B. one-celled plants
    C. crayfish and snails   D. large water plants
    E. insects falling in or washed in from the land

23. The principal food of our larger hawks is   23.____

    A. calves   B. chickens
    C. game birds   D. small rodents
    E. songbirds

24. The young of houseflies are   24.____

    A. caterpillars   B. cocoons
    C. small flies   D. gnats
    E. maggots

25. Of the following, the animal that is MOST dangerous to man in America is the   25.____

    A. black bear   B. housefly
    C. mountain lion   D. rattlesnake
    E. black widow spider

26. All of the following diseases are spread by animals EXCEPT   26.____

    A. bubonic plague   B. malaria
    C. scarlet fever   D. tularemia
    E. yellow fever

27. All of the following are parasitic diseases EXCEPT   27.____

    A. diabetes   B. malaria
    C. tuberculosis   D. typhoid fever
    E. streptococcic sore throat

28. A sharp blow in the front of the abdomen just below the ribs may cause a momentary   28.____
    stoppage of breathing because

    A. so much air has been knocked from one's lungs
    B. the secretion of adrenalin has been temporarily ended
    C. the portion of the autonomic nervous system which is centered in the solar plexus
       is affected
    D. the aveoli of the lungs have collapsed
    E. the diaphragm muscles are no longer stimulated by the cerebrum

29. In the control of disease, it has been found that   29.____

    A. all diseases can be prevented by vaccines or serums
    B. all communicable diseases can be cured by specific drugs
    C. effective treatment for all diseases is not known at the present time
    D. an individual who follows hygienic practices will avoid illness.
    E. a low-caloric diet should be given to all who are seriously ill

30. Children are not being successfully immunized to prevent   30.____

    A. chicken pox   B. measles
    C. mumps   D. pneumonia
    E. whooping cough

31. A disease that is highly infectious, incurable if not immediately treated and transmissible to unborn children is

    A. cancer
    B. measles
    C. syphilis
    D. tuberculosis
    E. infantile paralysis

31.____

32. The greatest danger from malaria is that it

    A. produces chills and a high fever
    B. attacks brain cells
    C. causes dysentery
    D. destroys red blood corpuscles
    E. upsets hormone distribution

32.____

33. Binocular vision is a type of eye functioning that

    A. is acquired at birth
    B. results in double vision
    C. is the simultaneous use of both eyes
    D. causes squinting
    E. is the result of discordant movements of the eyes

33.____

34. Infantile paralysis often causes immediate damage to

    A. blood vessels
    B. bones
    C. muscles
    D. the spinal cord
    E. connective tissues

34.____

35. In one type of treatment of hay fever, the patient is given, over a period of a month, increasing doses of the pollen that causes his allergy. This type of treatment resembles most closely

    A. the injection of antitoxin for curative purposes
    B. the Pasteur treatment for rabies
    C. vaccination against smallpox
    D. the toxoid treatment for tetanus
    E. the use of penicillin

35.____

36. When a person is confined to his bed by diphtheria,

    A. everything should be removed from the sickroom except the bed, table and chair
    B. a window should be kept open
    C. liquids should be given as the best nourishment
    D. anyone entering the room should wear a gown over the regular clothing
    E. the room should be fumigated immediately upon recovery

36.____

37. In many states, the health officer should be notified when a person has

    A. measles
    B. pellagra
    C. mumps
    D. scabies
    E. scurvy

37.____

38. Depilatories are used to

    A. relieve pain
    B. overcome constipation
    C. remove hair
    D. check perspiration
    E. remedy skin blemishes

39. The ultraviolet rays of the sun are especially beneficial in

    A. eczema
    B. measles
    C. rickets
    D. scabies
    E. scurvy

40. Safe drinking water in small quantities can be obtained quickly and economically

    A. from a spring
    B. by chlorination
    C. by distillation
    D. by filtration
    E. by exposure to the sun

41. The principal minerals that food should provide for building and preserving sound teeth are

    A. iodine and phosphorus
    B. iron and calcium
    C. calcium and phosphorus
    D. magnesium and iron
    E. phosphorus and iron

42. The enamel of one's permanent teeth is

    A. formed entirely before eruption
    B. formed entirely after eruption
    C. partially formed before eruption and added constantly after eruption
    D. entirely formed before eruption and added as needed to replace damage
    E. partially formed before eruption and added at certain periods through one's life

43. The vitamin that affects the clotting of the blood is

    A. ascorbic acid
    B. riboflavin
    C. thiamin
    D. vitamin D
    E. vitamin K

44. One function of the liver is the

    A. secretion of adrenalin
    B. formation of red blood cells
    C. temporary storage of glycogen
    D. digestion and absorption of starches
    E. absorption of fats from the intestinal tract

45. The principal function of red blood cells is to

    A. destroy disease germs
    B. carry oxygen to cells
    C. act as toxins in the blood stream
    D. cause the blood to coagulate
    E. give the blood a red color

46. The use of iodine in the body is most closely related to the functioning of the   46._____

    A. gall bladder   B. kidneys
    C. lymph nodes   D. pancreas
    E. thyroid

47. One function of the projections (villi) of the small intestine is to   47._____

    A. produce digestive hormones
    B. aid in the grinding of foods
    C. synchronize the peristaltic action of the intestine
    D. increase the absorptive surface of the intestine
    E. reverse peristaltic action

48. One function of sweat is to   48._____

    A. cleanse the pores   B. lubricate the skin
    C. nourish the hair   D. cool the body
    E. produce perspiration

49. An example of an enzyme is   49._____

    A. adrenalin   B. ptyalin   C. thiamin   D. thyroxine
    E. trichinosis

50. The acid found in our stomachs is _____ acid.   50._____

    A. acetic   B. formic   C. hydrochloric   D. nitric
    E. sulfuric

KEY (CORRECT ANSWERS)

1. E	11. A	21. C	31. C	41. C
2. C	12. C	22. B	32. D	42. A
3. E	13. D	23. D	33. C	43. E
4. A	14. B	24. E	34. D	44. C
5. C	15. B	25. B	35. B	45. B
6. E	16. E	26. C	36. D	46. E
7. B	17. C	27. A	37. A	47. D
8. C	18. D	28. C	38. C	48. D
9. B	19. A	29. C	39. C	49. B
10. A	20. D	30. D	40. B	50. C

TEST 3

DIRECTIONS: Each question or incomplete statement is followed by several suggested answers or completions. Select the one that BEST answers the question or completes the statement.

1. Petroleum consists MAINLY of

   A. carbon and hydrogen
   B. hydrogen and oxygen
   C. oxygen and nitrogen
   D. nitrogen and carbon
   E. carbon and oxygen

   1.____

2. If a strong solution of table salt is poured on the soil of a potted plant,

   A. much salt will diffuse into the juices of the plant
   B. the plant will be unaffected
   C. minerals dissolved in the plant juices will diffuse into the salt solution
   D. the plant will lose water through its roots
   E. root pressure will be increased and the plant will become turgid

   2.____

3. The MAIN function of humus in soil is to

   A. keep the soil "sweet"
   B. provide carbon dioxide for photosynthesis in the roots
   C. conserve moisture
   D. absorb nitrogen from the air
   E. live symbiotically with the plants

   3.____

4. Fungi procure their food

   A. by photosynthesis
   B. from the air
   C. from materials produced by other organisms
   D. from soil minerals
   E. by combining inorganic materials

   4.____

5. A grain of wheat is PRIMARILY

   A. a fertilized plant egg
   B. an embryo plant plus a food supply
   C. a developed pollen grain
   D. a miniature of the adult plant
   E. a food supply for the unfertilized plant egg

   5.____

6. An oak tree increases in diameter because of the growth that takes place

   A. in the bark
   B. just under the bark
   C. in the center of the trunk
   D. uniformly throughout the trunk
   E. in the size of each cell in the tree

   6.____

7. Grapefruit are so named because they

    A. are closely related to a species of tropical grapes
    B. grow in clusters
    C. are mutants of a domestic grape
    D. grow on trees whose leaves are almost indistinguishable from grape leaves
    E. are produced on vines

8. Of the following, the plant that requires two growing seasons to complete its life cycle is the

    A. bean   B. cabbage   C. corn   D. tomato
    E. watermelon

9. The flounder

    A. swims in its unique manner from birth
    B. has a symmetrical head
    C. has one eye that migrates to the opposite side of its head
    D. is a surface feeder
    E. is the main enemy of the oyster

10. One can drink water from a brook with his head lower than his feet because of the

    A. peristaltic action of the esophagus
    B. capillary action in the throat
    C. difference in pressure between the stomach and the atmosphere
    D. pumping action of the diaphragm
    E. valvular action of the larynx

11. Radioactive isotopes have been used in medicine to

    A. trace the course of certain compounds through the body
    B. cure anema
    C. determine the amount of phosphorus in the body
    D. supplement the bactericidal action of streptomycin
    E. make vaccines for the treatment of cancer

12. The effect of a specific antibody in the blood is to cause

    A. disintegration of white blood corpuscles
    B. destruction of all disease-producing bacteria
    C. disintegration of most bacteria
    D. destruction of specific bacteria
    E. rapid blood-clotting in wounds

13. Expressed in the centigrade scale, the average normal temperature of the human body is

    A. 37° C   B. 55° C   C. 68° C   D. 98° C   E. 212° C

14. The incubation period of a disease is the

    A. time required for the bacterium to hatch
    B. time from infection until the appearance of symptoms
    C. length of the life cycle of the infecting organism

D. period during which the patient should be confined to bed
E. length of exposure necessary to acquire a disease

15. As individual may do much to protect himself against hookworm in an infected area by   15.____

    A. being vaccinated against hookworm
    B. taking preventive medicine
    C. avoiding all pork
    D. eating only food that has been cooked under pressure
    E. wearing shoes

16. The iron lung is a device that   16.____

    A. replaces one lobe of the lungs
    B. blows air into the lungs
    C. raises and lowers the pressure on the outside of the body
    D. supplies pure oxygen to invalids
    E. increases peristaltic action

17. Sir Alexander Fleming is BEST known for his work in connection with the   17.____

    A. discovery of insulin
    B. development of the iron lung
    C. use of X-rays in the treatment of cancer
    D. prevention of yellow fever
    E. discovery of penicillin

18. Radioactive isotopes produced by atomic energy have already been used successfully in the   18.____

    A. removal of superfluous hair
    B. treatment of certain types of goiter
    C. prevention of tooth decay
    D. treatment of certain forms of mental disease
    E. treatment of water supplies to kill dangerous bacteria

19. When caring for an invalid in the home, one should remember that   19.____

    A. unless a person is ill, the body temperature is always 98. 6° F.
    B. the red arrow point on a clinical thermometer is at 100° F.
    C. the normal body temperature may vary as much as one and one-half degrees during the day
    D. a rectal temperature of 98° F. is considered normal
    E. the body temperature is usually lowest at about 4 p.m. and highest at about 3 a.m.

20. Which of the following statements is TRUE?   20.____

    A. Salivation is a sign that a baby is teething.
    B. After a baby has had an accidental fall, the mother should try to put it to sleep as soon as possible.
    C. Breast-fed babies usually have greater immunity to contagious diseases than bottle-fed babies have.

D. Thumb sucking is a sign that a baby is not getting enough to eat.
E. Infant mortality is higher in females than in males.

21. A disease to which a person is USUALLY permanently immune after recovering from an attack is

    A. influenza   B. malaria   C. pneumonia
    D. poliomyelitis   E. syphilis

22. Of the following, the BEST treatment for someone who looks as if he were about to faint is to

    A. have him sit down in a chair and close his eyes for a few minutes
    B. have him hold his arms above his head
    C. have someone take hold of him on either side and keep him walking
    D. have him sit down on the floor or ground with his head between his knees
    E. slap him vigorously on the back several times

23. Of the following, the BEST first-aid treatment for a person whose eyes have been exposed to irritating fumes is to

    A. flush the eyes with water from a drinking fountain
    B. put powdered boracic acid in the eyes
    C. apply cold towels to the eyes
    D. rub the eyes to stimulate the flow of tears
    E. rush the patient to the nearest physician

24. The MOST serious type of fatigue is induced by

    A. emotional strain
    B. mental work
    C. physical activity
    D. sedentary occupations
    E. inadequate sleep over several days

25. The BEST body position in going to sleep has been found to be

    A. on the abdomen   B. on the left side
    C. on the right side   D. flat on one's back
    E. any way that is comfortable

26. The use of a common towel by two or more persons may result in the spread of

    A. eczema   B. hives   C. impetigo   D. rickets
    E. shingles

27. Legally prohibiting expectoration in public places helps prevent

    A. cancer   B. pneumonia   C. scabies   D. tetanus
    E. typhoid fever

28. When in need of a stimulant, one may BEST use

    A. brandy   B. hot milk   C. orange juice   D. tea
    E. bicarbonate of soda in water

29. Toasted bread is more digestible than untoasted bread because the toasting process changes a part of the carbohydrate into

    A. dextrin   B. heparin   C. melanin   D. opsonin
    E. palmitin

30. Insufficient calcium in the diet of a child may cause

    A. bowlegs   B. impaired vision   C. infantile paralysis
    D. wryneck   E. tuberculosis of the bones

31. A generous supply of vitamin C may be included in a day's diet by using a sufficient quantity of

    A. broiled mackerel   B. stewed prunes
    C. pork chops   D. tomato juice
    E. whole wheat bread or cereals

32. Of the following, the food nutrient that provides energy in the diet is

    A. cellulose   B. iron   C. protein   D. riboflavin
    E. thiamin

33. Of the foods listed below, the one that will contribute the GREATEST number of calories to the diet is

    A. one cup of milk
    B. two cups of cabbage
    C. one-half cup of cornstarch pudding
    D. four tablespoonfuls of mayonnaise
    E. two medium-sized white potatoes

34. In case of high price or shortage of meat, other foods rich in protein may be used. The BEST substitute from the following list is

    A. egg plant   B. dark rice   C. spaghetti
    D. string beans   E. red kidney beans

35. The BEST of the following lunches for a two-year old child would be

    A. egg yolk, baked potato, whole wheat toast, chopped peas, milk
    B. cream soup, cabbage, graham crackers, custard, milk
    C. meat loaf, cabbage salad, toast, chocolate pudding, milk
    D. soft cooked egg, pineapple and raw carrot salad, toast, junket, milk
    E. creamed corn, toast, weak cocoa, custard

36. Which of the following statements is TRUE?

    A. One can become physically ill from ailments that are purely imaginary.
    B. A receding chin usually indicates a weak will.
    C. Good and bad personality traits are sometimes inherited.
    D. Believing that a thing is true often makes it true.
    E. A person's intelligence can always be improved through education

37. Which of the following would be injured if a baking soda solution were allowed to stand in it overnight?

   A. An earthenware casserole
   B. An enamel saucepan
   C. A pyrex double boiler
   D. An aluminum saucepan
   E. A stainless steel pressure saucepan

38. The illustration below represents a

   A. brad
   B. casing nail
   C. common nail
   D. cut nail
   E. finishing nail

39. A doorbell is USUALLY connected to the household circuit (A.C.) through a

   A. base plug
   B. condenser
   C. rectifier
   D. resistor
   E. transformer

40. An ordinary automobile storage battery consists of

   A. one large dry cell
   B. several dry cells
   C. one large wet cell
   D. several wet cells
   E. a chemical rectifier

41. The tool illustrated below is used MOST often by

   A. an electrician
   B. a machinist
   C. a printer
   D. a plumber
   E. a garage mechanic

42. The term "kiln dried" applies to

   A. linseed oil
   B. lumber
   C. plaster
   D. pottery
   E. cold-rolled steel

43. A "stud" in a frame building is a part of the

   A. ceiling
   B. floor
   C. foundation
   D. roof
   E. side wall

44. The joint shown below is a

   A. butt   B. dado   C. dovetail   D. half lap   E. rabbet

45. Which of the following prevents a saw from binding?

   A. set
   B. sharpness
   C. curve of back
   D. number of teeth
   E. thickness of blade

46. Two men are pulling on ropes attached to a rock. It is found that their resultant force is less than that used by either man. It MUST be that the forces are

    A. acting at less than 90° to each other
    B. acting at more than 90° to each other
    C. acting at 90° to each other
    D. both large
    E. both small

47. An observer is moving away from a vibrating object with the speed of sound. The observer will

    A. hear a note an octave higher
    B. hear a note an octave lower
    C. hear the same note but more faintly
    D. hear the same note emphasized
    E. not hear the emitted note

48. The extraction of nitrogenous wastes from the blood is the CHIEF function of the

    A. bladder   B. kidneys   C. large intestine
    D. liver   E. lungs

49. The surface of the earth has been changed the MOST by

    A. winds   B. glaciers   C. running water
    D. volcanos   E. chemical action of the atmosphere

50. Molds are to spores as green plants are to

    A. flowers   B. leaves   C. roots   D. seeds
    E. stems

KEY (CORRECT ANSWERS)

1. A	11. A	21. D	31. D	41. D
2. D	12. D	22. D	32. C	42. B
3. C	13. A	23. A	33. D	43. E
4. C	14. B	24. A	34. E	44. B
5. B	15. E	25. E	35. A	45. A
6. B	16. C	26. C	36. A	46. B
7. B	17. E	27. B	37. D	47. E
8. B	18. B	28. D	38. C	48. B
9. C	19. C	29. A	39. E	49. C
10. A	20. C	30. A	40. D	50. D

TEST 4

DIRECTIONS: Each question or incomplete statement is followed by several suggested answers or completions. Select the one that BEST answers the question or completes the statement.

1. The dinosaur was a prehistoric
   - A. amphibian
   - B. arthropod
   - C. mammal
   - D. primate
   - E. reptile

2. Evidence indicating that great climatic changes have occurred in the past is found in
   - A. the appearance of mountains
   - B. the delta of the Mississippi
   - C. coal deposits in Alaska
   - D. lava deposits
   - E. the records of the United States Department of Agriculture

3. A structure that helps to keep air pressure in the middle ear equal to atmospheric pressure is the
   - A. eardrum
   - B. Eustachian tube
   - C. Islands of Langerhans
   - D. nasal passage
   - E. semicircular canal

4. One factor NOT necessary for photosynthesis is
   - A. carbon dioxide
   - B. chlorophyll
   - C. free oxygen
   - D. sunlight
   - E. water

5. Carbon grains are an essential part of a
   - A. doorbell
   - B. radio loudspeaker
   - C. storage battery
   - D. transformer
   - E. telephone transmitter

6. A container of water is placed on a scale and the scale reading is 100 pounds. If a block of wood weighing 25 pounds is then floated half submerged in the water, the scale will read
   - A. 75 pounds
   - B. 87.5 pounds
   - C. 100 pounds
   - D. 112.5 pounds
   - E. 125 pounds

7. Most evidence seems to indicate that the first vertebrate animal to appear on the earth was the
   - A. amphibian
   - B. bird
   - C. fish
   - D. mammal
   - E. reptile

8. The earth's crust contains about 50% oxygen by weight. The next MOST abundant element in the earth's crust is
   - A. aluminum
   - B. calcium
   - C. hydrogen
   - D. iron
   - E. silicon

9. A large steel drum containing air at normal atmospheric pressure is found to float with 40% of its volume under water. When compressed air is forced into the drum until its pressure is doubled, the drum will

    A. float at the same level
    B. float higher in the water
    C. float lower in the water
    D. sink to a depth between the surface and the bottom
    E. sink to the bottom

9.____

10. When a bacterial cell is submerged in a strong salt solution, the cell shrinks because

    A. minerals enter the cell
    B. the cytoplasm within the cell decomposes
    C. the salt dissolves the cell wall
    D. the salt enters the cell
    E. water leaves the cell

10.____

11. Mosaic vision is characteristic of

    A. bacteria   B. bees
    C. earthworms   D. man
    E. robins

11.____

12. Ambergris, a substance used to make perfume, comes from

    A. an inflammation in the body of the sperm whale
    B. distilled attar of roses
    C. the hardened resin from pine trees
    D. the musk-producing organs of a deer
    E. the nectar-producing organs of the honeysuckle vine

12.____

13. Bloodplasma consists CHIEFLY of

    A. amino acids   B. fats   C. glucose   D. water
    E. urea and uric acids

13.____

14. Appendicitis is generally accompanied by

    A. daily fluctuation of red cell count
    B. high red cell count
    C. high white cell count
    D. low white cell count
    E. pain in the carotids

14.____

15. The dead red corpuscles in the blood stream are removed and decomposed by the

    A. heart   B. liver   C. lungs   D. small intestine
    E. white corpuscles

15.____

16. Auxins are

    A. growth hormones   B. insect poisons   C. new plastics
    D. new textiles   E. respiratory enzymes

16.____

17. On the desert the Arabs are able to keep water cool in earthenware jugs because

    A. particles of earthenware dissolve in the water and lower its temperature
    B. the attraction between the molecules of the jug and the water is a cooling process
    C. the change of some of the water to a vapor lowers the temperature
    D. the jug is a good conductor of heat
    E. the rough surface of the jug radiates heat more rapidly

18. An object weighs 10 pounds in air and floats in water with one half of its volume above the surface. The MINIMUM force that must be added to submerge the object is

    A. 5 pounds   B. 10 pounds   C. 20 pounds
    D. 31.25 pounds   E. 62.5 pounds

19. A hot stove poker is held near the face. The rays of light chiefly responsible for the sensation felt on the cheek are those of

    A. blue light   B. infrared light   C. red light
    D. ultraviolet light   E. white light

20. Plastic-coated screen is often used in place of glass in chicken coops and barns because

    A. glass filters out most of the infrared rays of sunlight
    B. glass filters out most of the ultraviolet rays of sunlight
    C. plastic filters out harmful rays of light
    D. plastic is far safer for the cattle or chickens since it will not shatter
    E. plastic transmits more of the rays of visible light

21. When smoke from a locomotive tends to settle to the ground, it may indicate that an area of rainy weather is approaching because

    A. the air is less dense and will not support the smoke particles
    B. the air is rising in a low pressure area
    C. the air is sinking near the low pressure area
    D. the smoke is sucked into the low pressure area
    E. there is less oxygen so that the smoke particles are not completely burned and are heavier

22. In order to overcome losses during long-distance transmission of electrical energy, it is common practice to

    A. decrease both the voltage and the current
    B. decrease the voltage and increase the current
    C. increase both the voltage and the current
    D. increase the voltage and keep the current constant
    E. increase the voltage and decrease the current

23. Oil is poured on water to reduce the height of waves because the

    A. added weight of the oil makes the waves break at a lesser height
    B. oil is a lubricant
    C. chemical action between oil and water produces a heavier substance
    D. oil fills up the troughs of the waves
    E. surface tension of the water will be weakened

24. The MOST penetrating of the following forms of radiation is

    A. heat
    B. infrared light
    C. the cosmic ray
    D. the X-ray
    E. ultraviolet light

25. A good index of the health of a community is its death rate from

    A. arteriosclerosis
    B. diphtheria
    C. influenza
    D. meningitis
    E. typhoid

26. Fehling's solution is added to a test tube containing a sample of breakfast cereal that has been heated in water. If the Fehling's solution turns brick red, the breakfast food PROBABLY contains

    A. animal fat
    B. grape sugar
    C. protein
    D. starch
    E. vitamin C

27. The part of the eye that corresponds to the diaphragm of the camera is the

    A. cornea
    B. iris
    C. lens
    D. pupil
    E. retina

28. The pneumothorax treatment is used in cases of

    A. cancer
    B. heart disease
    C. tuberculosis
    D. pneumonia
    E. paralysis of the upper thorax

29. In outer space, where there is no atmosphere, a jet-propelled rocket

    A. cannot be stopped
    B. cannot change its direction
    C. will not operate since there is no air against which the expelled gases can push
    D. will not operate since there is no air to supply oxygen for combustion of the fuel
    E. will operate more efficiently because there is no air resistance

30. A man has a cup of hot coffee, a teaspoonful of sugar, an ounce of cream. He desires to drink the combination at the lowest temperature possible at the end of three minutes. He should add the

    A. cream at once and the sugar in three minutes
    B. cream at once and the sugar slowly throughout the three-minute period
    C. sugar and cream at the end of three minutes
    D. sugar and cream immediately
    E. sugar at once and the cream slowly throughout the three-minute period

31. In one state, the average temperature on August 6 is USUALLY higher than on June 21. This is BEST explained by

    A. the fact that August 6 is midway between June 21 and September 21
    B. the fact that the humidity is higher on August 6
    C. the reason that accounts for 2 p.m. usually being warmer than noon
    D. the sun's rays being more vertical on August 6
    E. the sun being farther away on August 6 than June 21

32. Ordinary photographic film is developed under a ruby-colored light because the film is

    A. not sensitive to long wave lengths of visible light
    B. not sensitive to short wave lengths of visible light
    C. not sensitive to ultraviolet light
    D. not sensitive to visible light
    E. sensitive to all wave lengths of visible light

33. In a plant the semipermeable membrane which surrounds the cell is the

    A. cell membrane   B. cell wall   C. vacuole membrane
    D. nuclear membrane   E. cytoplasmic inclusion

34. Tobacco mosaic is due to

    A. a bacterium   B. a lack of iron   C. too much sun
    D. a virus   E. a lack of magnesium

35. When sheets are washed, bluing is sometimes added to the water because

    A. a chemical change called bleaching will occur
    B. it destroys most water-borne bacteria
    C. it is a water softener
    D. its color is complementary to yellow
    E. the soap is made less harsh

36. The HIGHEST clouds are

    A. alto-cumulus   B. cirrus   C. cumulus   D. nimbus
    E. stratus

37. Acetylcholine is a substance that controls the

    A. absorption of vitamins   B. action of nerves
    C. digestion of food   D. germination of seeds
    E. storage of fat

38. The PRINCIPAL function of the white blood cells is to

    A. act as toxins in the blood stream
    B. carry away waste products
    C. carry oxygen to the cells
    D. destroy disease germs
    E. produce antitoxins

39. There are indications that decay is retarded by treating the teeth of children with a compound of

    A. bromine   B. chlorine   C. fluorine   D. iodine
    E. sulfur

40. Poisons manufactured by bacteria are called

    A. molds   B. phagocytes   C. septics   D. toxins
    E. viruses

41. Aero-embolism is a body disturbance commonly known as

   A. appendicitis B. bends C. infantile paralysis
   D. pneumonia E. sugar diabetes

42. Diabetes is caused by the improper functioning of the

   A. adrenals B. digestive juices C. pancreas
   D. parathyroids E. thyroid

43. The air we exhale, compared to the air we inhale, contains

   A. less carbon dioxide B. less nitrogen
   C. more nitrogen D. more oxygen
   E. more water vapor

44. Studies of sleep by psychologists and health specialists indicate that

   A. a tired, stuporous feeling sometimes following a profound sleep is attributed to tossing too much
   B. adults reveal considerable individual differences in their need of sleep, but infants and pre-school children reveal insignificant differences at a given age
   C. best rest is obtained from sleep when the stomach is empty
   D. the typically healthy sleeper usually changes from one gross bodily position to another between twenty and forty-five times during eight hours of sleep
   E. young children show more movements in sleep than older children and adults

45. Edward Jenner perfected a method of making people immune to

   A. anthrax B. bubonic plague C. diphtheria
   D. smallpox E. yellow fever

46. A file clerk who has the habit of moistening her finger to facilitate the turning of pages can MOST easily break the habit by

   A. applying a bitter but harmless substance to her finger
   B. asking a co-worker to remind her when she puts her finger to her tongue
   C. making a practice of using the eraser of a pencil to turn pages
   D. placing a large sign in a conspicuous place on her desk
   E. putting a piece of adhesive plaster on her finger as a reminder

47. Ascorbic acid is the scientific name for

   A. a narcotic obtained from poppies
   B. a poisonous substance in tobacco
   C. acid in the stomach
   D. digitalis
   E. vitamin C

48. The HIGHEST concentration of oxygen is found in the

   A. hepatic vein B. jugular vein C. pulmonary artery
   D. pulmonary vein E. right auricle

49. A workman was injured by a blunt piece of flying steel. The wound, close to his eye, was dirty and lacerated but there was only slight bleeding. In giving first aid, his co-worker should

    A. apply a mild tincture of iodine and cover the wound with sterile gauze
    B. clean the wound carefully with alcohol and cover with sterile gauze
    C. cover the wound with sterile gauze and leave the cleaning to a physician
    D. remove the specks of dirt with a sterile swab before covering the wound with sterile gauze
    E. wash the wound carefully with soap and water and cover it with sterile gauze

50. Which one of the following statements concerning first aid is TRUE?

    A. A tourniquet should be loosened every 30 or 40 minutes to prevent stoppage of circulation and possible gangrene.
    B. It is essential to wash the hands before applying digital pressure to an open wound.
    C. It is useless to continue artificial respiration for more than one hour of there is no sign of returning consciousness.
    D. The pulse of a person suffering from shock is rapid and weak.
    E. Whiskey is a good stimulant to give a person bitten by a poisonous snake.

KEY (CORRECT ANSWERS)

1.	E	11.	B	21.	A	31.	C	41.	B
2.	C	12.	A	22.	E	32.	A	42.	C
3.	B	13.	D	23.	E	33.	A	43.	E
4.	C	14.	C	24.	C	34.	D	44.	D
5.	E	15.	B	25.	E	35.	D	45.	D
6.	E	16.	A	26.	B	36.	B	46.	C
7.	C	17.	C	27.	B	37.	B	47.	E
8.	E	18.	B	28.	C	38.	D	48.	D
9.	C	19.	B	29.	E	39.	C	49.	C
10.	E	20.	B	30.	C	40.	D	50.	D

TEST 5

DIRECTIONS: Each question or incomplete statement is followed by several suggested answers or completions. Select the one that BEST answers the question or completes the statement. *PRINT THE LETTER OF THE CORRECT ANSWER IN THE SPACE AT THE RIGHT.*

1. Of the following, the BEST source of vitamin E is 1.____

   A. citrus fruits
   B. cod liver oil
   C. halibut liver oil
   D. wheat germ oil
   E. milk and milk products

2. Which one of the following may be caused by a plant? 2.____

   A. amoebic dysentery B. influenza C. malaria
   D. ringworm E. yellow fever

3. Which one of the following parts of the circulatory system carries digested fats away from the intestines? 3.____

   A. arterial capillaries B. lacteals
   C. pancreatic duct D. pulmonary artery
   E. venal capillaries

4. At which one of the following points should digital pressure be applied to stop arterial bleeding in the hand or forearm? 4.____

   A. brachial B. carotid C. femoral D. subclavian
   E. temporal

5. The hormone that regulates the general metabolism of the body is 5.____

   A. adrenalin B. gastrin C. insulin D. pituitrin
   E. thyroxin

6. The small dipper seems to turn about the North Star once each day because 6.____

   A. all stars move in great circles on the celestial sphere
   B. the earth turns on its axis
   C. the North Star is the last star in the handle of the dipper
   D. the planets revolve around the sun
   E. the solar system rotates about a fixed star

7. The component of the atmosphere that shows the GREATEST percentage of variation is 7.____

   A. argon B. carbon dioxide C. nitrogen D. oxygen
   E. water vapor

8. Slate is to shale as marble is to 8.____

   A. feldspar B. gneiss C. limestone D. mica schist
   E. sandstone

113

9. A disease caused by the malfunction of the pancreas is

   A. coronary thrombosis   B. diabetes   C. gallstones
   D. rickets   E. tuberculosis

10. Respiration is to carbon dioxide as photosynthesis is to

    A. carbon dioxide   B. chlorophyll   C. oxygen
    D. starch   E. sunlight

11. When a machine that is 80% efficient does 1000 footpounds of work, the work input MUST be

    A. 80 foot-pounds   B. 800 foot-pounds
    C. 1000 foot-pounds   D. 1250 foot-pounds
    E. 1800 foot-pounds

12. A siphon is NOT used to empty the water out of the hold of a ship into the ocean because

    A. a siphon does not create a sufficient vacuum
    B. a siphon will not operate at sea level
    C. salt water is heavier than fresh water
    D. the air pressure is less on the ocean's surface than it is in the hold
    E. the hold is beneath the ocean's surface

13. A full moon might be seen

    A. faintly at noon
    B. high in the sky at sunset
    C. low in the east in the evening
    D. low in the east in the morning
    E. low in the west at midnight

14. A kerosene lamp burns with a yellow flame due to the

    A. burning of hydrogen
    B. complete burning of the hydrocarbons
    C. heating of the wick
    D. incandescence of unburned carbon particles
    E. natural color of any burning kerosene

15. On which one of the following days will a person's shadow be LONGEST at noon in the East?

    A. Christmas   B. Easter Sunday   C. Fourth of July
    D. Labor Day   E. Thanksgiving

16. Perfume is made by dissolving oils containing the essence of the desired odor in

    A. alcohol   B. banana oil   C. distilled water
    D. glycerin   E. volatile mineral oil

17. Which one of the following is produced naturally by living things?

    A. aspirin   B. atabrine   C. lysol   D. quinine
    E. sulfanilamide

18. Which one of the following terms is NOT associated with the others?

    A. beriberi   B. leukemia   C. rickets   D. scurvy
    E. xerophthalmia

19. Like most great caverns, the Howe Caverns of New York State

    A. are made of sandstone
    B. are the result of glaciation
    C. occur in limestone rock
    D. were formed by earthquakes
    E. were formed by wind erosion

20. The unrelated member of the following group is

    A. cyclotron   B. deuteron   C. electron   D. neutron
    E. positron

21. Fossils are MOST likely to be found in

    A. igneous rocks
    B. marble quarries
    C. metamorphic rocks
    D. D, ocean deeps
    E. sedimentary rocks

22. The watershed of a river has reference to

    A. its delta
    B. its flood plain
    C. the body of water into which the river drains
    D. the land from which water drains into the river
    E. the river and its tributaries

23. An increase of temperature from 10° C. to 30° C. is equivalent to an increase of

    A. 11 1/2° F.   B. 36° F.   C. 43 1/2° F.   D. 68° F.
    E. 86° F.

24. The body proper of all insects consists of three parts, namely, the head, the abdomen and the

    A. antennae   B. legs   C. shell   D. thorax
    E. wings

25. The rate of sugar storage in the liver may be studied by using radioactive

    A. calcium   B. carbon   C. carbon dioxide   D. iron
    E. nitrogen

26. A water table is

    A. a flat rock mass eroded by waves
    B. a rain gauge
    C. a river flood stage
    D. the sea level
    E. an underground water level

27. We can see only one side of the moon because the period of the moon's

    A. revolution about the earth equals that of the earth's revolution about the sun
    B. rotation is equal to its period of revolution about the earth
    C. rotation is equal to that of the earth's rotation

D. rotation is half that of the earth's rotation
E. rotation is twice that of the earth's rotation

28. The term that includes all others in the following group is   28._____

    A. absorption   B. assimilation   C. circulation
    D. digestion   E. nutrition

29. The unrelated member of the following group is   29._____

    A. adrenin   B. amylopsin   C. insulin
    D. parathormone   E. thyroxin

30. An object that weighs 500 pounds in air appears to lose 200 pounds when submerged in   30._____
    water to a depth of 10 feet. If the object is then lowered to a depth of 20 feet, its apparent
    weight will be

    A. 100 lb.   B. 200 lb.   C. 300 lb.   D. 400 lb.
    E. 500 lb.

31. The color of the sky is blue because   31._____

    A. blue light is reflected from the Heaviside layer
    B. cosmic rays transmit blue light
    C. dust particles are blue in color
    D. the short wave lengths of visible light are scattered most
    E. there is an excess of ultraviolet rays in the stratosphere

32. If you were placed in the middle of a room where the floor was perfectly frictionless, the   32._____
    BEST method to use in betting to a side wall would be to

    A. crawl over
    B. roll over
    C. throw an object horizontally
    D. walk over
    E. wave your arms violently up and down

33. A disease caused by a protozoan is   33._____

    A. arteriosclerosis   B. endocarditis   C. malaria
    D. poliomyelitis   E. tuberculosis

34. A one-cubic meter, closed, rigid tank contains air and 11 grams of water vapor at a tem-   34._____
    perature of 20° C. If the temperature of the confined air is raised to 35° C., which one of
    the following will result?

    A. The absolute himidity will rise.
    B. The absolute humidity will fall.
    C. The relative humidity will rise.
    D. The relative humidity will fall.
    E. No change will occur in either absolute or relative humidity

35. The use of a soda-acid type fire extinguisher is recommended for putting out fires involving burning

    A. dry chemicals
    B. fats or vegetable oils
    C. gasoline
    D. painted woodwork
    E. insulation on wires carrying 110-220 volts

36. The alloy, alnico, is widely used in making

    A. aluminum utensils
    B. cutting tools
    C. permanent magnets
    D. springs
    E. thermostats

37. A container is filled to the brim with ice water in which is floating an ice cube with 10 cc. of its volume above the surface. The specific gravity of ice is about 0.9. After the ice has completely melted,

    A. about one cc. of water will have overflowed
    B. about nine cc. of water will have overflowed
    C. about ten cc. of water will have overflowed
    D. the water level will have dropped
    E. the water level will have remained constant

38. A sextant is an instrument used to determine by a single observation the

    A. direction of true north
    B. elevation of a given place
    C. exact time at a given place
    D. latitude of a given place
    E. longitude of a given place

39. A 5-pound pail containing 25 pounds of water stands on a platform scale. A 4-pound piece of cork with a specific gravity of 0.25 is floated on the water. Weights are then placed on the piece of cork until it floats flush with the surface of the water. The platform scale now reads

    A. 30 lb.   B. 34 lb.   C. 37 lb.   D. 46 lb.   E. 50 lb.

40. The north pole of a magnet attracted one end of a freely swinging bar of metal marked *A*. This shows that the bar is

    A. made of a magnetic material
    B. made of iron
    C. made of iron with a south pole at *A*
    D. magnetized with a north pole at *A*
    E. unmagnetized

41. The corn plant produces its pollen and ovules

    A. at the same node
    B. in different rows
    C. on different plants
    D. on different flowering structures
    E. on the same flowering structure

42. Which one of the following prehistoric men appeared the LATEST chronologically?

    A. Cro-Magnon   B. Java   C. Neanderthal
    D. Peking   E. Piltdown

43. Tissues are to cells as organs are to

    A. blood   B. human beings   C. organisms   D. tissues
    E. vessels

44. The number of people who die each year from cancer is increasing because

    A. communicable diseases are better controlled and more people live longer
    B. it is a communicable disease
    C. it is an inherited disease
    D. malignant tumors are more prevalent than benign or harmless tumors
    E. medical science knows less about the disease than about any other disease

45. At noon on shipboard, a chronometer reads 10:00 p.m., Greenwich time. The longitude of the ship is

    A. 10° east   B. 150° east   C. 10° west   D. 100° west
    E. 150° west

46. In the East, hailstorms are MOST likely to occur in

    A. fall   B. late winter   C. midwinter   D. summer
    E. very early spring

47. An unused electric refrigerator was placed in a room which was surrounded with a perfect heat insulator. The refrigerator was put into opeation by connecting it to an external electrical circuit and at the same time its door was left open. During the first hour the temperature of the room would

    A. fall continuously
    B. fall somewhat and remain at this temperature
    C. fall somewhat and then return to its original temperature
    D. remain constant
    E. rise

48. The *Rh* factor is of importance in the study of

    A. fingerprinting   B. the acidity of a solution
    C. the blood   D. the determination of sex
    E. the resistance to infection

49. Which one of the following is the GREATEST advantage of growing up in a large family?

    A. Each member may be able to borrow articles from other members.
    B. Each member may be easily provided with recreation within his family circle.
    C. Each member may be required to give and receive financial support.
    D. Each member may have a chance to make adjustments to himself and to other people early in life.
    E. Each member may have fewer responsibilities.

50. Small arteries branch to form a network of capillaries. In turn, the capillaries unite to form

    A. alveoles   B. arteries   C. auricles   D. D, veins
    E. ventricles

KEY (CORRECT ANSWERS)

1. D	11. D	21. E	31. D	41. D
2. D	12. E	22. D	32. C	42. A
3. B	13. C	23. B	33. C	43. D
4. A	14. D	24. D	34. D	44. A
5. E	15. A	25. B	35. D	45. E
6. B	16. A	26. E	36. C	46. D
7. E	17. D	27. B	37. E	47. E
8. C	18. B	28. E	38. D	48. C
9. B	19. C	29. B	39. D	49. D
10. C	20. A	30. C	40. A	50. D

INTRODUCTION TO READING COMPREHENSION

The reading-comprehension question is now a universally accepted ingredient in aptitude, intelligence, general and mental ability, and achievement tests.

By its very nature, it is the most difficult of the question-types to comprehend and to cope with successfully, and, accordingly, it is usually weighted more heavily than all other questions on these examinations.

For the most part, tests of general aptitude and/or achievement draw the reading selections or *passages* from all the disciplines — literature, social studies, science, mathematics, music, art, etc. The student is not expected to, nor does he need to, have knowledge or proficiency in these fields. Rather, he is being tested on his understanding or his comprehension of the meaning of the specific passages presented, the theory being that his mental ability will be best tested by his reading power, not by his training or acquired knowledge in the different areas, since it may be reasonably expected that such training and/or knowledge will differ for many reasons among the candidates. All the information and material needed for answering the questions are, therefore, imbedded in the passages themselves. The power or skill of the student, then, is to be shown in the degree to which he succeeds in finding or inferring the answers to the questions from the information given in the reading material.

Historically, many colleges and universities, leaning on the theory of transfer of training, regard the reading comprehension factor as perhaps the most important of all in measuring scholastic aptitude since, according to this view, the ability to read with understanding and to go on from this point, is basic to all college and graduate work and research.

The factor of reading ability is a complex one which may be tested and measured at several discrete levels.

The easiest type of reading question is that which tests understanding of the material to be read — to list facts or details as described in the passage, to explain the meanings of words or phrases used, to clarify references, etc.

The next stage of difficulty is reached when the student is confronted with questions designed to show his ability to interpret and to analyze the material to be read, e.g., to discover the central thought of the passage, to ascertain the mood or point of view of the author, to note contradictions, etc.

The third stage consists of the ability to apply the principles and/or opinions expressed in the article, e.g., to surmise the recommendations that the writer may be expected to make later on or to formulate his stand on related issues.

The final and highest point is reached when the student is called upon to evaluate what he has read — to agree with or to differ with the point of view of the writer, to accept or to refute the evidences or methods employed, to judge the efficacy or the inappropriateness of different proposals, etc.

All these levels will be tested on the reading section of the Examination.

SUGGESTIONS FOR ANSWERING READING COMPREHENSION QUESTIONS

1. How is the candidate to proceed to answer the reading comprehension questions? First, scan the passage quickly, trying to gather at a glance the general import. Then, read the passage carefully and critically, <u>underlining with a pencil what are apparently leading phrases and concepts</u>.

Finally, read each question carefully, and seek the answer in definite parts - sentences, clauses, phrases, figures of speech, adverbs, adjectives, etc. - in the text of the passage.

2. Be sure to answer the questions <u>only</u> on the basis of the passage, and not from any other source. Answers may not be directly found in the text.

For the more difficult reading questions, answers are usually to be inferred or derived from the sense of one or <u>more</u> sentences, clauses, and even paragraphs.

3. Do not expect to find the bases for the answers in sequential parts of the textual material. The difficulty of questions is increased when the candidate is required to skip from one part of the passage to another without any order, i.e., question 1 may have its root in the last sentence of the paragraph, let us say, and question 5 may be based upon the second sentence, for example. This is a method of increasing the difficulty of the research and investigation required of the candidate.

4. When the question refers to a specific line, sentence, paragraph, or quotation, be sure to find this reference and to re-read it thoroughly. <u>The answer to such a question is almost certain to be found in or near this reference in the passage</u>.

5. Time for the reading question is limited, as it is for the examination as a whole. In other words, one must work speedily as well as effectively. The candidate, in seeking the answers to the reading questions, is not expected to go through all of the items in the thorough way presented in the sample questions above. That is, he has only to suit himself. It suffices, in order to attain to the right answer, to note <u>mentally</u> the basis for the answer in the text. There is no need to <u>annotate</u> your answer or to <u>write out</u> reasons for your answer. What we have attempted to do in the samples is to show that there is a definite and logical attack on this type of question, which, principally, consists of careful, critical reading, research and investigation, and evaluation of the material. One must learn to arrive at the correct answer through this process rather than through hit or miss tactics or guessing. There is no reading comprehension question, logically or fairly devised, which cannot be answered by the candidate provided he goes about this task in a systematic, sustained manner.

6. The candidate may be assisted by this advanced technique. Often, the general sense of the passage when fully captured, <u>rather than specific parts in the passage</u>, will lead to the correct answer. Therefore, it is most important that the candidate read the passage for total meaning first. This type of general understanding will be most helpful in answering those questions which have no specific background in the text but, rather, must be inferred from what has been read.

7. Beware of the following pitfalls:

    a. The categorical statement - You can almost be sure that any answer which uses the words <u>solely</u>, <u>wholly</u>, <u>always</u>, <u>never</u>, <u>at all</u> <u>times</u>, <u>forever</u>, etc., is wrong.

b.	The too-easy answer - When the question appears to be so simple that it can be answered almost word for word by reference to the text, be particularly on your guard. You will, probably, find that the language of the question may have been inverted or changed or that some important word has been added or omitted, so that you are being tested for alertness and attention to details. For example, if, in a passage, a comparison is made between Country A and Country B, and you are told that Country A has twice the area of Country B, and the question contains an item which states that *it is clear that the area of Country B is greater than Country A*, note how easily you can be beguiled into accepting this statement as true.

c.	Questions requiring that the candidate show his understanding of the main point of a passage, e.g., to state the central theme, or to suggest a worthy title, must be answered on that basis alone. You may be sure that other worthy possibilities are available, but you should examine your choice from the points of view of both appropriateness and breadth. For the most part, answers that are ruled out will contain one, but not both, of these characteristics.

d.	Make up your mind now that some, but not all, of the material in the various passages in the reading comprehension questions will be useful for finding the answer. Sometimes, passages are made purposely long to heighten the difficulty and to further confuse the harried candidates. However, do not disregard any of the textual material without first having given it a thorough reading.

e.	If the question requires that you give the writer's opinion or feelings or possible future action, do just that, and do not substitute your own predilections or antidotes. Similarly, do not make inferences if there exists in the text a clear-cut statement of facts. Base your answer, preferably, on the facts; make inferences or assumptions when they are called for, or as necessary.

f.	Do not expect the passages to deal with your subject field(s) alone. The passages offered will illustrate all the academic areas. While interest is a major factor in attaining to success, resolve now that you are going to wade through all the passages, in a thorough way, be they science or mathematics or economics or art. Unfamiliarity with a subject is no excuse on this type of test since the answers are to be based upon the reading passage alone.

In corollary fashion, should you encounter a passage dealing with a field with which you are familiar, do not permit your special knowledge to play a part in your answer. Answer only on the basis of the passage, as directed.

g.	The hardest type of reading question is the one in which the fifth choice presented is *none of these*. Should this phrase prove to be the correct answer, it would require a thorough, albeit rapid, examination of ALL the possibilities. This, of course, is time consuming and often frustrating.

h.	A final word of advice at this point. On the examination, leave the more difficult reading questions for the end. Try to answer those of lesser difficulty first. In this way, you will leave yourself maximum time for the really difficult part of the examination.

THE READING COMPREHENSION QUESTION ON THE GED TESTS

What has been said above has prime importance for, and application to, the examinations in the areas of social studies, natural sciences, and literary materials, respectively, as all of these tests are posed in the form of reading comprehension. That is, they consist of a selection of passages from the fields of social studies, natural sciences, and literary materials, respectively, at the high school level, and a number of questions testing the examinee's ability to comprehend and interpret the content of each passage.

As an entity, these tests purpose to determine the student's ability to interpret and to evaluate reading materials representative of those that he will have to read and study in his later school work. By means of this type of test, the student is called upon to demonstrate an expansive background of basic knowledge for it is obvious that a person's ability to interpret and evaluate printed information relative to any special subject depends for the most part upon how much he has already imbibed of the subject and the broad areas from which it has been selected. If the student possesses a wide background, he will be more likely to answer correctly the questions which call for a direct interpretation of the reading selection. A test of this type will thus require that an integrated body of knowledge be applied to particular problems, at the same time not placing any undue reward upon the form or manner in which the candidate's principles have evolved and not penalize him unduly for lack of ability to offer up any particular fact or set of facts where, in truth, another would serve the same general purpose.

These tests, then, are well suited for the task of determining the depth and power of the student's resources of substantial knowledge in the field tested. But the primary reason for using this type of test in this five-test battery is its particular efficacy and felicity in measuring and evaluating the generalized intellectual skills and abilities so necessary for the student for successful school work. These skills and abilities encompass the important aims of detecting errors and inconsistencies in logic; developing and applying generalizations; determining the adequacy of evidence; drawing inferences from data; noting implicit assumptions; searching out meanings not explicitly stated; forming value judgments; recognizing as such appeals to the emotions rather than to the intellect; perceiving and turning away the blandishments of the propagandists; detecting bias; and habituating oneself to the forms and methods of critical thinking.

INTERPRETATION OF READING MATERIALS IN THE SOCIAL STUDIES

INTRODUCTION

This Test consists of a number of selected passages from the field of the social studies and a number of questions, all of the multiple-choice type, testing the examinee's ability to comprehend and interpret the content of each passage. The emphasis is on demonstration of intellectual power rather than grasp of detailed content, the ability to use generalizations and concepts, and the power to comprehend, evaluate, and think clearly in terms of principles and ideas.

The candidate should note that this is a test of reading comprehension, and the answers for the most part are to be found in and by and through the text. Only a small portion of the questions is involved with or depends upon acquired basal or related information or knowledge.

The materials that follow have been planned to include, or to evolve, in equivalent form, quality, and degree of difficulty, all the aims set forth above for this test sector. The passages have been selected and presented, so far as possible, in ascending order of difficulty to achieve optimum self-instructional progression and maximum learning affect.

To achieve these purposes, ten (10) *Tests* are so offered, with answers, and with the answers fully explained, so that the candidate may learn how to go about answering the questions as well as the bases involved in attaining to the correct answers.

In addition, as a follow-up and as a reservoir for practice and drill and work-study, ten (10) additional *Tests* appear, in a similar gradation of difficulty and with an equal consistency. The correct answers are furnished for these questions.

Note: The questions in the *Tests* are presented for the most part in a five-item-choice form, which means that these questions are approximately 20% more difficult than the ones to be encountered on the Examination. This presentation should result in more extended effort and help to eliminate more surely any reliance on the element of guessing or any resignation into a mood of indifference to preparation.

The directions are approximately as follows, and these directions will govern the tests that follow:

DIRECTIONS: You have two hours for this test. As you answer the questions, you should omit any that seem unusually difficult until you finish the others.

This test consists of a number of short reading passages taken from textbooks and other writings in the social studies. The passages represent different methods of discussion and different points of view. Each passage is followed by a number of multiple-choice questions based on the passage. Read the passage first, and then answer the questions following it. Refer again to the passages as often as you find necessary in answering the question.

You will find that some of the questions will require considerable deliberation and frequent rereading of the passage. This is, in part, a test of your background in the social studies, but it is much more than just that. It is also a *study test* — a test of your ability to *dig out* the important meanings in what you read. The test will not penalize you seriously for having forgotten many of the detailed facts you once knew, if only you have retained the important generalizations and are able to use them intelligently in interpreting what you read.

Sample question and answers follow.

INTERPRETATION OF READING MATERIALS IN THE SOCIAL STUDIES

SAMPLE QUESTION

DIRECTIONS: In the passage that follows, each question or incomplete statement below is followed by several suggested answers or completions. Select the one that BEST answers the question or completes the statement. Base your choice in each case on the materials given and on your own understanding of the subject matter.

PASSAGE

Well, easily the most obvious badge of class in Britain is the accent of spoken language. Sociologists used to predict that the influence of radio would iron out regional accents and pronunciations and convert everyone into a passable imitation of a B.B.C. announcer. They have been proved wrong. In some strange ways, the standard London voices emerging from the wireless set have stiffened the resolution of the regions to maintain their regionalism. The old accents, the broad vowels of Yorkshire and Lancashire, the rich brogues of the West Country and the tortured staccato tones of the Cockney are heard as often as ever they were - and what's more they have more or less ousted spoken B.B.C. from the influential "telly." Most of our TV commercials use lower-middle class inflexions and strong regional accents to put across their message.

Quality and more value for money are clearly associated in the LMC mind with rugged, down-to-earth, nonsense language. During the war, the most effective broadcasters were Winston Churchill and J.B. Priestley, neither of whom used public-school accents. Churchill went out of his way to mispronounce such words as Nazi and Montevideo and spoke simply even when at his most rhetorical. Priestley employed a strong "Bruddersford" accent, as he has always done, and once again the message was strongly reinforced by the mode of delivery. The voice of authority is still that of John Citizen, the Man in the Street.

1. The advent of the B.B.C.

    A. standardized speech
    B. made people aware of the differences in accents
    C. revised the standards of English speech
    D. converted regional accents
    E. encouraged predictions from sociologists

1.____

In paragraph 1, it is mentioned that sociologists used to predict that regional accents would be influenced by the speech of the B.B.C. Therefore, Item E is correct. The paragraph further states that these predictions were proven wrong; therefore, Items A, B, and C must be incorrect. It is stated throughout the passage that regional accents were rather reinforced by the B.B.C. standard. Item B is not mentioned in the passage; however, it is safe to assume that people were always aware of the differences in accents.

2. The regional accent called Yorkshire

    A. stiffened the resolution of this region to change its speech habits
    B. is a kind of brogue
    C. has disappeared

2.____

D. contains broad vowels
E. is staccato

Item A is false because the passage states that the resolution was stiffened to MAINTAIN their speech habits. Item B refers to the West Country accent. Item E refers to Cockney. Item C is false because ...*Yorkshire...*, *Lancashire...the West Country ...the Cockney are heard as often as ever they were.* The passage also mentions the *broad vowels of Yorkshire.* Therefore, Item D is correct.

3. Most B.B.C. commercials are

    A. prohibited by the government
    B. considered contrary to the principles of B.B.C. broadcasting
    C. referred to as *telly*
    D. using upper-middle class accents
    E. using lower-middle class inflexions

3.____

The passage states (end of paragraph one), *Most of our TV commercials use lower-middle class inflexions....* Therefore, Item E is correct. Items A and B are not mentioned in the passage. Item C refers to an English colloquialism for television. Item D is false.

4. Why did Churchill occasionally mispronounce words?
Because

    A. he rose from the lower classes
    B. he didn't have an extensive education
    C. he wanted the majority of the people to heed him
    D. English pronunciation is often unlike American
    E. he used a public-school accent

4.____

Items A and B are false, aside from not being mentioned in the passage. The last paragraph of the passage explains why Item C is the correct one. It states that the voice of authority is the man in the street, that is, a voice which would use simple speech, a regional accent, and occasionally mispronounce words. Item D has nothing to do with the question. Item E is false: a public-school accent, in England, designates a higher standard of speech.

5. J.B. Priestley was

    A. a prominent member of Parliament
    B. a prominent industrialist
    C. the head of the B.B.C.
    D. a novelist
    E. an ambassador

5.____

J.B. Priestley was a prominent English playwright and novelist. Therefore, Item D is correct. Items A, B, C, and E are false.

6. The opposite of a *Bruddersford* accent (the combining of the names of two Yorkshire mill towns) might be called

6.____

A. Oxford   B. Cockney   C. Exeter   D. Oxbridge   E. Cambridge

There is an *Oxbridge* accent, also a portmanteau word (PORTMANTEAU WORD, a word made by telescoping or blending two other words, as BRUNCH for BREAKFAST and LUNCH), signifying the accents of Oxford and Cambridge. It is upper-class and, therefore, the opposite of the accent which derives its name from the two mill towns. Therefore, Item D is correct. Items A, B, C, and E are false.

EXAMINATION SECTION
TEST 1

PASSAGE

Secretary of State Richard Olney in 1895 was only stating the truth when he insisted that all basic political power in the Caribbean was in the hands of the United States, but in asserting this view, he used the infuriating word "fiat" - which annoyed both the British and the Latin Americans. Theodore Roosevelt, in creating the Republic of Panama, behaved no worse than the great W.E. Gladstone did in occupying Egypt; but Gladstone occupied Egypt with ostensible reluctance. (Henry Labouchere, the Liberal wit, said that what he objected to in the Grand Old Man was not his having the ace of trumps up his sleeve, but his assertion that God had put it there.) Theodore Roosevelt boasted of what he had done "to take the Canal," and his unfortunate candor was very expensive in cash and credit.

Then there is the question of the Senate. An examination of Molloy's great collection of treaties will show how late the British Foreign Office was in learning that a treaty with the Unites States is valid only if the Senate gives its consent. Again and again, European powers have made what they thought were hard bargains with the executive branch of the United States, only to have them rejected by the Senate. A great deal can be said in favor of many, if not all, of the Senate's actions, but the view expressed by John Hay that a treaty sent to the Senate has as much chance as a bull sent into the bull ring still survives in Europe if it no longer survives in the same form in the United States.

QUESTIONS

1. The author seems to be citing examples of

    A. successful U.S. diplomacy
    B. the need for better statesmen
    C. how certain U.S. statesmen have been diplomatically clumsy
    D. why Europe does not like the U.S.
    E. how the U.S. consistently mishandles foreign relations

2. In John Hay's view,

    A. treaties should not be made with foreign powers
    B. treaties should not be made by the executive branch of the government
    C. treaties should not have to be sent to the Senate
    D. all treaties made with other governments should be rejected by the Senate
    E. a treaty sent to the Senate has little chance of survival

3. Theodore Roosevelt, at one time,

    A. sent W.E. Gladstone to occupy Egypt
    B. stated that all political power in the Caribbean was in the hands of the U.S.
    C. was the Grand Old Man of the Democratic Party
    D. boasted of taking the Panama Canal
    E. infuriated both the British and the Latin Americans by his use of the word *fiat*

4. The author of this passage might be said to be writing in a vein

    A. of acceptance regarding past American blunders
    B. of criticism tempered with humor
    C. which is extremely unflattering to Europe

D. of ridicule
E. of malice

5. The author seems to be suggesting that

   A. European and Latin American countries are in disagreement with the U.S.
   B. the U.S. could be more diplomatically astute
   C. treaties should not be subject to both Senate and Executive approval
   D. Europe does not understand the U.S. system of ratifying treaties
   E. Theodore Roosevelt was not one of the best Presidents of the U.S.

6. Theodore Roosevelt was famous for having said

   A. "The business of America is business"
   B. (In reference to isolationalism) "River, stay, 'way from my door"
   C. "Speak softly and carry a big stick"
   D. "The only thing we have to fear is fear itself"
   E. "This generation has a rendezvous with destiny"

KEY (CORRECT ANSWERS)

1. C	4. B
2. E	5. B
3. D	6. C

EXPLANATION OF ANSWERS

1. The CORRECT ANSWER IS C. The author is not making any general statement, but citing certain cases. Therefore, B, D, and E must be considered too general. And since the author is citing cases of an unsuccessful nature, A is, of course, false.

2. In the last sentence of the last paragraph occurs John Hay's comparison of the Senate and the bull ring. This view indicates that E MUST BE THE CORRECT ANSWER. He did not comment on the treatment of treaties by either branch of the government.

3. The CORRECT ANSWER IS D, as shown in the last sentence of Paragraph 1. Items B and E refer to Richard Olney. While he is referred to in the passage as the Grand Old Man, he was not a Democrat..

4. Closer to the tone of the passage than the possibilities of A, D, or E is the answer stated in B. D and E are rather strong as descriptions of the passage, while A is too weak. C is completely false. The CORRECT ANSWER, THEN, IS B.

5. Items C and E are not stated or suggested at all in the passage. Items A and D are too extreme in their conclusions. B, THEN, WOULD SEEM TO BE THE MOST FITTING ANSWER.

    5._____

6. A was said by President Coolidge; D and E by Franklin Delano Roosevelt; C WAS SAID BY THEODORE ROOSEVELT AND IS THE CORRECT ANSWER.

    6._____

TEST 2

PASSAGE

The position Makarios holds in Cyprus is the result of his own skillful maneuvers. It is a position which he has built up by Byzantine wiliness, by clever use of other personalities, of the press, of the emotions of the people he knows so well. When other governments, driven to desperation by the Cyprus problem, drop hints that were Makarios to be overthrown the problem could quickly be solved, they are talking dangerous nonsense. Makarios is a man of his people, with their strengths and their weaknesses. If the Cyprus problem is to be solved, he is the man who must be convinced that the solution is just, he is the man whose confidence must be gained, for in Cyprus he alone will be able to convince and retain the confidence of his people.

Makarios explains the relationship between himself and his people this way: "The Archbishop of Cyprus is elected by the whole people. Ours is the only church in the world where this happens. He is elected to be the religious and national leader. I, therefore, enjoy the confidence of the vast majority of my people. I can convince the people. I am not a party leader; I have no army to force them to follow me: I express the will of the people and the people follow me. I just do what I think right."

Makarios does not himself dismiss the thesis that were he removed, the Cyprus problem could be more quickly solved. He admits that he is a stubborn man and that this stubbornness has already thwarted both the Americans and the British in imposing their ideas of a settlement. "I am stubborn. I cannot do what I do not believe in."

QUESTIONS

1. Makarios, President and Archbishop of Cyprus, gained his position

    A. by a Byzantine coup
    B. by consent of the populace
    C. through the press
    D. by playing upon emotionalism
    E. through strategic use of his armies

2. The author of the passage indicated a belief that Makarios

    A. was in danger of being overthrown
    B. was actually a dictator
    C. should not head both church and state
    D. was representative of the average Cypriote
    E. did not enjoy the confidence of his people

3. The British had been thwarted in imposing their ideas by

    A. the Americans   B. the Cypriote army
    C. party leadership   D. Makarios
    E. NATO

4. The Cypriote Orthodox Church is unique in that it(s)

    A. has its own army
    B. is not wholly separate from affairs of state

C. head is appointed
D. Archbishop is elected by the whole people
E. religious leader is not its national leader

5. Cyprus is an island which belongs to (the)

   A. Greece
   B. Turkey
   C. Malta
   D. British Commonwealth
   E. Enosis

6. Corcyra, an adjacent Grecian island, is acknowledged to be immortalized in the literary work of

   A. THE TEMPEST
   B. ELECTRA
   C. MEDEA
   D. ETRUSCAN PLACES
   E. OEDIPUS REX

KEY (CORRECT ANSWERS)

1. B   4. D
2. D   5. D
3. D   6. A

EXPLANATION OF ANSWERS

1. The passage states Makarios is a *man of his people* and retains the confidence of his people. The passage further states, *"The Archbishop of Cyprus is elected by the whole people."* Therefore, though C and D may have influenced their decision, he holds his office by consent of the people. THE CORRECT ANSWER, THEN, IS B.

2. Towards the end of the first paragraph, Makarios is deemed to be *a man of his people.....with their strengths and weaknesses,* WHICH WOULD MAKE ITEM D CORRECT. The writer refers to the talk of his being overthrown as *dangerous nonsense.* He does not express any opinion on Items B and C, and refutes Item E.

3. The passage states that both the Americans and the British have been thwarted in imposing their ideas, and, we must presume, have been so thwarted by Makarios. THEREFORE, THE ANSWER IS D. He says, in the passage, *"I am not a party leader...,"* discounting C as a possible answer. B and E are not mentioned.

4. D IS THE CORRECT ANSWER and is stated in the quotation in Paragraph 2, where Makarios says, *"...Ours is the only church in the world where this happens."* Item B is a correct statement regarding the Church, but is not a unique fact; Items A, C, and E are false.

    4._____

5. The Cypriotes elected in 1961 to become members of the British Commonwealth of Nations. It has rejected its political ties with Greece; THEREFORE, THE CORRECT ANSWER WOULD BE D. (Enosis, Item E, is the Greek word for *union,* referring, in this case, to the union of Greece and Cyprus.)

    5._____

6. Shakespeare's THE TEMPEST is said to have derived its locale from Corcyra, WHICH RENDERS ITEM A CORRECT. (And there exists in THE TEMPEST a name which is an anagram for Corcyra.) D is a travelogue about Greece written by D.H. Lawrence but is not specifically related to Corcyra; nor are answers B, C, and E.

    6._____

TEST 3
PASSAGE

The old argument about the respective merits of career and non-career appointments has little relevance. Today and in the future, most ambassadors will come from the career service - the proportion is now about two out of three - but there will still be room for candidates with special qualifications brought in from outside - as witness General Taylor. There is no place, however, as Ambassador Samuel Berger, recent envoy to Korea, has said, for a "non-career man who brings neither interest, nor aptitude, nor professional skills" to the job.

Over the years, successful ambassadors have come from many different backgrounds and occupations. If any generalization is valid, it may be that a solid foundation in some specialty is an asset, for mastery of a particular field often seems to lend a person added depth and confidence. The Foreign Service has tried to give young officers opportunities to specialize, but, on the whole, too few have been allowed to spend enough time in one place or in one type of work or to take advanced studies. Today, qualifications in the social sciences, in economics or in military affairs are highly desirable.

Yet, when all is said and done, the important thing is that an ambassador be a cultivated man who, in the best sense, is wise in the ways of the world, with the maturity of judgment that comes from varied experience, and with reserves of know-how and courage to call upon in a pinch.

QUESTIONS

1. It is found to be an asset that an ambassador have

    A. interest
    B. depth
    C. some specialization
    D. as many languages as possible
    E. confidence

2. One reason the officers of the foreign service have NOT become proficient in any one field is

    A. the concentration required is incompatible with the temperament of the typical ambassador
    B. they have too much to do
    C. their work demands a general knowledge
    D. they concentrate on one type of work
    E. they move around too much

3. An ambassador should be

    A. highly civilized
    B. well-liked
    C. reliable
    D. a linguist
    E. courageous

4. Successful ambassadors, prior to their appointment, are enlisted from

    A. the best universities
    B. varied backgrounds
    C. men active in Washington
    D. Cabinet members
    E. industry

5. Fundamentally, an ambassador is

A. totally responsible for our *image* abroad
B. responsible for any uprisings that might occur in the country to which he is appointed
C. the President's personal agent
D. guaranteed diplomatic immunity
E. fulfilling a social as well as political role

6. His traditional role is 6.____

A. that of teacher
B. to promote industry
C. to see that people form the best possible impression of the U.S.
D. that of a negotiator
E. that of a propagandist

KEY (CORRECT ANSWERS)

1. C   4. B
2. E   5. C
3. A   6. D

EXPLANATION OF ANSWERS

1. *"A solid foundation in some specialization is an asset,"* states the author. Answers B and E are mentioned as beneficial, but they are the by-products of NUMBER C, WHICH IS THE CORRECT ANSWER. 1.____

2. The ANSWER IS CONTAINED IN PARAGRAPH 2, SENTENCE 3. B and C might be considered valid answers were it not for the more specific inclusion of Answer E, which is taken directly from the passage. 2.____

3. The last paragraph describes a cultivated man: wise, mature, experienced, courageous. It states that this is *the important thing.* Such a man would be termed highly civilized. THUS, THE ANSWER IS A. The other items, particularly E, courageous, are assets but are merely parts of the *whole-cultivated* or civilized. 3.____

4. THE OPENING SENTENCE OF PARAGRAPH 2 CONTAINS THE ANSWER: IT IS ITEM B. While any of the other answers presented may count as factors in the selection of an ambassador, no particular one is favored. 4.____

5. C IS THE CORRECT ANSWER. For any one man to fulfill the requirements of Answers A and B would be impossible. D and E are true factually regarding ambassadors, but hardly describe their fundamental role. 5.____

6. D IS THE ANSWER HERE. He is not a teacher nor is he that which is stated in B. C and E are superficial duties compared to the vital act of negotiator or arbiter. 6.____

TEST 4
PASSAGE

Unless all the warning signals are wrong, this year we are really in for it. The mudslinging, the personal attacks, and the smears that always accompany a national election threaten in the next few weeks to submerge completely the voices of reasoned debate. Once again, as Lord Bryce declared, we are going to be treated to "the spectacle of half the honest men supporting for the leadership of the nation a person whom the other half declare to be a knave."

A knave, did he say? No mere knave. A thief, a cheat, a fixer of elections, a fake, a phony, a dodger of military duty, an inciter of riots, a coddler of Communists - and a man who is certain to be the victim of another heart attack.

Or: a crypto-Fascist, a warmonger, an extremist, a nuclear adventurer, a fool, a frustrated dictator, a simpleton, a racist, a fallout fancier, a know-nothing, a menace to little girls eating ice cream cones - and a man subject to recurrent nervous breakdowns.

All these epithets have been hurled at President Johnson or Senator Goldwater already. And the real smear season - the final frenzied few weeks of the campaign - is still to come.

Even before the cannonading began, Bruce L. Felknor, executive director of the Fair Campaign Practices Committee, the 10-year-old private agency that attempts to referee election battles, predicted that this would be an "exceptionally rough" campaign. He said that the "unusual polarization of opinion" - exemplified by Senator Gold-water's determination to provide "a choice, not an echo" - has given this campaign an encompassing emotional intensity rare in national politics.

QUESTIONS

1. The author states that mudslinging

    A. is always accompanied by warning signals
    B. is the worst sort of personal attack
    C. is dishonest
    D. was denounced by Lord Bryce
    E. always accompanies a national election

2. While Lord Bryce uses the word *knave*, the author implies that

    A. he really means a thief
    B. usually half the nation denounces the man running for office
    C. were Lord Bryce living today he would find other words
    D. today such a word would be considered mild
    E. men running for office can inspire riots

3. The *spectacle* referred to in the passage is the

    A. political campaign speeches
    B. election
    C. political parties

D. reasoned or unreasoned debate
E. manner in which the people express their choice

4. In which of the following comparisons made by the author is the parallelism of the characteristics MOST satisfactory?

   A. A cheat and an extremist
   B. The victim of a heart attack and a man subject to nervous breakdowns
   C. A phony and a fallout fancier
   D. An inciter of riots and a crypto-Fascist
   E. A fake and a fool

5. Why does the author feel that personal attacks threaten to submerge reasoned debate? Because

   A. they are incompatible with one another
   B. people are swayed by such attacks
   C. a man who will denounce and attack personally is incapable of reason
   D. valid personal attacks may disqualify an otherwise suitable candidate
   E. the persons seeking to defame through personal attack may thereby promote public sympathy for the opposition through vile or illogical defamation

6. What does the author mean by the term *nuclear adventurer*? A man who

   A. would be inclined to experiment in the search for more effective nuclear weapons
   B. would seek to employ nuclear discoveries to maintain the peace
   C. would be adventurous and imaginative in recruiting scientists to better our nuclear position in the arms race
   D. would probably spend too much of the taxpayers' money on the building of unnecessary planes and bombs
   E. might act without sufficient forethought and consultation and possibly plunge the world into a nuclear war

KEY (CORRECT ANSWERS)

1. E   4. B
2. D   5. A
3. E   6. E

EXPLANATION OF ANSWERS

1. This is a common sense question answered directly in the passage. It is also the theme of the article. THE CORRECT ANSWER IS E. While C and D might be considered indirectly correct through deduction, they are not stated in the passage.

2. The author uses the quotation in Paragraph 1 directly to contrast with the stronger terminology of Paragraph 2. The clue to the correct answer is contained in the second sentence of Paragraph 2, THE ONLY POSSIBLE ANSWER THEN BEING D. C is misleading because the author's attention is focused on the changes in the times and in words, not in conjecture on the words Lord Bryce might use today.

3. The *spectacle* referred to in the quotation is concerned with .... *half the honest men....leadership of the nation-.... to be a knave.* Therefore, THE CORRECT ANSWER IS E. While A and C seek to condition the response of the people, they, themselves, are not the *spectacle*.

4. THE ONLY ANSWER WHICH STATES SIMILAR CHARACTERISTICS IS B. The other pairs of epithets bears no relationship to one another.

5. The author implies that the smear personal attack is unreasonable and absurd, thus making it impossible to stem from, or to exist alongside, reasonable argument. A, THEN, IS THE ONLY POSSIBLE CORRECT ANSWER. While B and E may be true, they are not in direct relation to the question.

6. Though this information is not specifically contained in the passage, it should be reasonably surmised that the term stated is an epithet, which disqualifies A, B, and C. The threat contained in E is far stronger and more extreme than the description in D. THEREFORE, E IS THE CORRECT ANSWER.

TEST 5
PASSAGE

The permanent system, which went into force in 1920, includes essentially all the elements of immigration policy that are in our law today. The immigration statutes now establish a system of annual quotas to govern immigration from each country. Under this system, 156,987 quota immigrants are permitted to enter the United States each year. The quotas from each country are based upon the national origins of the population of the United States in 1920.

The use of the year 1920 is arbitrary. It rests upon the fact that this system was introduced in 1924, and the last prior census was in 1920. The use of a national origins system is without basis in either logic or reason. It neither satisfies a national need nor accomplishes an international purpose.

In an age of interdependence among nations, such a system is an anachronism, for it discriminates among applicants for admission into the United States on the basis of accident of birth.

Because of the composition of our population in 1920, the system is heavily weighted in favor of immigration from northern Europe and severely limits immigration from southern and eastern Europe and from other parts of the world.

A qualified person born in England or Ireland who wants to emigrate to the United States can do so at any time. A person born in Italy, Hungary, Poland, or the Baltic states may have to wait many years before his turn is reached.

One writer has listed six motives behind the act of 1924. They were: (1) postwar isolationism; (2) the doctrine of the alleged superiority of Anglo-Saxon and Teutonic "races"; (3) the fear that "pauper labor" would lower wage levels; (4) the belief that people of certain nations were less law-abiding than others; (5) the fear that entrance of many people with different customs and habits would undermine our national and social unity and order.

QUESTIONS

1. The immigration quota in effect then was based upon the

    A. current population of the United States
    B. population of the United States in 1920
    C. act of 1921
    D. population of the United States in 1929
    E. nationalities living at present in the United States

2. The author of the passage seems to feel that our immigration system is

    A. necessary
    B. illogical
    C. understandable
    D. inevitable
    E. though not completely fair, the only one possible at this time

3. Which of the reasons listed in parentheses at the end of the passage indicates why a person of English birth may (or may not) enter the United States?

   A. (1)   B. (2)   C. (3)   D. (4)   E. (5)

4. Why is the immigration system an anachronism?
   Because

   A. where it was once of value, it no longer is
   B. it dated back to 1920
   C. it favors immigration from southern and eastern Europe
   D. it limits immigration from northern Europe
   E. of our independence of other nations

5. A quota is

   A. a changing estimate
   B. a proportional part or share
   C. something that is quoted
   D. a number or amount
   E. a bid or offer so named or published

6. An emigrant is one who

   A. enters one country from another
   B. seeks residence in the United States
   C. migrates
   D. leaves a country for residence elsewhere
   E. enters and settles in another country

KEY (CORRECT ANSWERS)

1. B   4. B
2. B   5. B
3. B   6. D

EXPLANATION OF ANSWERS

1. At the end of Paragraph 1, the passage states, *"The quotas from each country are based upon the population of the United States in 1920."* THEREFORE, THE CORRECT ANSWER IS B. Since Items A, C, D, and E refer to events that have taken place since 1920, they are false. Item D indicates the year the permanent system went into force. Item C is not mentioned. Item A is not mentioned in relation to the immigration quota and what it is based upon; nor is item E.

2. The author states (Paragraph 2), *"The use of a national origins system is without basis in either logic or reason."* THEREFORE, THE CORRECT ANSWER IS B. From the quotation, the reader may assume that Items A, C, and E are false. Nowhere is Item D mentioned.

3. THE CORRECT ANSWER IS B. The passage states: *"(2) the doctrine of the alleged superiority of the Anglo-Saxon and Teutonic 'races'";* this statement immediately follows the flat declaration that *"A qualified person born in England....who wants to emigrate to the United States can do so at any time."* Items C, D, and E are contradictory to Item B. Item A is contradictory and irrelevant.

4. The author states, in Paragraph 3, that our present system is an anachronism because it is based on what was true of our population in 1920. THEREFORE, B IS THE CORRECT ANSWER. Item A is not correct because the author does not indicate that it was ever of value. Items C and D are false statements. And in Paragraph 3, the author speaks of the *interdependence* among nations, discounting E.

5. Item C refers to a quotation. Item E refers to a quotation of another kind, i.e., the stock market. Item D is incomplete and incorrect. THE CORRECT ANSWER, THEN, IS B. Item A is false because a quota is unchanging in its percentage effect.

TEST 6
PASSAGE

In Stalin's time, a leader removed from the Soviet power pyramid was tried, imprisoned, or executed, or became an "unperson" - disappearing not only physically but from all Soviet history and reference books.

Under Nikita Khrushchev, things changed. When "Khrush" got rid of "Bulge" (Premier Bulganin) and his other rivals in 1957, the worst he did was to accuse them of being "antiparty" and send them into obscurity.

Week before last, when Mr. K's own time came, there was a throwback of sorts to the Russia of Koestler's "Darkness at Noon." Official secrecy on how he was removed remained complete. The new "B and K" team of Leonid Brezhnev, 57, party First Secretary (and hence Number One) and Aleksei Kosygin, 60, Premier, conducted itself at public functions for the three latest Soviet cosmonauts as though the "dearly beloved Nikita Sergeyevitch" of the past seven years no longer existed. Books about him disappeared from bookstores; portraits of him still remaining on store counters, could not be bought.

The rigidly controlled Soviet press rested on its brief announcement of 11 days ago that Mr. Khrushchev had been relieved of his duties at his own request due to advancing age (he was 70) and failing health. And, by early last week, it became clear that this way of disposing of leaders would no longer suffice - not for the foreign Communist parties, with their new and less subservient relationship with Moscow, nor, possibly, for the Russian people, thawed out partially from political terror and less susceptible to myths and mysteries.

QUESTIONS

1. When Khrushchev's position as Soviet leader terminated,

    A. he was imprisoned
    B. he was accused of being *antiparty*
    C. there was complete official secrecy regarding the manner
    D. Brezhnev and Kosygin spoke well of him
    E. he was sent into obscurity

2. He was replaced as First Secretary by

    A. Brezhnev
    B. Kosygin
    C. Nikita Sergeyevitch
    D. Bulganin
    E. Brezhnev and Kosygin

3. Books written about Khrushchev

    A. unlike those in Stalin's period, did not disappear
    B. remained, unsold, on the bookshelves
    C. are currently being rewritten
    D. disappeared from the bookstores
    E. shared the same fate as his portraits

4. The author seems to be of the opinion that, regarding Khrushchev,

   A. his age and health made it impossible for him to maintain his position
   B. the Russian people have accepted his absence without question
   C. foreign branches of the party will cease to ask questions
   D. the party will have to elaborate on its eleven-day-old statement
   E. the people are too susceptible to political terror to demand further information or explanation

5. Stalin, after his death, was replaced by

   A. Mikoyan and Bulganin
   B. Molotov and Khrushchev
   C. Gromyko and Malenkov
   D. Beria, Khrushchev, and Malenkov
   E. Aleksei Adzubei and Marshal Zhukhov

6. In 1962, Khrushchev suffered a defeat when he

   A. withdrew troops from Vietnam
   B. had to abandon his farm programs as disastrous
   C. made a diplomatic break with China
   D. had to answer charges of nepotism
   E. was forced to withdraw missiles from Cuba

KEY (CORRECT ANSWERS)

1. C   4. D
2. A   5. D
3. D   6. E

EXPLANATION OF ANSWERS

1. Item A relates to the Stalinist period, and Items B and E relate to the Khrushchev period. Item D is inaccurate because he was not spoken of by these men. And in Paragraph 3, it is stated that *"official secrecy on how he was removed remained complete."* THE ANSWER, THEN, IS C.

2. Khrushchev held two positions, that of First Secretary and Premier. He was replaced as First Secretary by Brezhnev (Paragraph 3, sentence 3), and as Premier by Kosygin (Item B). THEREFORE, THE CORRECT ANSWER IS A. Item D, Bulganin, was his predecessor, and Item C, Nikita Sergeyevitch, are actually Khrushchev's first two names.

3. In the last sentence of Paragraph 3, the author states: *Books about him disappeared from bookstores...."* THIS INDICATES THAT D IS THE CORRECT ANSWER. Portraits of him (reference to Item E) remained in the stores but could not be bought (last clause of the last sentence of Paragraph 3), thus indicating that Item E is false. Item A is false because the books DID disappear. There is no mention made in the passage of their being rewritten, thus eliminating Item C. And the passage further indicates that they did NOT remain on the bookshelves, thus discounting B.

4. The last portion of the final paragraph makes clear the author's opinion that *this way of disposing of leaders would no longer suffice.* The final paragraph clearly refutes the acceptability of Items A, B, C, and E. THE CORRECT ANSWER HERE IS D.

5. Item E, Adzubei, was Khrushchev's son-in-law and the former editor of IZVESTIA, the official government newspaper. THE CORRECT ANSWER IS D, the *troika* of Beria, Khrushchev, and Malenkov. Beria was soon thereafter put to death, and Malenkov was deposed after approximately two years in power.

6. THE CORRECT ANSWER IS ITEM E. In the *nuclear crisis* of November, 1962, President Kennedy, of the United States, demanded the removal of all missiles from Cuba by the Russians. In a gigantic test of nerves, Khrushchev gave in. One year later, Kennedy was dead, the victim of an assassin's bullet. Tow years later, Khrushchev was out of power, peacefully deposed by the other party leaders. Item A, B, C, and D are not true.

TEST 7
PASSAGE

He is half the size of an American soldier and twice as disciplined. He does not smoke or drink. He shuns fish and meat and shrinks from contact with women.

To many exasperated Westerners, he seems bent on losing in Saigon any advantage the soldier wins on the battlefield. He believes that only his strategy will bring peace to Vietnam, that he will succeed where soldiers are bound to fail. His religion teaches humility and reconciliation, but he is jealous of his new political power and defiant in his demands.

He is a Buddhist priest. Like some Black clergymen in the United States, he has come to the forefront of a struggle that is recasting (1965) the shape of his country. He toppled one government in 1963. This(1965) year, he shook another until its military leader approached his temple as chastened as a novice seeking instruction.

In one sense, each priest exemplifies the movement. Since they united to overthrow President Ngo Dinh Diem, the Buddhists have spoken with a single voice.

QUESTIONS

1. In the passage, the author makes a comparison between

    A. a Black man and a clergyman
    B. a priest and a Buddhist
    C. the battlefield and Saigon
    D. a soldier and a priest
    E. the Buddhists and President Diem

2. The Buddhist priest, on matters of military strategy,

    A. looks to the United States
    B. trusts the Vietnamese soldiers
    C. trusts the American soldiers
    D. belives only in himself
    E. disbelieves in toppling governments

3. In matters of food, he is

    A. a vegetarian
    B. constantly fasting
    C. as disciplined as his countrymen
    D. disinterested
    E. a consumer of fish and meat only

4. The author indicates there is a contradiction between the Buddhists'

    A. religion and their political demands
    B. humility and their belief in reconciliation
    C. desire to recast the shape of their government and their toppling of governments
    D. strategy and their announced political aim
    E. jealousy of their political power and their new demands

5. Until 1963, Vietnam was ruled by

    A. a Buddhist, Thich Tam Chau
    B. a Roman Catholic Archbishop
    C. Nguyen Khanh
    D. *Big Minh*
    E. Ngo Dinh Diem

6. A coup d'etat refers specifically to the overthrow of an existing government by

    A. stuffing the ballot boxes
    B. civil war
    C. dynastic legitimization
    D. a decisive blow
    E. a revolutionary small group

KEY (CORRECT ANSWERS)

1.	D	4.	A
2.	D	5.	E
3.	A	6.	E

EXPLANATION OF ANSWERS

1. The passage begins with a comparison between an American soldier and a Buddhist priest. THUS, D IS THE PROPER COMPLETION OF THE STATEMENT. The battlefield and Saigon (Item C) are not compared but, rather, the soldier and the priest in relation to them. There is a comparison made between a Black clergyman and a Buddhist priest, but not in the vein of Items A and B. There is no comparison such as Item E suggests in the passage.

2. In Paragraph 2 of the passage, the author states, *"He believes that only his strategy will bring peace to Vietnam";* and further that *"he will succeed where soldiers are bound to fail."* In Paragraph 3, the reader finds *"....he toppled one government in 1963."* Therefore, Items A, B, C, and E may be discarded, and D IS THE CORRECT ANSWER.

3. The reader is told (in Paragraph 1) that, *"....he shuns fish and meat."* This means he must be a consumer of such other foods as fruits, vegetables, etc., ESTABLISHING A AS THE CORRECT ANSWER. There is no mention made of the eating habits of his countrymen. And his diet, though disciplined, is not referred to as one of *constantly fasting* (Item B). Items C and D are not mentioned in the passage, and Item E is denied.

4. The last sentence in Paragraph 2 states, *"His religion teaches humility and reconciliation but he is jealous of his new political power and defiant in his demands."* THIS CONTRADICTION WOULD INDICATE THAT A IS THE CORRECT ANSWER. The other combinations of answers (Items B, C. D, and E) are actually consistent with one another, and not contradictory.

    4.____

5. The rule of Vietnam by President Ngo Dinh Diem, a Catholic layman, was overthrown in 1963 by a bloody military coup led by General Minh and General Khanh. ITEM E IS, THEREFORE, THE CORRECT ANSWER. Item A refers to the present (1965) Buddhists' chief political spokesman. Items A, B, C, and D are false. Item B refers to President Diem's brother, who was the Roman Catholic Archbishop of Vietnam.

    5.____

6. A *coup d'etat* is the violent overthrow of an existing government by a small group. That is, it signifies the overthrow and displacement of the leaders, rather than that of the system of government itself. E IS, THEREFORE, THE CORRECT ANSWER. Item D refers to a *coup de grace,* administering the final blow (or death) to a losing cause (or a dying person). Items A, B, and C are incorrect. General Khanh (Item C), a military leader, was apparently the real power in Vietnam then in 1965. *Big Minh* (Item D) refers to General Minh, who served briefly in a primary role after the deposition of Diem but who has now been relegated to a secondary place by General Khanh.

    6.____

TEST 8
PASSAGE

He won his unique place in history by what he did between the ages of 65 and 70. This is a stage of life at which most people have already retired and relaxed their grip. A lifetime's opportunity at 65! How many of us could have taken advantage of this at that age? But, at 65, Churchill was just ready to get going. In his 60's, he was what most of us are in our 40's. He was at the height of his powers.

In the trajectory of a human life, there is a brief span in which the unspent vigor of youth overlaps with the accumulated experience and wisdom of maturity. For most of us, if this brief golden moment comes at all, it comes between 40 and 50. Churchill's golden moment came 20 years farther on in life than usual. This was fortunate for Britain and for the world, and it was fatal for the Nazis and for Germany.

Some people who are famous today were virtually unknown during their lifetime. Mendel, the discoverer of the laws of genetics, had to wait till a whole generation had passed before he suddenly leaped into fame. Churchill's leap into fame was sudden, like Mendel's, but fortunately Churchill did not have to wait so long to receive his due. He had become supremely famous within a few days of taking over the Government of Britain in the dark and desperate situation in which Britain found herself in the summer of 1940. Churchill then became famous immediately, all over the world, and it is noteworthy that he became as famous in the United States as everywhere else.

This is noteworthy considering what Churchill's major achievement was. It was Churchill who foiled Germany's attempt to conquer the world, and the American people - so it seems to a European observer – have not even yet realized how near Germany came, twice within Churchill's lifetime, to accomplishing her evil ambition. Americans seem never to have taken the deadly German menace to human freedom so much to heart as they have taken the less formidable Communist menace.

QUESTIONS

1. Churchill had in common with Mendel

    A. a generation's wait before recognition
    B. a sudden leap into fame
    C. the fact that they both became famous within a few days of their accomplishments
    D. the fact that they both became famous for political reasons
    E. a similar attitude toward fame

2. The MOST unusual thing about Churchill's accomplishments in relation to his age was:

    A. In his 40's, he was what most of us are in our 60's
    B. What he had already accomplished by the time he was 65
    C. What he did between the ages of 65 and 70
    D. What he accomplished after the age of 70
    E. Churchill's *golden moment* came 20 years earlier than usual

3. What was MOST striking about Churchill's career?

   A. He foiled Germany's attempt to conquer the world.
   B. He became as famous in Europe as in America.
   C. Americans never seemed to take the German menace so seriously as the Communist one.
   D. He became as famous in the United States as everywhere else.
   E. He never achieved so much fame in America as he did in Europe.

3._____

4. The author feels there is a brief, important span of life which comes

   A. when certain elements of youth and maturity merge
   B. between 40 and 50
   C. with unspent youth
   D. with accumulated experience
   E. with the wisdom of maturity

4._____

5. Since the people of America considered Churchill every bit as important as the people of Europe, this was probably because

   A. Germany was as close to domination of America as it was to domination of Europe
   B. America never took the German menace to freedom so seriously as the Europeans
   C. the Americans recognized that their destiny, too, was at stake
   D. he had such emotional impact
   E. Germany had gained control of all Europe except for Britain

5._____

6. During the Second World War, Churchill was

   A. a leading member of Parliament
   B. England's Prime Minister
   C. First Lord of the Admiralty
   D. a prominent author of several books
   E. a member of the Cabinet

6._____

KEY (CORRECT ANSWERS)

1. B   4. A
2. C   5. C
3. D   6. B

EXPLANATION OF ANSWERS

1. Paragraph 3 states that *"Churchill's leap into fame was sudden, like Mendel's..."* And this was, apparently, the only thing they had in common. THEREFORE, B IS THE CORRECT ANSWER. Item A applies to Mendel alone, NOT to Churchill. Items C, D, and E are false.

2. *"He won his unique place in history by what he did between the ages of 65 and 70"* begins the passage. THEREFORE, C IS CLEARLY THE CORRECT ANSWER. Item A is incorrect because the reverse is actually stated in the passage. Items B, D, and E are false.

3. The author points out (at the end of Paragraph 3) how noteworthy it was that Churchill became as famous in the United States as he did everywhere else, albeit this was NOT his major achievement. THEREFORE, THE CORRECT ANSWER IS D. Item A is, according to the author, Churchill's major achievement, but it is not the correct answer here because it is not what the question calls for. Item B is incorrect. It is actually a reversal of Item A. Item E is false. Item C is stated in the passage but is not related to the question.

4. THE CORRECT ANSWER IS A and is explained at the beginning of Paragraph 3. This is a better answer than B because it is more specific. Items C, D, and E are only part of the correct answer and so are incomplete.

5. THE CORRECT ANSWER IS C. Item A is incorrect; Germany was not so close to the domination of America. Item E is true but is not the reason for, or the answer to, the statement. Item D is irrelevant. Item B is possibly true but does not satisfactorily complete the statement.

6. During World War II, Churchill was Prime Minister of England. He did hold all the other posts mentioned in Items A, C, and E, but PRIOR to World War II. He was a journalist and writer of books, Item D, but that was not his primary function during the war. THE CORRECT ANSWER, THEN, IS B.

TEST 9

PASSAGE

In the long, fabled history of China, many of her leaders have, like Mao Tse-tung, pushed their way by iron will and shrewdness from humble beginnings to supreme power. In one of his poems, Mao implied that none who has ruled China in the past, not even the pitiless Chin Emperor, Shih Huang Ti, nor the great Han Wu Ti, is his equal. Mao's estimate of himself was an index to the vanity and self-confidence of this one-time country bumpkin who not only wielded more power over China's swarming millions than any of his predecessors but aspired as well to power on a world scale.

The success that was to be his seemed already in Mao's sharp, reflective eyes and assured manner when this writer last saw him in Yenan in the winter of 1945. He received visiting foreign correspondents in the rustic building that was headquarters in bleak, northwest China for the Chinese Communist party. A big man with a round face, high cheekbones, and a shock of black hair combed straight back, he was dressed in a long-sleeved padded gown. Pictures showed him older, a little heavier, but with the same sharp, distant, dreamy look in his eyes that he had in Yenan. Aloofly, politely, he greeted us and then excused himself for more pressing duties, leaving the tedious details of explaining Chinese Communist views to Liu Shao-chi, then, as now, his right-hand man.

QUESTIONS

1. In 1945, Mao Tse-tung gave the impression of

   A. a man from humble beginnings
   B. a poet
   C. realistic self-confidence
   D. a man who had no wish for domination beyond China
   E. self-assurance

2. Mao felt himself to be the equal of

   A. Liu Shao-chi
   B. no one
   C. any of China's past Emperors
   D. Han Wu Ti
   E. Shih Huang Ti

3. The passage was taken from an article containing an interview with Mao. This interview took place in

   A. Cambodia   B. Manchuria   C. Yenan
   D. Canton   E. southwest China

4. A rather surprising disclosure, considering Mao's position, was that he

   A. was not humble
   B. did not feel himself greater than Han Wu Ti
   C. received visitors in a rustic building
   D. had written poems
   E. wore a long-sleeved padded gown

5. A part of China within his jurisdiction was

   A. Macao
   B. Kunming
   C. Hong Kong
   D. Formosa
   E. Laos

6. Mao's political philosophy of government was

   A. socialistic
   B. capitalistic
   C. that of a representative republic
   D. communistic
   E. democratic

KEY (CORRECT ANSWERS)

1. E   4. D
2. B   5. B
3. C   6. D

EXPLANATION OF ANSWERS

1. The author seems to feel that Mao had an excess of self-confidence which was not realistic. Also, the reader is told he *"...aspires as well to power on a world scale"* (end of Paragraph 1). The answer is contained in the first sentence of Paragraph 2 where the author speaks of Mao's *self-assured manner.* Obviously, he did not give the impression of a man from humble beginnings (Item A). THE CORRECT ANSWER, THEN, IS E. Item C is incorrect because a wish for such power does not seem realistic. Item D is false because the reverse is true. Item B is neither mentioned nor implied in relation to the impression Mao gave.

2. The passage states, *"In one of his poems, Mao implied that none who has ruled China in the past.....is his equal."* This leads us to discard Item C. THEREFORE, THE CORRECT ANSWER IS B. Liu Shao-chi (Item A) is his right-hand man. The other men (Items D and E) are past Emperors of China.

3. In Paragraph 2, the author states, *"He received visiting foreign correspondents.....in Yenan."* THEREFORE, C IS THE CORRECT ANSWER, and Items A, B, and D are false. Yenan is in northwest China, states the passage, discounting E.

4. The rustic building was headquarters for the Chinese Communist party, and is, therefore, not the correct answer. This discounts Item C. However, the reader is told in the first paragraph that Mao DOES write poems. THEREFORE, THE CORRECT ANSWER IS Items A and B are false statements. Item E is true but hardly a surprising disclosure.

5. THE CORRECT ANSWER TO QUESTION 5 is B. Kunming is a city in China. Item A, Macao, is a Portuguese possession. Item C, Hong Kong, is a British Crown Colony. Laos is an independent country, discounting E. Item D, Formosa, is not within the jurisdiction of Mao, and so is false.

5.____

6. China is now under Communist rule. THEREFORE, THE CORRECT ANSWER IS D. Items A, B, C, and E are false.

6.____

TEST 10
PASSAGE

On Sunday morning, November 24, arrangements were made for Oswald's transfer from the city jail to the Dallas County jail, about 1 mile away. The news media had been informed on Saturday night that the transfer of Oswald would not take place until after 10 A.M. on Sunday. Earlier on Sunday, between 2:30 and 3 A.M., anonymous telephone calls threatening Oswald's life had been received by the Dallas office of the FBI and by the office of the county sheriff. Nevertheless, on Sunday morning, television, radio, and newspaper representatives crowded into the basement to record the transfer. As viewed through television cameras, Oswald would emerge from a door in front of the cameras and proceed to the transfer vehicle. To the right of the cameras was a "down" ramp from Main Street on the north. To the left was an "up" ramp leading to Commerce Street on the south.

The armored truck in which Oswald was to be transferred arrived shortly after 11 A.M. Police officials then decided, however, that an unmarked police car would be preferable for the trip because of its greater speed and maneuverability. At approximately 11:20 A.M., Oswald emerged from the basement jail office flanked by detectives on either side and at his rear. He took a few steps toward the car and was in the glaring light of the television cameras when a man suddenly darted out from an area on the right of the cameras where newsmen had been assembled. The man was carrying a Colt .38 revolver in his right hand and, while millions watched on television, he moved quickly to within a few feet of Oswald and fired one shot into Oswald's abdomen. Oswald groaned with pain as he fell to the ground and quickly lost consciousness. Within 7 minutes, Oswald was at Parkland Hospital where, without having regained consciousness, he was pronounced dead at 1:07 P.M.

QUESTIONS

1. The news media were

    A. not informed of the transfer
    B. given the wrong time
    C. not present
    D. informed of the transfer
    E. informed that the transfer would take place on Saturday

2. To facilitate maneuverability, the police

    A. barred the press
    B. used an unmarked car
    C. used an armored truck
    D. flanked Oswald as he emerged from the basement
    E. announced the time of the transfer

3. Oswald died of

    A. a succession of shots fired
    B. one shot in the head
    C. one shot in the abdomen
    D. one shot from a Colt .32 revolver
    E. one shot fired from a rifle

2 (#10)

4. The armored truck arrived 4.____

    A. at 11:20 A.M.
    B. before Oswald emerged from the basement jail office
    C. about 10:00 A.M.
    D. at exactly 1:07 P.M.
    E. shortly before 2:30 A.M.

5. In relation to the television cameras, Commerce Street was 5.____

    A. to the left of the *up* ramp
    B. leading from Main Street
    C. leading from a *down* ramp
    D. to the left
    E. to the right

6. Oswald was shot when he 6.____

    A. had left the glaring light of the TV cameras
    B. took a few steps toward the car
    C. emerged from the basement
    D. entered the car
    E. emerged from the jail office

7. Oswald was 7.____

    A. an assassin
    B. an alleged assassin
    C. a murderer in the first degree
    D. a murderer in the second degree
    E. insane

8. The report containing the passage is popularly known as the _____ Report. 8.____

    A. Kennedy   B. Dallas   C. Oswald
    D. Warren   E. Presidential

KEY (CORRECT ANSWERS)

1.	D	5.	D
2.	B	6.	B
3.	C	7.	B
4.	B	8.	D

EXPLANATION OF ANSWERS

1. The news media were informed of the transfer on Saturday, discounting Items A and E. They were given the correct time, discounting B. Also, they were present at the transfer, eliminating Item C. ITEM D IS THE CORRECT ONE, as stated in the second sentence of the first paragraph.

2. The passage states (second sentence, second paragraph), *"Police officials decided... an unmarked car would be preferable...because of its greater speed and maneuverability."* THEREFORE, ITEM B IS CORRECT. Item A is false. Item C indicates a discarded choice. Items D and E are true in themselves but had nothing to do with facilitating maneuverability; therefore, they are incorrect in this context.

3. The passage states that (second paragraph, third sentence from end), *"....he....fired one shot into Oswald's abdomen."* THEREFORE, ITEM C IS CORRECT. Item D is incorrect because, actually, *"The man was carrying a Colt .38 revolver...."* Items A, B, and E are false.

4. *"The armored truck arrived shortly after 11:00..."* states the passage in Paragraph 2, sentence one. Item A is the time Oswald emerged from the basement. Item C was the announced time of the transfer. Item D was the time of his death. Item E is the time the police received anonymous telephone calls. ITEM B IS, THEREFORE, CORRECT.

5. Item A is false because the street was not to the left of the ramp. Item B is false because Main St. and Commerce St. are not mentioned as connecting. Item C is false because the *down* ramp led from the cameras to Main St. ITEM D IS CORRECT as found in the last sentence of Paragraph 1. Item E is false; the right led to Main St.

6. Item A is false because the cameras were still on him. ITEM B IS CORRECT because it is the last moment referred to in the passage before the description of the shooting. Item C is false, as is Item E, because movements are detailed beyond that point. Item D is false because Oswald was shot before he got to the car.

7. Oswald did not live to stand trial. In view of this and because of the absence of complete proof, Oswald must be technically termed the ALLEGED assassin of President Kennedy. THEREFORE, ITEM B IS CORRECT. Items A, C, and D are false. Item E can now neither be proved nor disproved.

8. The report was issued by a commission headed by Earl Warren, Chief Justice of the Supreme Court. ITEM D IS CORRECT. Items A, B, C, and E are incorrect.

EXAMINATION SECTION
TEST 1

PASSAGE

By far, the best-known industry in Steuben County is the manufacture of glass. Just after the Civil War, the Flint Glass Company moved from Brooklyn to Coming, One reason why the company chose to settle in Coming was that the railroad from Pennsylvania to Corning brought coal for fuel at a low cost. In the early days, the company made lantern chimneys, bottles, and such familiar products. Later, it began making electric light bulbs. Now it manufactures all kinds of glass products. It makes Pyrex, a kind of glass that resists heat so well that it is used for cooking and baking. The company also makes glass wool, which is used for insulation and other purposes, and glass bricks, out of which the walls of some modern buildings are built.

1. The Flint Glass Company moved to Corning because it

    A. would be exempt from local taxes
    B. had been promised free land for its buildings
    C. could obtain coal cheaply
    D. could make glass bricks there

2. Glass wool, made in Corning, is used for

    A. insulation
    B. low cost fuel
    C. manufacturing lantern chimneys
    D. making electric blankets

3. Since its early days in Corning, the number and variety of the products of the glass industry have

    A. decreased   B. remained about the same
    C. increased slightly   D. increased greatly

4. The county in which Corning is located is

    A. Chautauqua   B. Cortland   C. Seneca   D. Steuben

5. Pyrex is used for

    A. antifreeze   B. cooking utensils
    C. curtain material   D. refrigeration

KEY (CORRECT ANSWERS)

1. C
2. A
3. D
4. D
5. B

TEST 2

PASSAGE

While Admiral Dewey was waiting in Manila Bay, exciting events were happening in the Atlantic. Soon after the start of the war, a Spanish fleet under Admiral Pascual Cervera set sail from the coast of Spain. An American fleet under Admiral William T. Sampson set out to give battle to Cervera's fleet. On May 19, Cervera's fleet came to anchor in the Cuban harbor of Santiago. Sampson's fleet quickly took up its position just outside the channel in order to blockade the harbor, which was too well defended by forts for the Americans to sail in. An American army was landed on the coast a few miles south of Santiago. On July 1-2, this force captured the outer defenses of the city at San Juan Hill and began a siege of Santiago. One of the regiments of volunteers that took part in the charge at San Juan Hill had been recruited by Theodore Roosevelt, who was second in command. The victory of the American army caused the Spaniards to give up hope. The Spanish commander in Cuba ordered Admiral Cervera to put to sea and save his fleet if he could. On July 3, Cervera, with his ships under full steam, started out of Santiago Harbor.

1. The paragraph describes a campaign in the

    A. War of 1812
    B. Mexican War
    C. Civil War
    D. Spanish-American War

2. At the time of the Cuban campaign, a new regiment was recruited by

    A. Cervera   B. Dewey   C. Roosevelt   D. Sampson

3. The American victory at San Juan Hill caused the enemy to

    A. lose confidence
    B. surrender unconditionally
    C. retreat to San Juan Hill
    D. enter Santiago

4. The war was fought

    A. only in the Atlantic Ocean
    B. only in the Pacific Ocean
    C. on both land and sea
    D. off the coast of Tripoli

5. Sampson's fleet tried to

    A. keep Cervera's fleet from entering the harbor
    B. blockade Santiago Harbor
    C. attack San Juan Hill
    D. prevent the United States regiment from entering the battle

KEY (CORRECT ANSWERS)

1. D
2. C
3. A
4. C
5. B

TEST 3

PASSAGE

In the generation after Appomattox, the pattern of our present society and economy took shape. Growth - in area, numbers, wealth, power, social complexity, and economic maturity - was the one most arresting fact. The political divisions of the republic were drawn in their final form, a dozen new states were admitted to the Union, and an American empire was established. In a space of forty years, population increased from thirty-one to seventy-six million, fifteen million immigrants - an ever-increasing proportion of them from southern and eastern Europe - poured into the Promised Land, and great cities like New York, Chicago, Pittsburgh, Cleveland, and Detroit doubled and redoubled their size. In swift succession, the Indians were harried out of their ancient haunts on the high plains and in the mountains and valleys beyond and herded into reservations, the mining and cattle kingdoms rose and fell, the West was peopled and farmed, and by the end of the century, the frontier was no more. Vast new finds of iron ore, copper, and oil created scores of great industries; small business grew into big business.

1. Which one of the following terms BEST describes the period discussed?

    A. Expansion   B. Conservation   C. Regulation   D. Isolation

2. The policy of the Federal government toward the Indians was to

    A. break up the tribal governments
    B. disenfranchise the Indians
    C. educate all Indian children in public schools
    D. remove them to reservations

3. An IMPORTANT factor in the industrial development that followed the Civil War was the

    A. diversification of agriculture
    B. development of new mineral resources
    C. rapid transformation of farmers into industrial workers
    D. development of a colonial empire

4. The last stage in the development of the West was accomplished by

    A. Indians   B. farmers   C. ranchers   D. miners

5. Which one of the following statements is made concerning the United States during the period described in the paragraph? The United States

    A. established an empire
    B. secured special interests in the oil wells and copper mines of Mexico
    C. developed a policy of dollar diplomacy
    D. advocated the open-door policy

6. Which one of the following statements concerning the frontier is made in the paragraph?

    A. After the admission of twelve states, expansion ceased.
    B. An outstanding characteristic of the frontier people was their intense nationalism.
    C. At the end of the 19th century, the frontier came to an end.
    D. The frontier was most important in shaping our present society.

KEY (CORRECT ANSWERS)

1. A
2. D
3. B
4. B
5. A
6. C

TEST 4

PASSAGE

If George Washington could have visited the United States in the 1840's, his thoughts might have run somewhat like this:

"I find it hard to believe that over 20,000,000 people now live in the United States, and that towns have been built beyond the Mississippi River. In my day, there were only 4,000,000 people, and most of these lived along the Atlantic Coast. Can this great city be New York, where I took the oath of office as President? The city I knew had 60,000 inhabitants; today, they tell me, it is the largest city in the New World and has a population of 500,000. What is this engine belching smoke and sparks which carries people across the countryside? When I traveled from Mount Vernon to New York in 1789, I depended on horses. I see factories where machines spin thread to weave it into cloth. Who ever heard in my day of a machine that could spin eighty threads at one time? Here is a boat run by steam which travels against the current of a river! In my time, we depended on the wind to drive our boats. Who would have believed that this country could change so greatly in fifty years!"

1. How much GREATER was the population of the United States in 1840 than in 1789?   1.____

   A. Twice as great
   B. Five times as great
   C. Twelve times as great
   D. Twenty times as great

2. George Washington was inaugurated in   2.____

   A. Boston
   B. Mount Vernon
   C. New York
   D. Philadelphia

3. A method of transportation used in the 1840's but not in Washington's time was the   3.____

   A. airplane   B. automobile   C. sailboat   D. railroad

4. The changes described in the paragraph took place within a period of about _____ years.   4.____

   A. 10   B. 20   C. 50   D. 70

5. In Washington's time, MOST of the people in the United States lived   5.____

   A. beyond the Mississippi
   B. along the eastern seaboard
   C. in the deep South
   D. in the Northwest

KEY (CORRECT ANSWERS)

1. B
2. C
3. D
4. C
5. B

TEST 5

PASSAGE

In philosophy, the New Deal was democratic, in method evolutionary. Because for fifteen years legislative reforms had been dammed up, they now burst upon the country with what seemed like violence but when the waters subsided, it was clear that they ran in familiar channels. The conservation policy of the New Deal had been inaugurated by Theodore Roosevelt; railroad and trust regulation went back to the eighties; banking and currency reforms had been advocated by Bryan and partially achieved by Wilson; the farm-relief program borrowed much from the Populists, labor legislation from the practices of such states as Wisconsin and Oregon. Even judicial reform, which caused such a mighty stir, had been anticipated by Lincoln and Theodore Roosevelt. And in the realm of international relations, the policies of the New Deal were clearly continuations of the traditional policies of strengthening national security, maintaining freedom of the seas, supporting law and peace, and championing democracy in the Western world.

1. All of the following are suitable titles for the selection EXCEPT

    A. The New Deal - an Evolution
    B. The Radical Program of the New Deal
    C. Precedents for the New Deal
    D. Conservatism in the New Deal

2. Many students of history do not agree that legislative reforms had been *dammed up* during the fifteen-year period preceding the New Deal.
   All of the following legislative measures were passed during this fifteen-year period EXCEPT the _____ Act.

    A. Norris-LaGuardia
    B. Reconstruction Finance Corporation
    C. Sherman Antitrust
    D. Agricultural Marketing

3. This selection traces the origin of many of the policies of the New Deal to all of the following EXCEPT

    A. former Presidents
    B. legislation of the Western states
    C. minority parties
    D. the Supreme Court

4. All of the following were indications of isolationism in the New Deal period EXCEPT the

    A. *cash-and-carry* policy
    B. Johnson Debt-Default Act
    C. Lima Conference
    D. *America First* organization

5. Abraham Lincoln, Theodore Roosevelt, and Franklin Roosevelt had all of the following policies in common EXCEPT

    A. trust regulation
    B. expansion of executive powers
    C. land reforms
    D. economic betterment of the common man

6. According to the selection legislative reforms of the New Deal are characterized by all of the following adjectives EXCEPT

    A. democratic
    B. evolutionary
    C. reactionary
    D. traditional

7. All of the following Presidents were associated with banking reforms EXCEPT

    A. Warren Harding
    B. Andrew Jackson
    C. Abraham Lincoln
    D. Woodrow Wilson

8. According to the selection, some legislative precedents for the New Deal were furthered in the United States by all of the following Presidents EXCEPT

    A. Abraham Lincoln
    B. Theodore Roosevelt
    C. Calvin Coolidge
    D. Woodrow Wilson

9. The student seeking primary source material on the New Deal farm program should consult

    A. THE WORLD ALMANAC
    B. the CONGRESSIONAL RECORD
    C. an encyclopedia of the social studies
    D. WHO'S WHO IN AMERICA

KEY (CORRECT ANSWERS)

1. B
2. C
3. D
4. C
5. A
6. C
7. A
8. C
9. B

TEST 6

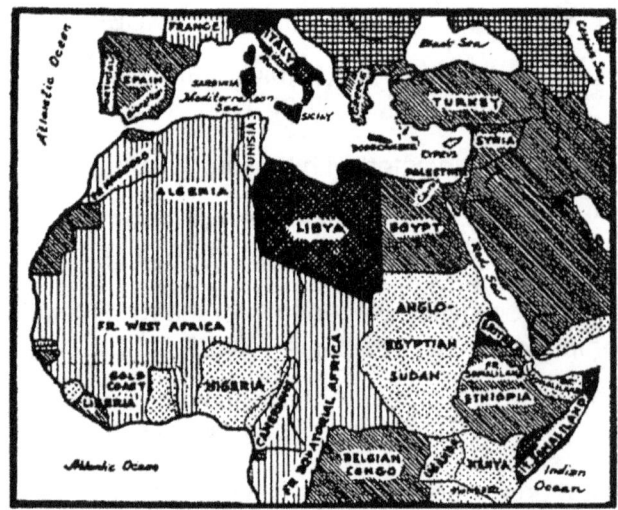

PASSAGE

London, August 14, 1948. A bankrupt empire was put for disposal in London this week. Although the empire, once the property of Italy, has few assets, bidding for the properties was spirited. Italy, despite her present domestic problems, was bidding strongly. Only Italy seemed to want the whole lot; others were angling for bits and pieces and odd parcels of the colonies. On the other hand, Great Britain, which wants the properties almost as badly as Italy, was bidding timidly as if she were afraid of running up the price too fast and too far.

The international auction sale was arranged last year when the winning powers in the recent war settled accounts with Italy. In the Italian peace treaty, Italy renounced all rights to her colonies. The Dodecanese promptly were ceded to Greece. In an annex to the treaty, the Big Four agreed that their Foreign Ministers should decide on the disposal of the other three colonies - Eritrea and Italian Somaliland on the east coast of Africa and Libya in North Africa. Failing a decision within one year, that is, by September 15, 1948, the Big Four agreed that they would hand over the problem to the United Nations General Assembly and abide by its verdict.

That year was nearly out when the deputies of the Big Four Foreign Ministers met, not to decide finally the future of the colonies, but merely to pass on recommendations to the Council of Foreign Minis- ters. When these deputies met last October, they sent out a four-power commission to investigate the situation in the colonies and the wishes of the inhabitants. Reports of that commission were in the hands of the deputies when they met this week.

1. The writer believes that the former Italian colonies   1.____

    A. have many fine resources
    B. are desired by some of the great powers
    C. are financially sound
    D. are strategically important to Russia

2. The Italian colonies in Africa include 2.____

   A. Ethiopia, Eritrea, Libya
   B. Italian Somaliland, Eritrea, Libya
   C. Eritrea, Libya, and the Dodecanese
   D. Ethiopia, Tripoli, and the Dodecanese

3. Italy's African colonies bordered on the 3.____

   A. Mediterranean Sea
   B. Indian Ocean
   C. Atlantic Ocean and Red Sea
   D. Red Sea, Mediterranean Sea, and Indian Ocean

4. The MOST appropriate title for the article would be 4.____

   A. PROBLEMS OF WORLD EMPIRES
   B. FATE OF ITALY'S AFRICAN EMPIRE UNDECIDED
   C. FOUR POWERS INVESTIGATE ITALY'S COLONIES
   D. ITALY'S WEALTH IN AFRICA

5. Libya lies 5.____

   A. east of Algeria   B. east of Egypt
   C. north of Egypt   D. west of Tunisia

6. The author of the article 6.____

   A. thinks that the colonies will be restored to the natives
   B. says the colonies will be given to the Arabs
   C. predicts that the colonies will be returned to Italy
   D. makes no prediction as to the action of the United Nations Assembly

7. MOST of Libya's boundaries bordered on 7.____

   A. possessions of the French Empire
   B. possessions of the British Empire
   C. the sea
   D. independent countries

8. If the Big Four cannot agree upon the disposition of the Italian colonies, they will refer the problem to the 8.____

   A. International Court of Justice
   B. Trusteeship Council
   C. General Assembly of the United Nations
   D. Security Council of the United Nations

9. The author of the article states that 9.____

   A. the colonies were disposed of in the Italian peace treaty
   B. Greece received all the Italian colonies
   C. the Big Four were first assigned disposal of the colonies
   D. the United Nations Assembly would have to approve the disposal of the colonies

10. The author names the following countries as bidders in the disposal of the remaining colonies

    A. France and the Netherlands
    B. Great Britain and France
    C. Italy and Portugal
    D. Great Britain and Italy

11. By a study of this map, a student could determine the

    A. number of air miles from Rome to Cairo
    B. most densely populated areas
    C. notable topographic features of Ethiopia
    D. boundaries and comparative areas

12. Of the following statements selected from the article, the one that is CLEARLY a statement of opinion is that

    A. the Dodecanese were ceded to Greece
    B. the Big Four agreed to hand over the problem to the United Nations under certain conditions
    C. the deputies met in October, 1947
    D. Great Britain was afraid of running the price up too fast and too far

KEYS (CORRECT ANSWERS)

1. B
2. B
3. D
4. B
5. A

6. D
7. A
8. C
9. C
10. D

11. D
12. D

TEST 7

PASSAGE

"We hold these truths to be self-evident: that all men and women are created equal; that they are endowed by their Creator with certain inalienable rights; that among these are life, liberty, and the pursuit of happiness...

"The history of mankind is a history of repeated injuries and usurpations on the part of man toward woman, having in direct object the establishment of an absolute tyranny over her. To prove this, let facts be submitted to a candid world.

"He has never permitted her to exercise her inalienable right to the elective franchise.

"He has compelled her to submit to laws, in the formation of which she had no voice...

"He has so framed the laws of divorce, as to what shall be the proper causes, and in case of separation, to whom the guardianship of the children shall be given, as to be wholly regardless of the happiness of women - the law, in all cases, going upon a false supposition of the supremacy of man, and giving all power into his hands...

"He has monopolized nearly all the profitable employments, and from those she is permitted to follow, she receives but a scanty remuneration. He closes against her all the avenues to wealth and distinction which he considers most honorable to himself. As a teacher of theology, medicine, or law, she is not known.

"He has denied her the facilities for obtaining a thorough education, all colleges being closed against her..."

RESOLUTIONS ADOPTED AT THE SENECA FALLS CONVENTION, 1848

1. This selection appeals for support of the movement for
    - A. temperance
    - B. women's rights
    - C. social security
    - D. child labor legislation

2. Which served as a model for this selection?
    - A. Federal Bill of Rights
    - B. Emancipation Proclamation
    - C. Mayflower Compact
    - D. Declaration of Independence

3. An *inalienable right* is BEST defined as a right that
    - A. cannot be taken away
    - B. is granted to women only
    - C. is granted to all except aliens
    - D. is guaranteed by the preamble to the Federal Constitution

4. Which right did women enjoy at the time of the Seneca Falls Convention?
    - A. The right to serve on juries
    - B. The right of assembly
    - C. Equal vocational opportunities
    - D. Equal rights before the law

5. Which problem of the Seneca Falls Convention remains a legal issue in the United States today?   5.____

    A. A voice in making laws
    B. College admission
    C. Equal pay for equal work in industry
    D. Exclusion from the practice of medicine

6. About how long after the Seneca Falls Convention was the right to the elective franchise (referred to in the selection) achieved by a constitutional amendment? _____ years.   6.____

    A. 5   B. 50   C. 75   D. 100

KEY (CORRECT ANSWERS)

1. B
2. D
3. A
4. B
5. C
6. C

TEST 8

FROM THE FOUR CORNERS OF THE COUNTRY

1. The cartoon suggests that in the 82nd Congress

   A. harmony prevailed
   B. more agreement existed on domestic issues than on foreign policy
   C. only the reactionary Democrats opposed Truman's foreign policy
   D. there was disagreement within both the Democratic and the Republican parties

2. The cartoon specifically refers to division within the Republican party over

   A. foreign policy
   B. inflation
   C. civil rights
   D. taxation

3. Which of the following are leaders of the two Republican groups represented in the cartoon?

   A. Taft and Acheson
   B. Dewey and Hoover
   C. Austin and Dulles
   D. Stassen and Lehman

4. We can conclude from the cartoon that in the 82nd Congress, there was

   A. little prospect that either group in the Democratic party will take a world-minded view
   B. no possibility of any important legislation
   C. no possibility that the President's recommendations will receive favorable consideration
   D. little likelihood of settling significant foreign policy issues on strict party lines

5. Which of the following conclusions drawn from the cartoon can be readily proved?

   A. There was a reaction group in the Democratic party.
   B. All isolationists came from the same part of the country.
   C. The 82nd Congress was evenly divided between Republicans and Democrats.
   D. The Republicans were more interested in foreign policy than in domestic issues.

KEY (CORRECT ANSWERS)

1. D
2. A
3. B
4. D
5. A

TEST 9

FAMILY INCOME BEFORE TAXES
United States, 1946 and 1953

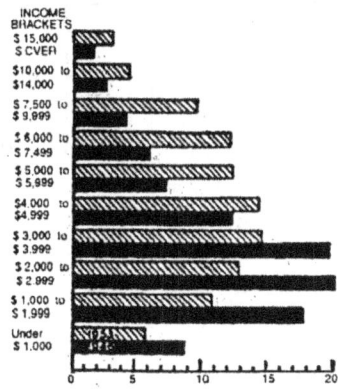

PERCENT OF FAMILIES

1. In 1953, the percent of families with incomes between $3000 and $3,999 was APPROXIMATELY

   A. 5%   B. 10%   C. 15%   D. 20%

2. In 1946, which income bracket included the largest percentage of families?

   A. $1,000 to $1,999   B. $2,000 to $2,999
   C. $3,000 to $3,999   D. $4,000 to $4,999

3. Which of these income brackets included a larger percentage of families in 1953 than in 1946?

   A. $1,000 to $1,999   B. $2,000 to $2,999
   C. $3,000 to $3,999   D. $4,000 to $4,999

4. In 1953, the percent of families with incomes less than $3,000 was about

   A. 30   B. 45   C. 60   D. 75

5. The average family income in 1953 was CLOSEST TO

   A. $1,500   B. $2,500   C. $4,500   D. $6,000

KEY (CORRECT ANSWERS)

1. C
2. B
3. D
4. A
5. C

TEST 10

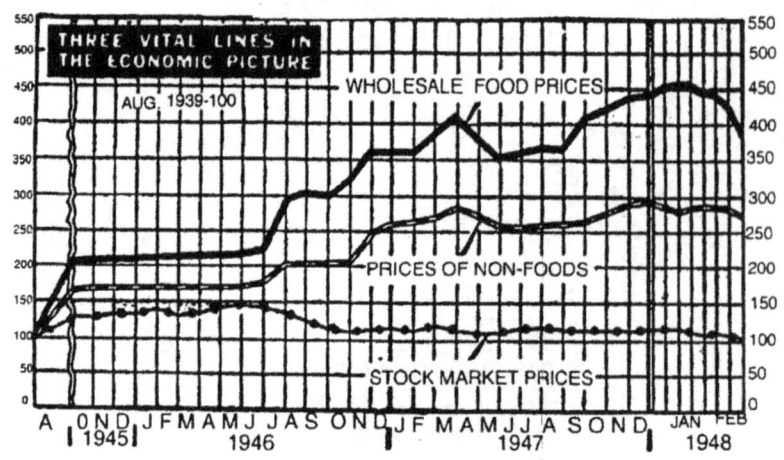

1. For the year 1948, the chart shows a _____ period.

   A. two-month   B. six-week   C. seven-week   D. eight-week

2. Throughout the period from October 1945 to February 1948, stock market prices

   A. rose sharply
   B. declined sharply
   C. remained comparatively steady
   D. fluctuated greatly

3. A comparison of wholesale food prices at the end of the second week in February 1948 with wholesale food prices in October 1945 shows an increase of APPROXIMATELY _____ points.

   A. 50   B. 100   C. 200   D. 300

4. In the period covered by the graph, wholesale food prices declined sharply

   A. once   B. twice   C. three times   D. four times

5. The prices of non-food items reached their highest peak in

   A. March 1946   B. December 1946
   C. March 1947   D. December 1947

6. For the period shown in 1948, all items

   A. rose   B. remained the same
   C. declined   D. fluctuated greatly

7. The month in which the GREATEST increase in wholesale food prices occurred was

   A. July 1946   B. October 1946
   C. September 1947   D. December 1947

8. The same wholesale order of groceries that cost $100 in August 1939 cost approximately $450 in

   A. November 1946   B. March 1947
   C. December 1947   D. January 1948

KEY (CORRECT ANSWERS)

1. C   6. C
2. C   7. A
3. C   8. D
4. B
5. D

Interpretation of Reading Materials in the Natural Sciences

Introduction

The basis of this test, as in the case of Test: <u>Interpretation of Reading Materials in the Social Studies</u> and Test: <u>Interpretation of Literary Materials,</u> lies in the comprehension and interpretation of selected passages in the field of the natural sciences at the high school level. The examinee then answers a series of multiple-choice questions of the four-item type relating to the selection, for which a total time of two (2) hours is given. At the present time, about seven (7) passages appear on the Examination, containing approximately sixty-five (65) questions.

The candidate should note that this is a test of reading comprehension and that the answers for the most part are to be found in and by and through the text. Only a small portion of the questions is involved with or depends upon acquired basal or related information or knowledge.

The Tests that follow have been planned to include, or to evolve, in equivalent form, quality, and degree of difficulty, all of the aims set forth above for this sector. The passages have been selected and presented, so far as possible, in ascending order of difficulty to achieve optimum self-instructional progression and maximum learning affect.

To achieve these purposes, ten (10) Tests are so offered, with answers, and with the answers fully explained, so that the candidate may learn how to go about answering the questions as well as the bases involved in attaining to the correct answers. The book thus becomes a complete self-instructional programmed vehicle.

In addition, as a follow-up and as a reservoir for practice and drill and work-study, ten (10) additional passages appear, in a similar gradation of difficulty and with an equal consistency. The correct answers are furnished for these questions.

Note: The questions in the Tests are presented for the most part in a five-item-choice form, which means that these questions are approximately 20% more difficult than the ones to be encountered on the Examination. This presentation should result in more extended effort and help to eliminate more surely any reliance on the element of guessing, or any resignation into a mood of indifference to preparation.

The directions for Test: <u>Interpretation of Reading Materials in the Natural Sciences</u> are approximately as follows, and these directions will govern the Tests that follow:

DIRECTIONS: You have two hours for this test. As you answer the questions, you should omit any that seem unusually difficult until you finish the others.

Your answers to the exercises in this test are to be recorded in the space at the right.

This test consists of a number of short reading passages taken from textbooks and other materials in the natural sciences. Each passage is followed by a number of multiple-choice questions based on the passage. Read the passage first and then answer the questions following it. Refer again to the passage as often as you find necessary in answering the questions.

You will find that some of the questions will require considerable deliberation and frequent rereading of the passage. This is in part a test of your background of general knowledge in the natural sciences, but it is much more than just that. It is also a *study test* - a test of your ability to *dig out* the important meanings in what you read. This test will not penalize you seriously for having forgotten many of the detailed facts you once knew, if only you have retained the important generalizations and are able to use them intelligently in interpreting what you read.

Sample question and answers follow.

SAMPLE QUESTIONS

DIRECTIONS: In the passage that follows, each question or incomplete statement below is followed by several suggested answers or completions. Select the one that BEST answers the question or completes the statement. Base your choice in each case on the materials given and on your own understanding of the subject matter.

PASSAGE

Last week an amateur archaeologist reported that he had deciphered the meaning of scratches that appear on thousands of mammoth tusks, reindeer bones, cave walls, and other relics of the last ice age.

He thinks they are calendars and other notations revealing a surprisingly high level of intelligence and sophistication among men of that period. His finding, published in the journal SCIENCE, has already produced a ripple of excitement in the academic world. It seeks to show that many of the perplexing inscriptions were calendars delineating lunar months.

In part because the ice age weather was plentiful in rain, snow, and fog, he says, the ancient sky-gazers were unable to pin down the length of the month with precision. Even to the present-day observers without special equipment, it is difficult to determine with certainty just when the moon is full. Hence, the inscriptions, dating back as much as 35,000 years, show months of 29, 30, and 31 days. The author of the article is Alexander Marshack, a science writer. His analyses are to be published at length next year.

1. The scratches discovered by the archaeologist appeared

    A. on calendars   B. in the first ice age
    C. on reindeer bones   D. on stones
    E. on small tusks

According to the passage (paragraph one), the scratches appeared on thousands of mammoth tusks (discounting E), reindeer bones, and cave walls. Therefore, Item C is correct. There is no mention made of stones, discounting D. The scratches represented what we today call calendars; therefore, item A is incorrect. And they are of the last ice age, discounting B.

2. Why did the men of that period have difficulty ascertaining the length of a month? Because

   A. they had a primitive intelligence
   B. the inscriptions were perplexing
   C. they didn't understand the concept of the lunar month
   D. it was difficult to determine when the moon was full
   E. there were no *sky-gazers*

2.____

Item A is false because the passage states (paragraph two) that the men had a high level of intelligence. The inscriptions had been perplexing to the archaeologists; therefore, B is false. They did refer to the moon as a guide, discounting C. Item E is incorrect because the passage mentions *sky-gazers*. Item D is the correct answer and is explained in the last paragraph of the passage.

3. The weather of the period was plentiful in

   A. sunshine
   B. fog
   C. hurricanes
   D. hail
   E. storms

3.____

The weather was plentiful in rain, snow, and fog, states the passage (paragraph 3). Items A, C, D, and E, though they may have occurred, are not mentioned in the passage. Item B is correct.

4. Their estimation of a lunar month

   A. was absurd by present-day standards
   B. fell short by quite a few days
   C. was completely inaccurate
   D. was very close to the estimate of today
   E. was actually an impossibility because they had no special instruments or equipment

4.____

The months were estimated as containing 29, 30, and 31 days (paragraph 3 of the passage). Therefore, the correct item is D. Items A, B, and C are false. Item E is incorrect because they were able to form an estimate of a lunar month without any special equipment.

5. The equinoxes occur on

   A. June 21st and December 21st
   B. March 22nd and September 22nd
   C. June 22nd and March 22nd
   D. September 22nd and December 22nd
   E. March 21st and September 23rd

5.____

Item E is correct. Equinox refers to the two lines each year when the sun crosses the equator, and day and night are everywhere of equal length. Items A, B, C, and D are false.

6. The solstices occur on

    A. June 21st and September 21st
    B. March 22nd and September 21st
    C. June 22nd and December 22nd
    D. September 21st and December 23rd
    E. March 21st and September 23rd

Solstices refer to the two points on the ecliptic at which the distance from the celestial equator is greatest, and which is reached each year by the sun about June 22nd and December 22nd. Therefore, Item C is correct. Items A, B, D, and E are false.

INTERPRETATION OF READING MATERIALS IN THE NATURAL SCIENCES
EXAMINATION SECTION
TEST 1

PASSAGE

Less than 100 years ago, a fabulous *new era* of medicine—or so it was supposed to be—was ushered in by the *wonder drugs*, the germkillers extraordinary. Here, it seemed, were the ultimate weapons that could rout hordes of pestilential bugs. Once and for all, there was to be an end to the menace of dozens of infectious diseases. It was a heady dream—but it grossly underestimated the enemy.

The infections are still with us. The bugs have been fighting back. Their counter-attacks, indeed, have sometimes been so vicious that scientists have been forced to go to new lengths to try to repulse them. The battle today seesaws.

One of the latest examples of bug turnabout was noted a few weeks ago when tuberculosis experts met at an isoniazid *reunion* luncheon to take a look at that drug-ten years after it had been hailed as the conqueror of TB and after the first desperately ill patients to receive it got up out of their beds and danced exuberantly in hospital corridors. Currently, as many as 6 percent of TB patients are beyond help by isoniazid—infected with strains of tubercle bacilli impervious to the drug—and resistance to isoniazid is growing.

The trend, not yet calamitous, follows explosive epidemics produced by *hospital staph* bacteria that sneer at penicillin and many other antibiotics. There have been-and continue to be-troubles with numerous other disease organisms despite, and even because of, antibiotics.

As early as 1954, University of Michigan physicians, noting the ability, evident even then, of some germs to live with highly vaunted antibiotics, suggested that *man may be sitting on a time bomb, capable of *** shattering the illusion of medical miracles****.

1. What is meant by the statement in the passage that *man may be sitting on a time bomb*?   1.____

    A. The *bugs* may progressively develop resistances to the drugs.
    B. The idea of medical miracles is an illusion.
    C. There is a great chance that TB could develop into a more difficult disease to treat.
    D. As the *bugs* get stronger, the disease becomes more prevalent.
    E. One day the miracle drugs which have been discovered will cause more harm than good.

2. *The bugs have been fighting back,* states the passage.   2.____
   This means:

    A. Higher doses of a particular drug become required.
    B. Patients develop an immunity to the disease.
    C. The *bugs* increase in number as a result of the drug.
    D. Some people have no reaction to the antibiotics.
    E. As the drugs become stronger, so do the *bugs*.

3. *Wonder drugs* are not the ultimate weapon because
    A. it remains for a drug to be discovered which the *bugs* cannot fight
    B. they only treat one disease, not all
    C. they are limited to certain people, i.e., many are allergic
    D. they sometimes carry their own diseases, with which they replace the ones they cure
    E. scientists deny the existence of a foreseeable day when the *ultimate weapon* against disease can be evolved

4. Wonder drugs were discovered
    A. by Jonas Salk
    B. 20 years ago
    C. less than five decades ago
    D. over a century ago
    E. as a by-product of research done in nuclear physics

5. *Animalcules* is another word for
    A. antibiotics   B. bacteria   C. drugs
    D. penicillin   E. oreomycin

6. Scientists realistically predict the day when
    A. there will be no more disease
    B. better drugs will be made
    C. the *bugs* may develop a resistance to all antibiotics
    D. antibiotics will not be needed to cure disease
    E. all bacteria will be conquered

KEY (CORRECT ANSWERS)

1. A   4. C
2. E   5. B
3. A   6. C

EXPLANATION OF ANSWERS

1. CORRECT ANSWER: A

   B is irrelevant; C is not stated; D is not stated or implied; E is pure conjecture and not inferred in the passage.

2. CORRECT ANSWER: E

   Items A and D are sometimes true but bear no relation to the question. C is false. Patients may develop an immunity to the antibiotics, but never to the disease. Therefore, B is false. The proper answer is E: *The battle today seesaws* (last sentence of the second paragraph).

3. CORRECT ANSWER: A

   While B and C are factually true, they do not satisfactorily complete the statement. D is scientifically unknown as yet. Item E is false. The correct answer is A (see the last sentence of the first paragraph).

4. CORRECT ANSWER: C

   The opening sentence is *Less than 50 years ago....a....'new era'....was ushered in by the 'wonder drugs'*. Therefore, C is the correct answer. The other answers are false.

5. CORRECT ANSWER: B

   Animalcules is a synonym for bacteria. Therefore, B is the proper answer. The other answers are completely incorrect as they are the substances which fight bacteria.

6. CORRECT ANSWER: C

   Though scientists are working constantly to perfect superior drugs, it has been their experience that the *bugs* are progressing in strength faster than the drugs can be improved. (See, particularly, the last paragraph.) Therefore, the correct answer is C.

TEST 2
PASSAGE

BILLINGS, Mont. — A 60-year-old Montanan traced on a map the other day the boundaries of the Bob Marshall Wilderness Area. As he lifted his finger, a smile creased his face. He said:

That's it. It has been pretty well explored for minerals, but you never can tell when somebody might want to try something again. Let's hope nobody can touch it now. It's something that should have been done long ago.

His reference was to the creation of the National Wilderness Preservation System, as set down in Public Law 88577, which went into effect September 3. The act is the compromise of a long and bitter fight to carve out of the national forests and other Federal lands a system that will, in the words of the legislation, *secure for the American people of present and future generations the benefits of an enduring resource of wilderness.*

The compromise was between conservationists and those who would put forest resources to commercial and other-than-wilderness uses.

It pins this down by its definition that a wilderness, *in contrast with those areas where man and his own works dominate the landscape, is hereby recognized as an area where the earth and the community of life are untrammeled by man, where man himself is a visitor who does not remain.*

1. The National Wilderness Preservation System was of great interest because it

    A. went into effect September 3
    B. was a compromise
    C. preserved an important resource
    D. worked hand-in-hand with commerce
    E. allowed for other-than-wilderness uses

2. What is meant by the statement ... *somebody might want to try something again?*

    A. It might be tapped for minerals
    B. Some party might damage the property.
    C. The property's resources might be tapped for commercial purposes.
    D. Building might take place.
    E. The general public might cause forest fires or sanitation problems.

3. *Untrammeled* means

    A. not trampled on
    B. not traveled
    C. something uninvestigated by man
    D. something abused by man
    E. something left in its original condition

4. After reading the passage, one gets the impression that the author

    A. appreciates the beauty of nature
    B. understands the needs of commerce in relation to natural resources
    C. is engaged in a bitter fight

2 (#2)

      D. will secure for the American people an enduring wilderness
      E. is on the side of the conservationists

5. A good title for this passage would be   5.____

    A. THE BOUNDARIES OF THE WILDERNESS
    B. EXPLORING FOR MINERALS
    C. SAVING THE WILDS
    D. HOW COMMERCE MAKES USE OF NATURAL RESOURCES
    E. THE WILDERNESS

6. The TVA, a conservation act, was enacted during the Presidency of   6.____

    A. Theodore Roosevelt   B. Woodrow Wilson
    C. Dwight D. Eisenhower   D. Franklin D. Roosevelt
    E. Harry Truman

KEY (CORRECT ANSWERS)

1. C	4. E
2. C	5. C
3. E	6. D

EXPLANATION OF ANSWERS

1. CORRECT ANSWER: C

   Item C is the correct answer, and it is clearly delineated in the quotation contained in paragraph 3, viz., ... *secure for the American people ... an enduring resource of wilderness.*

2. CORRECT ANSWER: C

   When the speaker says, *It has been pretty well explored for minerals, but you never can tell when somebody might want to try something again,* he is referring to a similar possibility of an exploitation by industry. This would designate C as the proper answer. Though B, D, and E are possible occurrences, he is not, in this statement, referring to these.

3. CORRECT ANSWER: E

   The last clause of the passage indicates that A, B, and C are incorrect because man can visit a wilderness area and leave it *untrammeled*. D is incorrect because it infers the opposite of the word's correct meaning.

4. CORRECT ANSWER: E

   The passage is not about the author's love of nature or the needs of commerce, nor does his work match the events or aims suggested in C and D. E would be most suited to his position on natural resources, and is the correct answer.

5. CORRECT ANSWER: C

   The best answer presented here would be C. The theme of the passage is in no way related to items B and D. A and E could be considered, but C is much more directly related to the passage.

6. CORRECT ANSWER: D

   The correct answer is D, Franklin Roosevelt (1933).

TEST 3
PASSAGE

Where others saw unrelated, individually created flowers or birds or people, he saw a mass of altering, dissolving, and interrelated forms flowing onward through earth's history. Living creatures were like cloud shapes contorted by the winds of time. As it happens, the years have proved him right.

What made Darwin a scientist? Let us ask again in particular because by modern school standards and measurements he was not a very good pupil, let alone a candidate for genius. His career was undecided; he dawdled and misspelled words, enraged his father and, giving up a career in medicine, was packed off to Cambridge with the notion that he might at least learn enough to become a country parson.

We cannot analyze Darwin's entire life, but we can say that his quoted letter to Joseph Hooker is enormously important and revelatory. Charles Darwin was a millionaire of facts but they happened not to be the facts in which the schools of his day were interested. Indeed, he spoke of his Cambridge studies as *next thing to intolerable.* As a result, his formal educational career was no measure of his real capacities. Later, as he remembered his experience in South America, he was to speak of lonely desert travels in which *the whole of my pleasure was derived from what passed in my mind.*

Yet the influences at work upon him were not all of a solitary character. His grandfather Erasmus had entertained evolutionary ideas about which Charles had learned as a youth; a kindly botanist, John Henslow, had obtained for him his post as naturalist on the Beagle. On the outward voyage to South America, Darwin had read Sir Charles Lyell's PRINCIPLES OF GEOLOGY and been convinced by Lyell's then-heretical views that the earth was extremely ancient—a necessary prelude to grasping the slow pace of plant and animal evolution.

1. As opposed to the individually created flowers or birds, Darwin saw

    A. living creatures
    B. masses of altering and dissolving cloud shapes
    C. interrelated forms
    D. people
    E. winds of time

2. The reader can assume from the passage that the author feels a formal education is

    A. necessary even for a candidate for genius
    B. what made Darwin a scientist
    C. not always a measure of real capacities
    D. necessary for a scientist
    E. not able to help a pupil beyond his potential

3. His first ideas about evolution may well have come from

    A. his grandfather
    B. Joseph Hooker
    C. John Henslow
    D. PRINCIPLES OF GEOLOGY
    E. his voyage to South America

2 (#3)

4. Sir Charles Lyell's ideas were   4._____

    A. about animal evolution
    B. about plant life
    C. unaccepted by his period
    D. Darwin's primary inspiration
    E. extremely ancient

5. A work of Darwin's is   5._____

    A. ZOOLOGY OF THE VOYAGE OF THE BEAGLE
    B. ON THE TENDENCY OF VARIETIES TO DEPART INDEFINITELY FROM THE ORIGINAL TYPE
    C. TRAVELS ON THE AMAZON AND THE RIO NEGRO
    D. THE BOTANIC GARDEN
    E. ZOONOMIA

6. The famous Scopes trial brought him into conflict with   6._____

    A. William Jennings Bryan   B. Clarence Darrow
    C. the State of Tennessee   D. J.T. Scopes
    E. the State of Kentucky

KEY (CORRECT ANSWERS)

1. C   4. C
2. C   5. A
3. A   6. C

EXPLANATION OF ANSWERS

1. CORRECT ANSWER: C

   He saw, states the passage (sentence 1), *altering, dissolving, and interrelated forms flowing onward through earth's history.* And as he saw these things, he was envisioning the relationships of all living things. He seemed to see, implies the author, no one thing independent of another. C, then, is the proper answer.

2. CORRECT ANSWER: C

   Judging from Darwin's various failures and indecisions discussed in paragraph 2, the reader can only accept C as the correct completion of the statement. While A, D, and E are probably acceptable statements in themselves, they have nothing to do with the man about whom the author is writing. B, apparently, is not the opinion of the author.

3. CORRECT ANSWER: A

   The evolutionary ideas about which he learned as a youth came from his grandfather long before, presumably, his many other influences. Therefore, A must be the correct answer.

4. CORRECT ANSWER: C

   The last paragraph mentions *Lyell's then-heretical views . . . .* Therefore, C is the only possible answer. Item D is not indicated in the passage, and A, B, and E are false.

5. CORRECT ANSWER: A

   Items D and E were works of Erasmus Darwin, grandfather of Charles. Items B and C are the works of Alfred Russell Wallace. Item A is the work of Charles Darwin-his work on the Beagle mentioned in the passage and is the correct answer.

6. CORRECT ANSWER: C

   Scopes was charged with teaching Darwinian evolution in violation of a state law forbidding such instruction. The state was Tennessee, and the correct answer is C. Clarence Darrow was attorney for the defense and William Jennings Bryan, attorney for the prosecution.

TEST 4
PASSAGE

The most fascinating thing about a greenhouse is the opportunity provided for growing unusual plants. A greenhouse gardener need not limit himself to the plants he once grew in his home. He can branch out to plants from all over the world–depending on the temperature maintained in the greenhouse.

In a greenhouse where the temperature is kept just above freezing, alpine plants can be grown. Edelweiss, bottle gentian, creeping phlox, and columbines like Aquilegia akitensis and A. flabellata are just a few of the candidates. A book on rock gardening or a catalogue from a specialist nursery will suggest many other plants. A practical advantage to growing these cold-greenhouse plants is the saving on wintertime fuel bills.

Under warmer conditions, many kinds of dwarf shrubs will be fun to grow. Do not overlook some of the berried kinds like pyracantha Victory, which is hardy outdoors only about as far north as Zone 7. Tender shrubs and trees such as kumquat, calamondin orange, and dwarf lemon are satisfying to grow, for they will often have flowers and fruit at the same time.

The charming wax plant, Hoya oarnosa, develops beautifully in a warm greenhouse. Others are hibiscus, lantana, oleander, and osmanthus or sweet olive.

1. According to the passage, kumquat is a

   A. sturdy shrub
   B. dwarfed plant
   C. tender shrub
   D. fruit
   E. form of berry

2. An oleander develops

   A. in a warm greenhouse
   B. in a cold greenhouse
   C. outdoors in a southern climate
   D. well in the home
   E. in a northern climate

3. The advantage to growing plants like edelweiss in the wintertime is

   A. they are far more attractive plants than most
   B. they are too fragile for summer cultivation
   C. temperature
   D. the saving on fuel bills
   E. that they are an alpine plant

4. A good title for the passage might be

   A. HOW TO GROW NORTHERN PLANTS
   B. HOW TO GROW TROPICAL PLANTS
   C. THE FLORIDIAN PLANTS: HIBISCUS, OLEANDER, LANTANA
   D. HOW TO GROW CITRUS IN A GREENHOUSE
   E. CANDIDATES FOR A GREENHOUSE

5. Broadly, the subject covered in the passage would come under the heading of

   A. botany
   B. nurseries
   C. gardens
   D. rock gardening
   E. pyracantha

6. A flowering plant, discovered by an American traveling in Mexico, and destined to become our most popular Christmas plant, thanks to the temperature control of the green house, is the

   A. mistletoe
   B. philodendron
   C. poinsettia
   D. rhododendron
   E. hibiscus

KEY (CORRECT ANSWERS)

1. C	4. E
2. A	5. A
3. D	6. C

EXPLANATION OF ANSWERS

1. CORRECT ANSWER: C

Paragraph 3, sentence 3, contains the description of a kumquat as a *tender shrub,* indicating C as the correct answer.

2. CORRECT ANSWER: A

Paragraph 4 contains the completion of the statement. It mentions Hoya carnosa as needing a warm greenhouse and goes on to state that, of other plants needing the same environment, one is oleander. Thus, the answer is A. Though an oleander will flourish outdoors in a southern climate, this is not indicated by the author in the passage.

3. CORRECT ANSWER: D

The last sentence of paragraph 2 states that edelweiss is a cold-greenhouse plant and such plants are a *saving on wintertime fuel bills.* Therein lies its practical advantage. C and E could be considered adequate answers if the requirements only of the plant were the consideration, but D is the better answer because of the word *advantage* in the question (inferring that which is an advantage to the grower).

4. CORRECT ANSWER: E

Though A, B, C, and D are all mentioned in the passage, the all inclusive title in item E presents the best possible choice and is the correct answer.

5. CORRECT ANSWER: A

Botany being the science discussed in the passage is the most enveloping choice and, therefore, the best answer. Thus, the answer is A. B, C, D, and E, were they to be catagorized, would all come under the heading of A since they are all parts of the whole-botany.

6. CORRECT ANSWER: C

Joel R. Poinsett, an American diplomat, discovered the flowering plant, poinsettia, in 1851, and it has since become our most popular Christmas plant. Thus, the answer is C.

TEST 5
PASSAGE

In a provocative series of experiments, a team of scientists at Western Reserve University in Cleveland has developed techniques to remove the brain of a monkey from its body and keep it alive for many hours. Bare except for two small bits of bone to help support it, the nerves and blood vessels that once connected it to the monkey's body severed, the brain is suspended above a laboratory table. Attached to it are the tubes of a mechanical heart to maintain its blood supply; from it run wires to recording instruments. Their measurements of its electrical activity not only show that it remains alive but even suggest that sometimes this isolated brain is conscious.

While the immediate goal of the team, headed by Dr. Robert J. White, is the development of methods for obtaining answers to basic questions related to the physiology of the brain, one cannot help being fascinated by less specifically scientific, but perhaps more profoundly philosophic, considerations. Can the truly *detached minds* of the Cleveland monkeys really be conscious? If so, conscious of what?

Sensation, for example, is an important ingredient of the conscious state. Does biological science give us any clues as to what sensations, if any, the conscious incorporeal brains of the Western Reserve monkeys could have felt? After all, the nerves that normally carry to the brain indications of touch, taste, odor, light, and sound were all cut, and the associated sensory organs were far removed. Does this mean that, during its conscious periods, the isolated monkey brain floated in a sensory void, with no flashes of touch, pain, sight, or sound to remind it of the kind of existence it once knew?

1. What is used by the scientists to support the brain?

    A. Nerves and blood vessels that once connected it to the monkey's body
    B. Two small bits of bone
    C. A mechanical heart
    D. A laboratory table
    E. The tubes of the mechanical heart

2. The suggestion that the brain is sometimes conscious comes from

    A. the measurements on the recording instruments
    B. associated sensory organs
    C. the memory of the kind of existence it once knew
    D. the maintenance of its blood supply
    E. the mechanical heart

3. By the term *incorporeal brains,* the author means

    A. brains without nerves
    B. brains with mechanical tubes
    C. brains in a sensory void
    D. that the brain, though isolated, has artificial support
    E. disembodied brains

4. The author states that the brain can be kept alive

   A. indefinitely
   B. until it normally expires corporeally
   C. until the mechanical heart fails
   D. a few minutes
   E. for many hours

5. Scientists, by such experiments as these, are PROBABLY trying to determine

   A. how certain parts of the brain can be mechanically replaced
   B. how the brain feels and thinks
   C. whether the brain of a monkey is superior to the human brain
   D. how they might duplicate this experiment with a human brain
   E. how long brains can be kept alive without their bodies

6. A part of the brain called the brainstem is

   A. the seat of mental activity
   B. the coordinator of muscular activity
   C. an extension of the spinal cord
   D. the mantle that fits the skull
   E. controller of voluntary action and the senses

7. The cerebral cortex is

   A. divided into two equal hemispheres
   B. that part of the brain through which all nerve impulses are channeled
   C. that part which controls breathing
   D. that part which controls heartbeat
   E. that part which generates feelings, i.e., hunger, anger, pleasure

KEY (CORRECT ANSWERS)

1. B
2. A
3. E
4. E
5. B
6. C
7. A

3 (#5)

EXPLANATION OF ANSWERS

1. CORRECT ANSWER: B

    It is stated in paragraph 1 that the brain is *bare except for two small bits of bone to help support it*. The answer, then, is B. Items C and E refer to things connected to the brain but not supporting it.

2. CORRECT ANSWER: A

    Item C is stated as a question in the passage and goes unanswered. However, item A is stated in the last sentence of paragraph 1 and is the correct answer. Items D and E are artificial appendages on which the recording instruments depend, but cannot, themselves, estimate or measure consciousness.

3. CORRECT ANSWER: E

    Incorporeal means without a body, or a disembodied brain. Therefore, E is the correct answer. The other answers are characteristic of (or related to) the brain described in the passage but do not relate to the term *incorporeal*.

4. CORRECT ANSWER: E

    In sentence 1, paragraph 1, the author states there are techniques to *remove the brain. . . . and keep it alive for several hours*. Item E, then, is the correct answer. C is not correct because, should a mechanical heart fail, it would be replaced, and the brain would continue its *life course* for the prescribed length of time.

5. CORRECT ANSWER: B

    The correct answer is B (see paragraph two-*basic questions related to the physiology of the brain*). Item E, the scientists have obviously ascertained; items A, C, and D are neither mentioned nor implied in the passage.

6. CORRECT ANSWER: C

    Items A, D, and E relate to the cerebral cortex. Item B refers to the cerebellum.

7. CORRECT ANSWER: A

    Items B, C, D, and E refer to functions of the brainstem. Item A, which describes the make-up of the cerebral cortex, is the correct answer.

TEST 6
PASSAGE

The highest honors bestowed in the world of science were given last Thursday to an American, two Russians, and a British woman.

The Nobel Prize in physics was shared by Dr. Charles H. Townes, now provost of the Massachusetts Institute of Technology, and Drs. N.G. Basov and A.M. Prokhorov of the Soviet Union. The three men, during the early nineteen fifties, paved the way for a major invention: the maser. Dr. Townes also helped show how the maser principle could be applied to light, resulting in discovery of the laser.

The Nobel Prize in chemistry went to Mrs. Dorothy C. Hodgkin of Great Britain for her work in deciphering the structure of such complex molecules as those of penicillin and vitamin B-12. The latter is vital in treating a fatal form of pernicious anemia. Its structure was spelled out after eight years of work. *Never before,* the award announcement said, *has it been possible to determine the precise structure of so large a molecule.*

The analyses were performed by shining x-rays through crystals of the substance in question and recording the manner in which the rays were diffracted by the crystal structure.

Applied light was first achieved by Dr. Townes and his colleagues at Columbia University at a radar or *microwave* frequency. Hence, they called it *microwave amplification by stimulated emission of radiation,* or, more briefly, the maser, from the initials of these words.

When the same principle was applied to the production of intense light, it was called an optical maser or *laser*

One of the earliest applications of the maser was to increase many-fold the sensitivity of radar systems used to detect distant missiles.

1. The invention of the maser

    A. occurred in Great Britain
    B. made it possible to determine the precise structure of a molecule
    C. was related to the work of Drs. Basov, Townes, and Prokhorov
    D. was the work of Mrs. Dorothy C. Hodgkin
    E. was the work of Dr. Charles H. Townes

2. Vital in treating a form of pernicious anemia is

    A. deciphering the structure of complex molecules
    B. vitamin B-12
    C. the analysis performed by shining x-rays through crystals
    D. recording the manner in which the rays are defracted
    E. penicillin

3. The *laser* got its name from the

    A. microwave amplification by stimulated emission of radiation
    B. initials of its earliest application
    C. initials of the principle of the laser applied to light

D. application of the maser to increase the sensitivity of radar systems
E. optical laser

4. The Nobel Prize in physics was

   A. given for the work of deciphering the structure of molecules
   B. given for the invention of the laser
   C. given to Mrs. D.C. Hodgkin
   D. shared
   E. given to Drs. Basov and Prokhorov

5. The above passage might be found in a(n)

   A. scientific journal dealing with nuclear physics
   B. article on the detection of missiles
   C. brochure from the Massachusetts Institute of Technology
   D. article in a medical journal on the treatment of pernicious anemia
   E. article on Nobel Prize winners

6. A word MOST CLOSELY related to amplification is

   A. stimulation   B. enlargement
   C. emission   D. light
   E. radiation

KEY (CORRECT ANSWERS)

1. C   4. D
2. B   5. E
3. C   6. B

EXPLANATION OF ANSWERS

1. CORRECT ANSWER: C

   Paragraph 2 states, *The three men...paved the way for a major invention: the maser.* The correct answer, therefore, is item C. Item B relates to the work of Mrs. Hodgkin (item D), who lives in Great Britain (item A). Item E is incomplete and, therefore, false.

2. CORRECT ANSWER: B

   The answer is contained in paragraph 3, where it is stated,...*such complex molecules as those of penicillin and B-12. The latter is vital in treating...pernicious anemia.* The correct answer, then, is B. Item A relates to the work of Mrs. Hodgkin, as do items C and Item E is incorrect.

3. CORRECT ANSWER: C

   The laser is an optical maser (item E), but it got its precise name from the initials of the principle of the maser (item A) applied to light; that is, item C, which is the correct answer. The earliest application of the laser (item B) was item D and has nothing to do with the laser.

4. CORRECT ANSWER: D

   The prize was given to Drs. Basov, Prokhorov, and Townes. It was shared by these three men; therefore, the correct answer is D. E is incorrect because it is incomplete. The prize in Chemistry was given to Mrs. Hodgkin, item C. As for items A and B, if the reader were to check for the reason that the prize was given, he would find that it was the invention of the maser, discounting both A and B.

5. CORRECT ANSWER: E

   The correct answer, and the most inclusive one, regarding the source of the passage is item E. Item A is obviously false, as is C. B and D refer to things mentioned in the passage but not the substance or the main theme of it.

6. CORRECT ANSWER: B

   Item B is the correct meaning of amplification and, thus, the correct answer for the question. Items A, B, C, and E are incorrect.

TEST 7
PASSAGE

Thus for most of the earth's history, life, in the form of primitive algae, fungi, and bacteria, had little more than a toehold in these pools. The oldest fossil evidence of such algae dates back two or three billion years, yet diverse, large scale life forms did not appear in the fossil record until some 600 million years ago.

It is this sudden appearance of diverse life that has puzzled scientists. The assumption has been that the earlier record was destroyed or that previous life forms did not have shells or skeletons hard enough to leave a record. Yet soft plants and animals also leave their prints in the sands of time and they, too, were absent.

What really happened, according to the new hypothesis, was that when volcanic growth produced continents, and hence shallow pools of considerable extent, the pond-bottom plants slowly raised the oxygen content of the air until, at one percent of the present level, it was sufficient to filter out almost all the lethal ultraviolet. The latter, henceforth, could poison only the top few inches of the oceans and life, which had been hardly more than microscopic, erupted in all evolutionary directions.

The eruption of oceanic life increased photosynthesis and the oxygen level rose high enough to make the dry land habitable. This led to great forests and photosynthesis became so extensive that there was perhaps ten times as much oxygen in the air as today. The carbon dioxide of the air, that acts like the glass of a green-house in keeping the earth warm, was depleted, and the Permian ice ages of 250 million years ago resulted.

1. An example of algae is

   A. a form of mushroom plant
   B. fossiliferous
   C. seaweed
   D. a form of bacteria
   E. cryptogamous plants

2. The scientists were puzzled because

   A. of the production of shallow pools
   B. of the evidences of fossiliferous life prior to 600 million years ago
   C. they did not feel that the oldest forms of life did not have hard shells or skeletons
   D. they did not think volcanic growth produced continents
   E. they did not understand how plants could lower the oxygen content of the air

3. Continents were produced by

   A. fermentation
   B. a high level of oxygen
   C. photosynthesis
   D. volcanic growth
   E. the Permian ice ages

4. How could the ultraviolet poison only the top few inches of the oceans and life? Because

   A. salt water reflects the rays
   B. ultraviolet rays are poisonous to certain ocean plants
   C. the pond-bottom plants raised the oxygen content of the air
   D. the pond-bottom plants acted as a filter
   E. ultraviolet cannot penetrate below the ocean's surface

5. Ultraviolet rays are

   A. the strongest rays of the sun
   B. rays within the violet of the visible spectrum
   C. the rays of the sun which promote growth
   D. rays beyond the violet of the visible spectrum
   E. those rays which are attracted by salt or fresh water

6. Photosynthesis is the

   A. growth from within plant or animal life
   B. process by which plants manufacture food for their growth with the aid of light
   C. impulse of fluids to mix and become diffused through each other
   D. tendency of elements to pass through one another with unequal rapidity
   E. pressures produced by osmosis

KEY (CORRECT ANSWERS)

1. C 4. D
2. B 5. D
3. D 6. B

3 (#7)

EXPLANATION OF ANSWERS

1. CORRECT ANSWER: C

   Algae is a subaqueous plant, that is a plant growing beneath the water. Therefore, the answer would be C. Items A and E are fungi. Item B, fossiliferous, means *containing or bearing fossils.* Item D is incorrect because algae is a form of plant life.

2. CORRECT ANSWER: B

   The answer to this question is to be found in paragraph 1, towards the end, and the beginning of paragraph 2. Items A and D are accepted concepts. Item E is a false statement, as is C. Item B is the correct answer.

3. CORRECT ANSWER: D

   At the beginning of paragraph 3, it is mentioned that *volcanic growth produced continents.* Therefore, item D is the correct answer, aside from being the only direct statement made about the production of continents. Items A, C, and E are not mentioned in relation to the production of continents.

4. CORRECT ANSWER: D

   The pond-bottom plants slowly raised the oxygen content of the air...until it was sufficient to filter out almost all the lethal ultraviolet states the passage in paragraph 3. Therefore, item D is the correct answer. A and E are false statements. Item C is true but not pertinent. Item B is misleading.

5. CORRECT ANSWER: D

   Ultraviolet rays are those short rays beyond the violet of the visible spectrum. A, B, C, and E are not applicable to ultra-violet rays.

6. CORRECT ANSWER: B

   Items C and D relate to the process of osmosis. Items A and E are incorrect.

TEST 8
PASSAGE

The discovery and use of metals was one of the crucial steps that put mankind on the long road to modern civilization.

New clues to the discovery were reported last week. They suggest that men were taking the first steps toward use of metal a millennium earlier than the dawn of real metallurgy. The clues are little bits of copper that appear to have been cold-hammered into shape as pins, a drill, and a sharply bent hook nearly 9,000 years ago by an artisan in one of man's earliest villages.

The copper specimens were discovered last summer by a team excavating an ancient village site at Cayonu, in southeastern Turkey.

Co-directors of the expedition that made the discoveries were Prof. Hale Cambel, from the University of Istanbul, and Prof. Robert J. Braidwood of the Oriental Institute and Department of Anthropology, University of Chicago.

In a telephone interview last week, Professor Braidwood said all the evidence indicates that the stone dwelling in which the tools were found was nearly 9,000 years old.

In the Shanidar Valley of northern Iraq, scientists from Columbia University independently have found a specimen that also seems to be cold-hammered copper and suggests the same conclusion as that reached by Professor Braidwood and his colleagues.

1. The discovery of the cold-hammered copper specimens was made

   A. in southwestern Turkey
   B. 9,000 years ago
   C. in Istanbul
   D. in the Shanidar Valley
   E. on the African continent

2. Why does the author suggest that metal was used before the dawn of real metallurgy? Because

   A. The scientists found evidences of copper
   B. The scientists found evidences of cold-hammers
   C. There was evidence of life in the site at Cayonu
   D. They assumed that people must have lived in Cayonu 9,000 years ago
   E. The scientists found copper worked into certain forms

3. Metallurgy is the

   A. discovery of metals
   B. discovery of minerals that could be worked into metals
   C. discovery of ore
   D. art of working metals
   E. application of metals to the body

4. A millennium is _____ years.

   A. thousands of
   B. a few thousand
   C. several thousand
   D. a thousand
   E. an incalculable number of

5. The dominant religion of Turkey today is 5.____

    A. Hinduism   B. Hebrew
    C. Islam   D. Buddhist
    E. Greek Orthodox

6. The capital of Turkey today is 6.____

    A. Istanbul   B. Ankara
    C. Constantinople   D. Smyrna
    E. Izmir

KEY (CORRECT ANSWERS)

1.	D	4.	D
2.	E	5.	C
3.	D	6.	B

EXPLANATION OF ANSWERS

1. CORRECT ANSWER: D

   A place, apart from Cayonu, where scientists found cold-hammered copper specimens is the Shanidar Valley, item D, which is the correct answer. Istanbul is the location of the university of one of the scientists (item C). And Cayonu is in southeastern Turkey, thus discounting item A. Item B refers to the age of the specimens. Item E is false.

2. CORRECT ANSWER: E

   The evidences that the scientists found were copper that had been cold-hammered into different shapes, indicating E as the correct answer. A and B are insufficient or incomplete answers. C does not represent enough evidence, nor does D.

3. CORRECT ANSWER: D

   Metallurgy is *the art of working metals.* It has nothing to do with the discovery of or the existence of metal substances, discounting items A, B, and C, but rather with such activities as smelting, refining, parting, etc. Thus, the correct answer is D. Item E is incorrect.

4. CORRECT ANSWER: D

   A millennium is a thousand years. Thus, the answer is D. Items A, B, C, and E are incorrect.

5. CORRECT ANSWER: C

   The dominant religion of Turkey is Islam. The other choices are practiced in Turkey, but have very small followings throughout the country.

6. CORRECT ANSWER: B

   Turkey's capital is Ankara, item B, which is the correct answer. Constantinople, item C, was the former name and the former capital; it was replaced by the name, Istanbul, in the 20's. Izmir is the present-day name for Smyrna, a change which was made coincidentally with that for Constantinople.

TEST 9
PASSAGE

A radically new concept of evolution is being discussed in scientific circles. As presented by two Texans, it would explain the chief puzzle in the record of life's history on earth: the sudden appearance, some 600 million years ago, of most basic divisions of the plant and animal kingdoms.

There is virtually no record of how these divisions came about. Thus, the entire first part of evolutionary history is missing.

The theory says that evolution of a large proportion of the diverse species that have inhabited the earth–plants, fish, trees, and so forth–took place in two gigantic *revolutions* of comparatively short duration.

There is now general agreement that the earth was born as barren of an atmosphere as is the moon today, but volcanoes poured out gases, including an abundance of water vapor - enough to fill the oceans and produce an envelope of *air.*

It is agreed that the early air was radically different from that of today. Volcanoes do not produce oxygen gas, and the early air was dominated by hydrogen compounds. Hence, it was transparent to ultraviolet sunlight that no longer reaches the earth. Recent observations in space have documented the nature of sunlight before filtering by the atmosphere. It is clearly rich in wavelengths of ultraviolet that are lethal to all known forms of life.

This light not only penetrated the original air, but even pierced the top 15 to 30 feet of the oceans.

Since oceanic water circulates, any drifting life would have been carried into the layer bathed in ultraviolet. Hence, it seems unlikely to Drs. Berkner and Marshall that life could have originated in the oceans. Instead, they believe it probably sprang forth independently on the bottoms of numerous deep pools, possibly warmed by the volcanic activity widespread at that time.

1. The earth, at its beginning,

    A. contained craters like the moon
    B. was barren
    C. was fertile
    D. had animal and plant life only in its oceans
    E. had only plants, fish, and trees

2. The doctors mentioned in the passage seem to believe that

    A. life could have originated in the oceans
    B. life came about as the volcanoes poured out gases
    C. a gigantic revolution took place before a large proportion of the diverse species could inhabit the earth
    D. life sprang forth from numerous deep pools
    E. oceanic water, at the beginning, did not circulate

3. How was the volcanic air different from that of today?

   A. It did not come from volcanoes.
   B. The gases did not contain water vapor.
   C. It was dominated by oxygen.
   D. Ultraviolet light could easily penetrate it.
   E. It was not dominated by hydrogen compounds.

4. The air of today can filter ultraviolet rays because

   A. there are no more volcanoes
   B. they are absorbed by the earth
   C. of its oxygen content
   D. of its hydrogen content
   E. the ocean absorbs them

5. The BEST definition of an hypothesis is a(n)

   A. theory or formula derived by inference
   B. tentative assumption made in order to draw out and test its logical or empirical consequences
   C. assumption made in the form of a concession
   D. interpretation of a practical situation or condition taken as the ground for action
   E. statement of order and relation in nature that has been found to be invariable under the same conditions

6. In relation to the content of the passage, the BEST definition of air is the(a)

   A. mixture of invisible gases which surround the earth
   B. surrounding or pervading influence
   C. medium of transmission
   D. compound of 2 parts hydrogen and 1 part oxygen
   E. volcanic gas

KEY (CORRECT ANSWERS)

1. B   4. C
2. D   5. B
3. D   6. A

EXPLANATION OF ANSWERS

1. CORRECT ANSWER: B

   The earth was born as barren of an atmosphere as is the moon today, states the passage in paragraph 4. The only difference was that it had volcanoes which poured out gases, which in turn produced oceans and air. But since the correct answer must refer to the earth at its beginning (refer back to the question stem), B is the only possible answer. Item A is not mentioned. Item C does not refer to the earth at its beginning. Item E took place much later, during the *revolutions* mentioned in paragraph 3. Item D is not stated in the passage.

2. CORRECT ANSWER: D

   At the end of the passage, the two doctors are mentioned as believing that life *probably sprang forth independently on the bottoms of numerous deep pools.* Therefore, D is the correct answer. E is a false statement. The doctors did not believe A or B. C is false because two *gigantic revolutions* took place, according to paragraph 3.

3. CORRECT ANSWER: D

   Volcanic air was transparent to ultraviolet sunlight because it did not produce oxygen gas and was dominated by hydrogen compounds (paragraph 5). Item E is false. It did contain hydrogen compounds. C is false because the reverse is true.
   Items A and B are incorrect because the opposites are true.

4. CORRECT ANSWER: C

   It is the oxygen content in the air which filters out the ultra-violet rays before they reach the earth or the oceans. Therefore, the correct answer is C, and can be found in paragraph 5. Items A, B, and E have nothing to do with the ability of the air to filter the rays. Hydrogen, mentioned in item D, is transparent to ultraviolet rays.

5. CORRECT ANSWER: B

   Item E refers to a law. A and C are insufficient as definitions. D is a broad definition but not so precise as item B, which is the most accurate definition presented, and the correct answer.

6. CORRECT ANSWER: A

   Since the passage is concerned with natural science, item A is far superior to items B and C. Items D and E are incorrect. The correct answer, then, is A.

TEST 10
PASSAGE

Some 25,000 infants suffocate each year in the United States alone. The infants, most of them premature, turn blue and choke and die.

They die from something that is not to this day in most current medical directories, dictionaries, or guides. It is a mysterious condition called hyaline membrane disease. Many years ago this disease killed Patrick Bouvier, the younger son of John F. Kennedy, and it usually kills about half of the infants it strikes.

About 2,000 of the nation's pathologists met in Miami this week for the joint annual session of the College of American Pathologists and the American Society of Clinical Pathologists. They heard a report suggesting that a cure for hyaline membrane has been found.

It was through a series of autopsies of 150 infants who died of hyaline membrane disease that the new treatment for this disease evolved.

The study was done by a Louisville pathologist, Dr. Daniel Stowens, Director of Laboratories at Children's Hospital.

From his autopsies, Dr. Stowens determined that babies who are victims of hyaline membrane disease had too much water in their bodies. The baby's major organ systems may be all right. But they attempt to get rid of the water through the lungs. This clogs these organs and prevents the normal absorption of oxygen into the blood. So the babies die.

There are many complicated theories about how hyaline membrane disease blocks the lungs. The new simple theory had led to a simple therapy.

It is the use of two epsom salts enemas. The first enema clears away the mucus; the second, which relies on epsom salts' affinity for water, draws fluid away from the lungs.

Dr. Stowens reported that gasping and choking babies have been dramatically relieved of their symptoms in a matter of a few minutes after the treatment. In the last eight months, 28 babies suffering from hyaline membrane disease have been treated by epsom salts enemas in five Louisville hospitals, and all are reported to be alive today.

1. The babies who are victims of hyaline membrane disease die because they

    A. are organically defective
    B. absorb oxygen into the blood
    C. lack sufficient water in their system
    D. get rid of excess water through their lungs
    E. do not attempt to get rid of the excess water in their system

2. Before the new method of treating the disease was dis covered, it

    A. was always fatal
    B. killed half the infants it struck
    C. killed 25,000 infants a year all over the world
    D. killed 2,000 infants in the United States every year
    E. killed 150 infants a year

3. The success of the new method seems to

   A. be unpredictable
   B. be perfected
   C. involve some risk
   D. be disapproved of in some medical circles
   E. depend on the baby treated

4. The cause of death from hyaline membrane is

   A. the bloodstream
   B. the lungs
   C. the membrane
   D. suffocation
   E. the heart

5. Dr. Stowens might rightfully be compared to

   A. Dr. Spock
   B. the polio vaccine
   C. Dr. Teller
   D. Dr. Salk
   E. the hyaline membrane disease

6. Prior to the discovery of the therapy,

   A. there existed a simple theory about it
   B. hyaline membrane disease was not treated
   C. there was no theory on how to treat it
   D. the theories about causes were many and recondite
   E. there was a simple therapy

7. The new theory

   A. does not use epsom salts
   B. does not use water
   C. delivers fluid to the lungs
   D. relies on the affinity between epsom salts and water
   E. use various epsom salts enemas

8. With the new therapy, babies

   A. gasp and choke
   B. have been treated over the last 12 months
   C. are relieved of their symptoms in a matter of minutes
   D. are relieved of their symptoms in a few hours
   E. have now been treated in 28 hospitals

9. A pathologist is

   A. a doctor
   B. a specialist in children's diseases
   C. usually a pediatrician
   D. one versed in the nature of respiratory ailments
   E. one versed in the nature of diseases

KEY (CORRECT ANSWERS)

1. D   4. D   7. D
2. B   5. D   8. C
3. B   6. D   9. E

EXPLANATION OF ANSWERS

1. CORRECT ANSWER: D

   In the next to last sentence of paragraph 6, the reason is explained. The correct answer is D. Item B is incorrect because it is the prevention of the normal oxygen flow that leads to fatalities. C is incorrect because they have too much water in their system. Whether the baby is organically defective or not has nothing to do with the disease, discounting A. Item E is incorrect because the babies do make this attempt.

2. CORRECT ANSWER: B

   In the last sentence of paragraph 2, it is stated that the disease killed about half the infants it struck. Thus, the correct answer is B. 150 infants had autopsies performed (item E). 25,000 yearly in the United States died from it, discounting item C. Item A is false. The figure 2,000 in item D refers to the nation's pathologists.

3. CORRECT ANSWER: B

   It would seem, since all the babies treated are alive today, that Dr. Stowens' approach to the disease has been perfected and that the cure has been found. Therefore, the correct answer is B. Item D is not mentioned in the passage. And items A, C, and E are false.

4. CORRECT ANSWER: D

   The cause of death is suffocation. This is mentioned in the first sentence of the passage. The correct answer is D. Items A, B, C, and E are organs and parts of the body affected but not the cause of death. Item C refers to a part of the name of the disease.

5. CORRECT ANSWER: D

   Dr. Spock, a specialist in child growth and development, does not pioneer in the treatment of diseases, discounting A. Item C refers to a nuclear physicist. Item E refers to the disease Dr. Stowens sought to treat. But Dr. Salk, item D, found a way to treat polio successfully and, therefore, is the correct answer. Item B refers to the method he used.

6. CORRECT ANSWER: D

   The answer may be reached through paragraph 7, which ends in *The new simple therapy had led to a simple theory.* Before this, there were *many complicated theories about how ... disease blocks the lungs.* Therefore, item D is correct. (*Recondite* means complex, profound.) Item A is false; it occurred after the discovery of the therapy. Item B is false because it was treated. Item C is false; there were many theories. Item E is false although it contains a repetition of part of the statement appearing in the paragraph.

7. CORRECT ANSWER: D

   Item A is false because the opposite is stated in the passage. Item B is false for the same reason. Item C is false because fluid is drawn away from the lungs. Item D is correct because it is part of the second stage of the treatment (or therapy) indicated in paragraph 8. Item E is false because the two that are used do not justify the adjective *various*.

8. CORRECT ANSWER: C

Item A is false because that is what occurs before they are treated. Item B is false because they have been treated over the last 8 months. Item C is correct, as indicated in para-graph 9. Item D is false because a different length of time *(a few minutes)* is mentioned in the passage. Item E is false because the passage actually states that 28 babies have been treated in 5 hospitals.

9. CORRECT ANSWER: E

A pathologist is one versed in the nature of diseases. Therefore, E is the only possible answer and the correct one. Item A is insufficient. Items B, C, and D are false.

Interpretation of Reading Materials in the Natural Sciences

EXAMINATION SECTION
TEST 1

PASSAGE

The higher forms of plants and animals, such as seed plants and vertebrates, are similar or alike in many respects but decidedly different in others. For example, both of these groups of organisms carry on digestion, respiration, reproduction, conduction, growth, and exhibit sensitivity to various stimuli. On the other hand, a number of basic differences are evident. Plants have no excretory systems comparable to those of animals. Plants have no heart or similar pumping organ. Plants are very limited in their movements. Plants have nothing similar to the animal nervous system. In addition, animals cannot synthesize carbohydrates from inorganic substances. Animals do not have special regions of growth, comparable to terminal and lateral meristems in plants, which persist throughout the life span of the organism. And finally, the animal cell wall in only a membrane, while plant cell walls are more rigid, usually thicker, and may be composed of such substances as cellulose, lignin, pectin, cutin, and suberin. These characteristics are important to an understanding of living organisms and their functions and should, consequently, be carefully considered in plant and animal studies.

1. Which of the following do animals lack?

    A. Ability to react to stimuli
    B. Ability to conduct substances from one place to another
    C. Reproduction by gametes
    D. A cell membrane
    E. A terminal growth region

2. Which of the following statements is FALSE?

    A. Animal cell walls are composed of cellulose.
    B. Plants grow as long as they live.
    C. Plants produce sperms and eggs.
    D. All vertebrates have hearts.
    E. Wood is dead at maturity.

3. Respiration in plants take place

    A. only during the day
    B. only in the presence of carbon dioxide
    C. both day and night
    D. only at night
    E. only in the presence of certain stimuli

4. An example of a vertebrate is the

    A. earthworm   B. starfish   C. amoeba
    D. cow   E. insect

5. Which of the following statements is TRUE?

   A. All animals eat plants as a source of food.
   B. Respiration, in many ways, is the reverse of photosyn-thesis.
   C. Man is an invertebrate animal
   D. Since plants have no hearts, they cannot develop high pressures in their cells.
   E. Plants cannot move.

6. Which of the following do plants lack?

   A. A means of movement
   B. Pumping structures
   C. Special regions of growth
   D. Reproduction by gametes
   E. A digestive process

7. A substance that can be synthesized by green plants but not by animals is

   A. protein   B. cellulose   C. carbon dioxide
   D. uric acid   E. water

KEY (CORRECT ANSWERS)

1. E   5. B
2. A   6. B
3. C   7. B
4. D

TEST 2
PASSAGE

The discovery of antitoxin and its specific antagonistic effect upon toxin furnished an opportunity for the accurate investigation of the relationship of a bacterial antigen and its antibody. Toxin-antitoxin reactions were the first immunological processes to which experimental precision could be applied, and the discovery of principles of great importance resulted from such studies. A great deal of the work was done with diphtheria toxin and antitoxin and the facts elucidated with these materials are in principle applicable to similar substances.

The simplest assumption to account for the manner in which an antitoxin renders a toxin innocuous would be that the antitoxin destroys the toxin. Roux and Buchner, however, advanced the opinion that the antitoxin did not act directly upon the toxin, but affected it indirectly through the mediation of tissue cells. Ehrlich, on the other hand, conceived the reaction of toxin and antitoxin as a direct union, analogous to the chemical neutralization of an acid by a base.

The conception of toxin destruction was conclusively refuted by the experiments of Calmette. This observer, working with snake poison, found that the poison itself (unlike most other toxins) possessed the property of resisting heat to 100° C, while its specific antitoxin, like other antitoxins, was destroyed at or about 70° C. Nontoxic mixtures of the two substances, when subjected to heat, regained their toxic properties. The natural inference from these observations was that the toxin in the original mixture had not been destroyed, but had been merely inactivated by the presence of the antitoxin and again set free after destruction of the antitoxin by heat.

1. Both toxins and antitoxins ordinarily

    A. are completely destroyed at body temperatures
    B. are extremely resistant to heat
    C. can exist only in combination
    D. are destroyed at 180° F
    E. are products of nonliving processes

2. MOST toxins can be destroyed by

    A. bacterial action
    B. salt solutions
    C. boiling
    D. diphtheria antitoxin
    E. other toxins

3. Very few disease organisms release a true toxin into the bloodstream. It would follow, then, that

    A. studies of snake venom reactions have no value
    B. studies of toxin-antitoxin reactions are of little importance
    C. the treatment of most diseases must depend upon information obtained from study of a few
    D. antitoxin plays an important part in the body defense against the great majority of germs
    E. only toxin producers are dangerous

4. A person becomes susceptible to infection again immediately after recovering from

   A. mumps
   B. tetanus
   C. diphtheria
   D. smallpox
   E. tuberculosis

5. City people are more frequently immune to communicable diseases than country people are because

   A. country people eat better food
   B. city doctors are better than country doctors
   C. the air is more healthful in the country
   D. country people have fewer contacts with disease carriers
   E. there are more doctors in the city than in the country

6. The substances that provide us with immunity to disease are found in the body in the

   A. blood serum
   B. gastric juice
   C. urine
   D. white blood cells
   E. red blood cells

7. A person ill with diphtheria would MOST likely be treated with

   A. diphtheria toxin
   B. diphtheria toxoid
   C. dead diphtheria germs
   D. diphtheria antitoxin
   E. live diphtheria germs

8. To determine susceptibility to diphtheria, an individual may be given the _____ test.

   A. Wassermann
   B. Schick
   C. Widal
   D. Dick
   E. Kahn

9. Since few babies under six months of age contract diphtheria, young babies PROBABLY

   A. are never exposed to diphtheria germs
   B. have high body temperatures that destroy the toxin if acquired
   C. acquire immunity from their mothers
   D. acquire immunity from their fathers
   E. are too young to become infected

10. Calmette's findings

    A. contradicted both Roux and Buchner's opinion and Ehrlich's conception
    B. contradicted Roux and Buchner, but supported Ehrlich
    C. contradicted Ehrlich, but supported Roux and Buchner
    D. were consistent with both theories
    E. had no bearing on the point at issue

KEY (CORRECT ANSWERS)

1. D
2. C
3. C
4. E
5. D
6. A
7. D
8. B
9. C
10. D

TEST 3

PASSAGE

Sodium chloride, being by far the largest constituent of the mineral matter of the blood, assumes special significance in the regulation of water exchanges in the organism. And, as Cannon has emphasized repeatedly, these latter are more extensive and more important than may at first thought appear. He points out *there are a number of circulations of the fluid out of the body and back again, without loss.* Thus, for example, it is estimated that from a quart and one-half of water daily *leaves the body* when it enters the mouth as saliva, another one or two quarts are passed out as gastric juice, and perhaps the same amount is contained in the bile and the secretions of the pancreas and the intestinal wall. This large volume of water enters the digestive processes; and practically all of it is reabsorbed through the intestinal wall, where it performs the equally important function of carrying in the digestive foodstuffs. These and other instances of what Cannon calls *the conservative use of water in our bodies* involve essentially osmotic pressure relationships in which the concentration of sodium chloride plays an important part.

1. This passage implies that

    A. the contents of the alimentary canal are not to be considered within the body
    B. sodium chloride does not actually enter the body
    C. every particle of water ingested is used over and over again
    D. water cannot be absorbed by the body unless it contains sodium chloride
    E. substances can pass through the intestinal wall in only one direction

2. According to this passage, which of the following processes requires most water? The

    A. absorption of digested foods
    B. secretion of gastric juice
    C. secretion of saliva
    D. production of bile
    E. concentration of sodium chloride solution

3. A body fluid that is NOT saline is

    A. blood   B. urine   C. bile
    D. gastric juice   E. saliva

4. An organ that functions as a storage reservoir from which large quantities of water are reabsorbed into the body is the

    A. kidney   B. liver   C. large intestine
    D. mouth   E. pancreas

5. Water is reabsorbed into the body by the process of

    A. secretion   B. excretion C. digestion
    D. osmosis   E. oxidation

6. Digested food enters the body PRINCIPALLY through the

    A. mouth   B. liver   C. villi
    D. pancreas   E. stomach

219

7. The metallic element found in the blood in compound form and present there in larger quantities than any other metallic element is

    A. iron
    B. calcium
    C. magnesium
    D. chlorine
    E. sodium

8. An organ that removes water from the body and prevents its reabsorption for use in the body processes is the

    A. pancreas
    B. liver
    C. small intestine
    D. lungs
    E. large intestine

9. In which of the following processes is sodium chloride removed MOST rapidly from the body?

    A. Digestion
    B. Breathing
    C. Oxidation
    D. Respiration
    E. Perspiration

10. Which of the following liquids would pass from the alimentary canal into the blood MOST rapidly?

    A. A dilute solution of sodium chloride in water
    B. Gastric juice
    C. A concentrated solution of sodium chloride in water
    D. Digested food
    E. Distilled water

11. The reason why it is unsafe to drink ocean water even under conditions of extreme thirst is that it

    A. would reduce the salinity of the blood to a dangerous level
    B. contains dangerous disease germs
    C. contains poisonous salts
    D. would greatly increase the salinity of the blood
    E. would cause salt crystals to form in the bloodstream

KEY (CORRECT ANSWERS)

1. A
2. A
3. D
4. C
5. D
6. C
7. E
8. D
9. E
10. E

TEST 4
PASSAGE

In the days of sailing ships, when voyages were long and uncertain, provisions for many months were stored without refrigeration in the holds of the ships. Naturally, no fresh or perishable foods could be included. Toward the end of particularly long voyages, the crews of such ships became ill and often many died from scurvy. Many men, both scientific and otherwise, tried to devise a cure for scurvy. Among the latter was John Hall, a son-in-law of William Shakespeare, who cured some cases of scurvy by administering a sour brew made from scurvy grass and watercress.

The next step was the suggestion of William Harvey that scurvy could be prevented by giving the men lemon juice. He thought that the beneficial substance was the acid contained in the fruit.

The third step was taken by Dr. James Lind, an English naval surgeon, who performed the following experiment with 12 sailors, all of whom were sick with scurvy: Each was given the same diet, except that four of the men received small amounts of dilute sulfuric acid, four others were given vinegar, and the remaining four were given lemons. Only those who received the fruit recovered.

1. Credit for solving the problem described above belongs to

   A. Hall, because he first devised a cure for scurvy
   B. Harvey, because he first proposed a solution of the problem
   C. Lind, because he proved the solution by means of an experiment
   D. both Harvey and Lind, because they found that lemons are more effective than scurvy grass or watercress
   E. all three men, because each made some contribution

2. A good substitute for lemons in the treatment of scurvy is

   A. fresh eggs
   B. tomato juice
   C. cod-liver oil
   D. liver
   E. whole-wheat bread

3. The number of control groups that Dr. Lind used in his experiment was

   A. one   B. two   C. three   D. four   E. none

4. A substance that will turn blue litmus red is

   A. aniline
   B. lye
   C. ice
   D. vinegar
   E. table salt

5. The hypothesis tested by Lind was:

   A. Lemons contain some substance not present in vinegar
   B. Citric acid is the most effective treatment for scurvy
   C. Lemons contain some unknown acid that will cure scurvy
   D. Some specific substance, rather than acids in general, is needed to cure scurvy
   E. The substance needed to cure scurvy is found only in lemons

6. A problem that Lind's experiment did NOT solve was:

    A. Will citric acid alone cure scurvy?
    B. Will lemons cure scurvy?
    C. Will either sulfuric acid or vinegar cure scurvy?
    D. Are all substances that contain acids equally effective as a treatment for scurvy?
    E. Are lemons more effective than either vinegar or sulfuric acid in the treatment of scurvy?

7. The PRIMARY purpose of a controlled scientific experiment is to

    A. get rid of superstitions
    B. prove a hypothesis is correct
    C. disprove a theory that is false
    D. determine whether a hypothesis is true or false
    E. discover new facts

KEY (CORRECT ANSWERS)

1. E   5. D
2. B   6. A
3. B   7. D
4. D

TEST 5
PASSAGE

Photosynthesis is a complex process with many intermediate steps. Ideas differ greatly as to the details of these steps, but the general nature of the process and its outcome are well established. Water, usually from the soil, is conducted through the xylem of root, stem, and leaf to the chlorophyl-containing cells of a leaf. In consequence of the abundance of water within the latter cells, their walls are saturated with water. Carbon dioxide, diffusing from the air through the stomata and into the intercellular spaces of the leaf, comes into contact with the water in the walls of the cells which adjoin the intercellular spaces. The carbon dioxide becomes dissolved in the water in these walls, and in solution diffuses through the walls and the plasma membranes into the cells. By the agency of chlorophyl in the chloroplasts of the cells, the energy of light is transformed into chemical energy. This chemical energy is used to decompose the carbon dioxide and water, and the products of their decomposition are recombined into a new compound. The compound first formed is successively built up into more and more complex substances until finally a sugar is produced.

1. The union of carbon dioxide and water to form starch results in an excess of

   A. hydrogen
   B. carbon
   C. oxygen
   D. carbon monoxide
   E. hydrogen peroxide

2. Synthesis of carbohydrates takes place

   A. in the stomata
   B. in the intercellular spaces of leaves
   C. in the walls of plant cells
   D. within the plasma membranes of plant cells
   E. within plant cells that contain chloroplasts

3. In the process of photosynthesis, chlorophyl acts as a

   A. carbohydrate
   B. source of carbon dioxide
   C. catalyst
   D. source of chemical energy
   E. plasma membrane

4. In which of the following places are there the GREATEST number of hours in which photosynthesis can take place during the month of December?

   A. Buenos Aires, Argentina
   B. Caracas, Venezuela
   C. Fairbanks, Alaska
   D. Quito, Ecuador
   E. Calcutta, India

5. During photosynthesis, molecules of carbon dioxide enter the stomata of leaves because

   A. the molecules are already in motion
   B. they are forced through the stomata by the sun's rays
   C. chlorophyl attracts them
   D. a chemical change takes place in the stomata
   E. oxygen passes out through the stomata

6. Besides food manufacture, another useful result of photosynthesis is that it   6._____

    A. aids in removing poisonous gases from the air
    B. helps to maintain the existing proportion of gases in the air
    C. changes complex compounds into simpler compounds
    D. changes certain waste products into hydrocarbons
    E. changes chlorophyl into useful substances

7. A process that is almost the exact reverse of photosynthesis is the   7._____

    A. rusting of iron   B. burning of wood
    C. digestion of starch   D. ripening of fruit
    E. storage of food in seeds

8. The leaf of the tomato plant will be unable to carry on photosynthesis if the   8._____

    A. upper surface of the leaf is coated with vaseline
    B. upper surface of the leaf is coated with lampblack
    C. lower surface of the leaf is coated with lard
    D. leaf is placed in an atmosphere of pure carbon dioxide
    E. entire leaf is coated with lime

KEY (CORRECT ANSWERS)

1. C   5. A
2. E   6. B
3. C   7. B
4. A   8. C

TEST 6
PASSAGE

The British pressure suit was made in two pieces and joined around the middle in contrast to the other suits, which were one-piece suits with a removable helmet. Oxygen was supplied through a tube, and a container of soda lime absorbed carbon dioxide and water vapor. The pressure was adjusted to a maximum of 2 1/2 pounds per square inch (130 millimeters) higher than the surrounding air. Since pure oxygen was used, this produced a partial pressure of 130 millimeters, which is sufficient to sustain the flier at any altitude.

Using this pressure suit, the British established a world's altitude record of 49,944 feet in 1936 and succeeded in raising it to 53,937 feet the following year. The pressure suit is a compromise solution to the altitude problem. Full sea-level pressure cannot be maintained, as the suit would be so rigid that the flier could not move arms or legs. Hence, a pressure one-third to one-fifth that of sea level has been used. Because of these lower pressures, oxygen has been used to raise the partial pressure of alveolar oxygen to normal.

1. The MAIN constituent of air not admitted to the pressure suit described was   1._____

   A. oxygen   B. nitrogen   C. water vapor
   D. carbon dioxide E. hydrogen

2. The pressure within the suit exceeded that of the surrounding air by an amount equal to   2._____
   130 millimeters of

   A. mercury   B. water   C. air
   D. oxygen   E. carbon dioxide

3. The normal atmospheric pressure at sea level is _____ mm.   3._____

   A. 130   B. 250   C. 760   D. 1000   E. 1300

4. The water vapor that was absorbed by the soda lime came from   4._____

   A. condensation
   B. the union of oxygen with carbon dioxide
   C. body metabolism
   D. the air within the pressure suit
   E. water particles in the upper air

5. The HIGHEST altitude that has been reached with the British pressure suit is about   5._____
   _____ miles.

   A. 130   B. 2 1/2   C. 6   D. 10   E. 5

6. If the pressure suit should develop a leak, the   6._____

   A. oxygen supply would be cut off
   B. suit would fill up with air instead of oxygen
   C. pressure within the suit would drop to zero
   D. pressure within the suit would drop to that of the surrounding air
   E. suit would become so rigid that the flier would be unable to move arms or legs

7. The reason why oxygen helmets are unsatisfactory for use in efforts to set higher altitude records is that

   A. it is impossible to maintain a tight enough fit at the neck
   B. oxygen helmets are too heavy
   C. they do not conserve the heat of the body as pressure suits do
   D. if a parachute jump becomes necessary, it cannot be made while such a helmet is being worn
   E. oxygen helmets are too rigid

8. The pressure suit is termed a compromise solution because

   A. it is not adequate for stratosphere flying
   B. aviators cannot stand sea-level pressure at high altitudes
   C. some suits are made in two pieces, others in one
   D. other factors than maintenance of pressure have to be accommodated
   E. full atmospheric pressure cannot be maintained at high altitudes

9. The passage implies that

   A. the air pressure at 49,944 feet is approximately the same as it is at 53,937 feet
   B. pressure cabin planes are not practical at extremely high altitudes
   C. a flier's oxygen requirement is approximately the same at high altitudes as it is at sea level
   D. one-piece pressure suits with removable helmets are unsafe
   E. a normal alveolar oxygen supply is maintained if the air pressure is between one-third and one-fifth that of sea level

KEY (CORRECT ANSWERS)

1. B   6. D
2. A   7. D
3. C   8. E
4. C   9. C
5. D

TEST 7
PASSAGE

The formed elements of the blood are the red corpuscles or erythrocytes, the white corpuscles or leucocytes, the blood platelets, and the so-called blood dust or hemoconiae. Together, these constitute 30-40 percent by volume of the whole blood, the remainder being taken up by the plasma. In man, there are normally 5,000,000 red cells per cubic millimeter of blood; the count is somewhat lower in women. Variations occur frequently, especially after exercise or a heavy meal, or at high altitudes. Except in camels, which have elliptical corpuscles, the shape of the mammalian corpuscle is that of a circular, nonnucleated, bi-concave disk. The average diameter usually given is 7.7 microns, a value obtained by examining dried preparations of blood and considered by Ponder to be too low. Ponder's own observations, made on red cells in the fresh state, show the human corpuscle to have an average diameter of 8.8 microns. When circulating in the blood vessels, the red cell does not maintain a fixed shape but changes its form constantly, especially in the small capillaries. The red blood corpuscles are continually undergoing destruction, new corpuscles being formed to replace them. The average life of red corpuscles has been estimated by various investigators to be between three and six weeks. Preceding destruction, changes in the composition of the cells are believed to occur which render them less resistant. In the process of destruction, the lipids of the membrane are dissolved and the hemoglobin which is liberated is the most important, though probably not the only, source of bilirubin. The belief that the liver is the only site of red cell destruction is no longer generally held. The leucocytes, of which there are several forms, usually number between 7000 and 9000 per cubic millimeter of blood. These increase in number in disease, particularly when there is bacterial infection.

1. Leukemia is a disease involving the

    A. red cells
    B. white cells
    C. plasma
    D. blood platelets
    E. blood dust

2. *The erythrocytes in the blood are increased in number after a heavy meal.* The paragraph implies that this

    A. is true
    B. holds only for camels
    C. is not true
    D. may be true
    E. depends on the number of white cells

3. When blood is dried, the red cells

    A. contract
    B. remain the same size
    C. disintegrate
    D. expand
    E. become elliptical

4. Ponder is PROBABLY classified as a professional

    A. pharmacist
    B. physicist
    C. psychologist
    D. physiologist
    E. psychiatrist

5. The term *erythema,* when applied to skin conditions, signifies

    A. redness
    B. swelling
    C. irritation
    D. pain
    E. roughness

6. Lipids are insoluble in water and soluble in such solvents as ether, chloroform, and benzene.
   It may be inferred that the membranes of red cells MOST closely resemble

   A. egg white
   B. sugar
   C. bone
   D. butter
   E. cotton fiber

7. Analysis of a sample of blood yields cell counts of 4,800,000 erythrocytes and 16,000 leucocytes per cubic millimeter.
   These data suggest that the patient from whom the blood was taken

   A. is anemic
   B. has been injuriously invaded by germs
   C. has been exposed to high-pressure air
   D. has a normal cell count
   E. has lost a great deal of blood

8. Bilirubin, a bile pigment, is

   A. an end product of several different reactions
   B. formed only in the liver
   C. formed from the remnants of the cell membranes of erythrocytes
   D. derived from hemoglobin exclusively
   E. a precursor of hemoglobin

9. Bancroft found that the blood count of the natives in the Peruvian Andes differed from that usually accepted as normal. The blood PROBABLY differed in respect to

   A. leucocytes
   B. blood platelets
   C. cell shapes
   D. erythrocytes
   E. hemoconiae

10. Hemoglobin is probably NEVER found

    A. free in the bloodstream
    B. in the red cells
    C. in women's blood
    D. in the blood after exercise
    E. in the leucocytes

KEY (CORRECT ANSWERS)

1. B   6. D
2. D   7. B
3. A   8. A
4. D   9. D
5. A   10. E

TEST 8
PASSAGE

Chemical investigations show that during muscle contraction, the store of organic phosphates in the muscle fibers is altered as energy is released. In doing so, the organic phosphates (chiefly adenosine triphosphate and phospho-creatine) are transformed anaerobically to organic compounds plus phosphates. As soon as the organic phosphates begin to break down in muscle contraction, the glycogen in the muscle fibers also transforms into lactic acid plus free energy; this energy the muscle fiber uses to return the organic compounds plus phosphates into high-energy organic phosphates ready for another contraction. In the presence of oxygen, the lactic acid from the glycogen decomposition is changed also. About one-fifth of it is oxidized to form water and carbon dioxide and to yield another supply of energy. This time the energy is used to transform the remaining four-fifths of the lactic acid into glycogen again.

1. The energy for muscle contraction comes directly from the   1._____

    A. breakdown of the organic phosphates
    B. resynthesis of adenosine triphosphate
    C. breakdown of glycogen into lactic acid
    D. oxidation of lactic acid

2. Lactic acid does not accumulate in a muscle that is(has)   2._____

    A. in a state of lacking oxygen
    B. an ample supply of oxygen
    C. in a state of fatigue
    D. repeatedly being stimulated

3. The energy for the resynthesis of adenosine triphosphate and phosphocreatine comes from the   3._____

    A. oxidation of lactic acid
    B. synthesis of organic phosphates
    C. change from glycogen to lactic acid
    D. resynthesis of glycogen

4. The energy for the resynthesis of glycogen comes from the   4._____

    A. breakdown of organic phosphates
    B. resynthesis of organic phosphates
    C. change occurring in one-fifth of the lactic acid
    D. change occurring in four-fifths of the lactic acid

5. The breakdown of the organic phosphates into organic compounds plus phosphates is an _____ reaction.   5._____

    A. anabolic   B. aerobic
    C. endothermic   D. anaerobic

KEY (CORRECT ANSWERS)

1. A
2. B
3. C
4. C
5. D

TEST 9

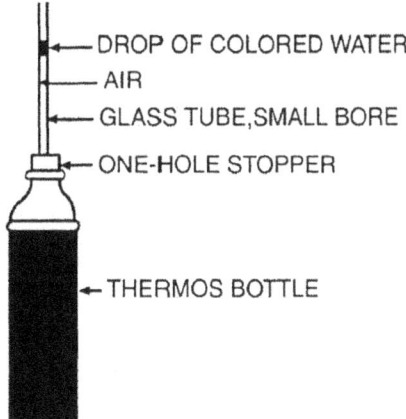

1. The device shown in the diagram above indicates changes that are measured more accurately by a(n)

    A. thermometer
    B. hygrometer
    C. anemometer
    D. hydrometer
    E. barometer

2. If the device is placed in a cold refrigerator for 72 hours, which of the following is MOST likely to happen?

    A. The stopper will be forced out of the bottle.
    B. The drop of water will evaporate.
    C. The drop will move downward.
    D. The drop will move upward.
    E. No change will take place.

3. When the device was carried in an elevator from the first floor to the sixth floor of a building, the drop of colored water moved about $\frac{1}{4}$ inch in the tube.
   Which of the following is MOST probably true?
   The drop moved

    A. downward because there was a decrease in the air pressure
    B. upward because there was an increase in the air pressure
    C. downward because there was an increase in the air temperature
    D. upward because there was an increase in the air temperature
    E. downward because there was an increase in the air temperature and a decrease in the pressure

4. The part of a thermos bottle into which liquids are poured consists of

    A. a single-walled, metal flask coated with silver
    B. two flasks, one of glass and one of silvered metal
    C. two silvered-glass flasks separated by a vacuum
    D. two silver flasks separated by a vacuum
    E. a single-walled, glass flask with a silver-colored coating

231

2(#9)

5. The thermos bottle is MOST similar in principle to 5.____

   A. the freezing unit in an electric refrigerator
   B. radiant heaters
   C. solar heating systems
   D. storm windows
   E. a thermostatically controlled heating system

6. In a plane flying at an altitude where the air pressure is only half the normal pressure at sea level, the plane's altimeter should read approximately _____ feet. 6.____

   A. 3000 B. 9000 C. 18000 D. 27000 E. 60000

7. Which of the following is the POOREST conductor of heat? 7.____

   A. Air under a pressure of 1.5 pounds per square inch
   B. Air under a pressure of 15 pounds per square inch
   C. Unsilvered glass
   D. Silvered glass
   E. Silver

KEY (CORRECT ANSWERS)

1. A 5. D
2. C 6. C
3. B 7. A
4. C

TEST 10

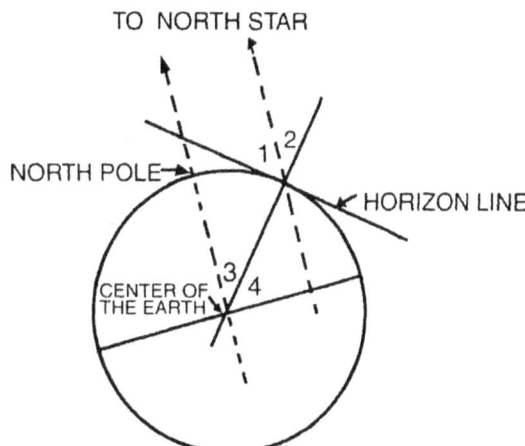

The latitude of any point on the earth's surface is the angle between a plumb line dropped to the center of the earth from that point and the plane of the earth's equator. Since it is impossible to go to the center of the earth to measure latitude, the latitude of any point may be determined indirectly as shown in the accompanying diagram.

It will be recalled that the axis of the earth, if extended outward, passes very near the North Star. Since the North Star is, for all practical purposes, infinitely distant, the line of sight to the North Star of an observer on the surface of the earth is virtually parallel with the earth's axis. Angle 1, then, in the diagram represents the angular distance of the North Star above the horizon.

Angle 2 is equal to angle 3, because when two parallel lines are intersected by a straight line, the corresponding angles are equal. Angle 1 plus angle 2 is a right angle and so is angle 3 plus angle 4. Therefore, angle 1 equals angle 4 because when equals are subtracted from equals, the results are equal.

1. If an observer finds that the angular distance of the North Star above the horizon is 30°, his latitude is _____ ° N.

   A. 15 B. 30 C. 60 D. 90 E. 120

2. To an observer on the equator, the North Star would be _____ the horizon.

   A. 30° above   B. 60° above   C. 90° above
   D. on   E. below

3. To an observer on the Arctic Circle, the North Star would be

   A. directly overhead   B. 23 1/2° above the horizon
   C. 66 1/2° above the horizon D. on the horizon
   E. below the horizon

2 (#10)

4. The distance around the earth along a certain parallel of latitude is 3600 miles. At that latitude, how many miles are there in one degree of longitude? _____ mile(s).

   A. 1 B. 10 C. 30 D. 69 E. 100

4._____

5. At which of the following latitudes would the sun be directly overhead at noon on June 21?

   A. $0°$ B. $23\ 1/2°S$ C. $23\ 1/2°N$ D. $66\ 1/2°N$ E. $66\ 1/2°S$

5._____

6. On March 21, the number of hours of daylight at places on the Arctic Circle is

   A. none B. 8 C. 12 D. 16 E. 24

6._____

7. The distance from the equator to the 45th parallel, measured along a meridian, is APPROXIMATELY _____ miles.

   A. 450 B. 900 C. 1250 D. 3125 E. 6250

7._____

8. The difference in time between the meridians that pass through longitude 45° E and longitude 105° W is _____ hours.

   A. 6 B. 2 C. 8 D. 4 E. 10

8._____

9. Which of the following is NOT a great circle or part of a great circle?

   A. Arctic Circle
   B. 100th meridian
   C. equator
   D. shortest distance between New York and London
   E. Greenwich meridian

9._____

10. At which of the following places does the sun set EARLIEST on June 21?

    A. Montreal, Canada
    C. Mexico City, Mexico
    E. Manila, P.I.
    B. Santiago, Chile
    D. Lima, Peru

10._____

KEY (CORRECT ANSWERS)

1. B   6. C
2. D   7. D
3. C   8. E
4. B   9. A
5. C   10. B

INTERPRETATION OF LITERARY MATERIALS

INTRODUCTION

The basis of this test lies in the comprehension and interpretation of selected passages, which may be prose or verse, and have been culled from American and English literature, classical and modern. The examinee then answers a series of multiple-choice questions of the four-item type relating to the selection. About one-third of the passages are poetry, and two-thirds are prose.

The following standards of literary interpretation form the major criteria of this test:

1. The ability to understand the literal and figurative meanings of words as used in the passage

2. The ability to glean facts and to grasp the main thought or theme

3. The ability to discern or to relate the purpose, the mood or tone, or the point of view of the passage or of its author

4. The ability to detect and to assess the use of simple literary techniques.

The candidate should note that this is a test of reading comprehension and that the answers for the most part are to be found in and by and through the text. Only a small portion of the questions is involved with or depends upon acquired basal or related information or knowledge.

The *Tests* that follow have been planned to include, or to evolve, in equivalent form, quality, and degree of difficulty, all of the aims set forth above for this sector. The passages have been selected and presented, so far as possible, in ascending order of difficulty to achieve optimum self-instructional progression and maximum learning affect.

To achieve these purposes, fifteen (15) *Tests* are so offered, with answers, and with the answers fully explained, so that the candidate may learn how to go about answering the questions as well as the bases involved in attaining to the correct answers. The book thus becomes a complete self-instructional programmed vehicle.

In addition, as a follow-up and as a reservoir for practice and drill and work-study, fifteen (15) additional passages appear, in a similar gradation of difficulty and with an equal consistency. The correct answers are furnished for these questions.

Note: The questions in the *Tests* are presented for the most part in a five-item-choice form, which means that these questions are approximately 20% more difficult than the ones to be encountered on the Examination. This presentation should result in more extended effort and help to eliminate more surely any reliance on the element of guessing, or any resignation into a mood of indifference to preparation.

Note: Poetry, as well as prose, furnishes the text of some of the passages. To those candidates who, for undefinable reasons, regard the poetry passage as more difficult or less comprehensible than the prose selection, this assurance is offered: It is not so. Both types of passages are equally difficult and equally comprehensible. For this reason, poetry selections appear herein and the answers are given, together with full explanations therefor.

The directions for Test - INTERPRETATION OF LITERARY MATERIALS are approximately as follows, and these directions will govern the *Tests* that follow.

DIRECTIONS: You have two hours for this test. As you answer the questions, you should omit any that seem unusually difficult until you finish the others.

Your answers to the exercises in this test are to be recorded on the separate answer sheet, which is loosely inserted in the test. Remove this answer sheet now; write your name and the other information called for in the blanks at the top of the answer sheet; then finish reading these directions. You may find that these questions will require you to read the selections much more carefully and analytically than you are accustomed to reading such materials, and that you will need to spend more time on many questions than is usually required in objective achievement tests. You may find that the best procedure to follow is to read the selection through once quite carefully; then read all of the questions based on the selection, answering on the first reading as many questions as you can answer easily. Then reread the selection as many times as is necessary the more difficult questions.

After the number on the answer sheet corresponding to that of each exercise, mark the ONE numbered space which designates the answer you have selected as correct.

Sample question and answers follow.

SAMPLE QUESTIONS

DIRECTIONS: In the passage that follows, each question or incomplete statement below is followed by several suggested answers or completions. Select the one that BEST answers the question or completes the statement. Base your choice in each case on the materials given and on your own understanding of the subject matter.

PASSAGE

Tiger, tiger, burning bright
In the forests of the night,
What immortal hand or eye
Could frame thy fearful symmetry?

1. The meter of the poem is 1.____

   A. iambic   B. anapestic   C. trochaic
   D. dactylic   E. spondaic

Item C is correct. The trochee consists of two syllables: one accented, followed by one unaccented. The other items, A, B, D, and E, present different combinations of accented and unaccented syllables.

An IAMB (Item A) is a metrical foot of two syllables, a short followed by a long, or an unaccented by an accented (U -), as in *Come live/with me/and be/my love*.

An ANAPEST (Item B) is a metrical foot of three syllables: two short followed by one long (quantitative meter), or two unstressed followed by one stressed (accentual meter). Thus, *for the nonce* is an accentual anapest.

A TROCHEE (Item C) is a metrical foot of two syllables: a long followed by a short, or an accented followed by an unaccented.

A DACTYL (Item D) is a metrical foot of three syllables: one long followed by two short, or, in modern verse, one accented followed by two unaccented $(-\cup\cup)$, as in *Géntly and húmãnly.*

A SPONDEE (Item E) is a metrical foot consisting of two long syllables or two heavy beats.

2. The words *Tiger, tiger* and the words *burning bright* represent

   A. allusion   B. couplet   C. antithesis
   D. simile   E. alliteration

Item E is correct. Alliteration is the commencement of two or more words of a word group with the same consonant or letter, for the purpose of effect. Item B represents successive rhyming lines. Item C is the contrasting of one idea against another. Item A is a form of reference. Item D is an expressed comparison.

3. The question asked in the poem is:

   A. Who could hold the tiger?
   B. Who could paint such a thing as a tiger?
   C. Who made the tiger?
   D. Who would dare go near a tiger?
   E. Who could describe a tiger?

Item C is correct. The word *frame* in the poem, in this case, means to fashion or mold. Items A, B, D, and E are incorrect.

4. The above lines of the poem represent a(n)

   A. ode   B. oxymoron   C. ottava rima
   D. sestet   E. quatrain

Item E is correct. A four-line stanza is termed a quatrain. Items A, B, C, and D are false.

An ODE (Item A) is a lyric poem, typically of elaborate or irregular metrical form and expressive of exalted or enthusiastic emotion.

OXYMORON is a rhetorical figure of speech by which a locution produces an effect by a seeming self-contradiction, as in *cruel kindness* or *to make haste slowly.*

OTTAVA RIMA, in prosody, is an Italian stanza of eight lines, each of eleven syllables (or, in the English adaptation, of ten or eleven syllables), the first six lines riming alternately and the last two forming a couplet with a different rime (used in Keats' ISABELLA and Byron's DON JUAN).

SESTET is the last six lines of a sonnet.

QUATRAIN is a stanza or poem of four lines, usually with alternate rhymes.

5. This famous poem was written by 5.____
   - A. Samuel Taylor
   - B. Alexander Pope
   - C. Alfred Tennyson
   - D. William Blake
   - E. John Milton

   William Blake wrote this poem. Therefore, item D is correct. Items A, B, C, and E are false.

6. Blake also wrote 6.____
   - A. SONGS OF INNOCENCE
   - B. ELEGY WRITTEN IN A COUNTRY CHURCHYARD
   - C. TO ALTHEA FROM PRISON
   - D. LYCIDAS
   - E. PARADISE LOST

   Item A was written by Blake. Item B by Thomas Gray; Item C by Richard Lovelace; Item D by Milton; Item E by Milton.

INTERPRETATION OF LITERARY MATERIALS

EXAMINATION SECTION
TEST 1

PASSAGE

Once he was established as a playwright with MAN AND SUPERMAN in 1905, he settled down to a swift, assertive prose style that was brilliant and unique, in plays as well as prefaces. He did not play tricks with the language. The sentence structure was not varied much, nor was the tension relieved by rhetoric. Shaw was solely concerned with communicating the energy of his mind.

He composed the preface to PYGMALION in Pitman shorthand, which his secretary then transcribed. That indicates the speed with which he wrote, and perhaps also accounts for the leanness of the style. He did not waste time on literary flourishes. Nothing was important except the idea. For ideas were his obsession. He took voluptuous pleasure in them. To him they were things, and he lived among them as most men wallow in creature comforts.

Ascetic and puritanical, he had no taste for any kind of debauches except intellectual arguments. BACK TO METHUSELAH, 418 pages long, was his most reckless orgy. A METABIOLOGICAL PENTATEUCH he called the play, thereby alienating both the reader and the playgoer. Although the play was produced by the Theatre Guild in 1922 and by Barry Jackson at the Birmingham Repertory Theatre, Shaw knew that it could never be popular with audiences, as MAN AND SUPERMAN had been. But as the foremost literary intellectual of his time, he could not refrain from making a Jovian statement about the human race-which was the preoccupation of his lifetime.

QUESTIONS

1. The author feels that Shaw's play BACK TO METHUSELAH, which he calls A METABIOLOGICAL PENTATEUCH, would alienate the reader and playgoer because

    A. it sounds too complex and confusing
    B. it would not appeal to the intellectual
    C. they would probably find it overlong and tedious
    D. it is obviously dated
    E. audiences prefer musicals to dramas

2. Shaw sometimes used shorthand because

    A. he used to be a secretary
    B. it enabled him to use literary flourishes quickly
    C. his style would then become lean and taut
    D. it was more suited to the speed of his thoughts
    E. it enabled him to sufficiently embellish his ideas

3. The play that was to establish Shaw as a playwright was

A. ST. JOAN B. DON JUAN IN HELL
C. MAN AND SUPERMAN D. PYGMALION
E. MAJOR BARBARA

4. Characteristics of Shaw, the playwright, and, probably, qualities of Shaw, the man, were   4.____

   A. ribald wit and scorn
   B. gregariousness and humor
   C. recklessness and belligerence
   D. mysticism and asceticism
   E. asceticism and puritanism

5. His prose style, if one were limited to one word, might BEST be described as   5.____

   A. assertive   B. biting   C. voluptuous
   D. intense   E. polished

6. *Shavian* is a   6.____

   A. word invented by Shaw
   B. word reserved exclusively for Shaw, the man and his works
   C. word applied to anything resembling the thought and humor of George Bernard Shaw
   D. word for works belonging to the period in which George Bernard Shaw lived and wrote
   E. derogatory term for Shaw's works

7. Two well-known works by Shaw are _____ and _____.   7.____

   A. ANTONY AND CLEOPATRA; SONNETS
   B. THE DAY OF THE RABBLEMENT; POMES PENYEACH
   C. CAESAR AND CLEOPATRA; ANDROCLES AND THE LION
   D. SAILOR OFF THE BREMAN; WELCOME TO THE CITY
   E. THE PLOUGH AND THE STARS; THE SILVER TASSIE

3 (#1)

KEY (CORRECT ANSWERS)

1. C
2. D
3. C
4. E
5. A
6. C
7. C

EXPLANATION OF ANSWERS

1. From the title and sub-title, the reader finds that the play deals with the first five books of the Old Testament (Pentateuch), transcends biology (metabiological), and dates back to the time of Methuselah. C is the correct answer.

2. In the passage, the author states that Shaw was not fond of flourishes or embellishments. This eliminates B and E. C is incorrect because his style would not be influenced by his method. Therefore, D must be the correct answer, particularly in view of the second sentence in the second paragraph, viz., *That indicates the speed with which he wrote....*

3. The correct answer is stated in the first sentence of the passage where the author writes, *Once he was established as a playwright with MAN AND SUPERMAN in 1905...* C is the correct answer.

4. The first sentence of paragraph 3 terms Shaw *ascetic and puritanical.* Though he possessed great humor and wit, they did not exist alongside the other qualities stated here. E is the correct answer.

5. In sentence 1, the author states that *...he settled down to a swift, assertive prose style that was brilliant and unique....* A is the correct answer. C and E are obviously not suited to Shaw. B and D are not mentioned in the passage.

6. *Shavian* is not another word for Shaw; the man, his works, nor his period. It is, rather, a term for that which resembles his thought. C is the correct answer.

7. Of the above, A lists the works of Shakespeare; B, James Joyce; C, G.B. Shaw; D, Irwin Shaw; and 5, Sean O'Casey. C is the correct answer.

TEST 2

PASSAGE

One day, a few years ago, during a lunch table discussion about eroticism and sin, Andre Malraux suddenly asked Andre Gide for his definition of a Christian. Gide, who had been visibly dazzled by Malraux' torrential discourse-he has a habit of illustrating such discourses by carrying on a kind of aerial dogfight with a smoking cigarette-hesitated a moment and then remarked, with that quiet verbal hand-wringing which was so peculiarly his: "I feel I am going to be flunked again."

Things have changed a good deal since then. If Gide were alive today, it would be easy enough for him to turn the tables on his former examiner by awarding Malraux a D-or, at best, an inglorious C-plus-for his stewardship as Minister of Cultural Affairs.

Let us be fair to Malraux. No man in France, with the possible exception of Charles de Gaulle, has been more a victim of his own myth. The French, ever since Joan of Arc, have tended to believe in miracles, and Malraux is only the latest in a long series of heroes who seemed ideally suited to fill the bill. If France's culture was imperiled by bureaucratic paralysis, bourgeois complacency or public apathy, then what man was better fitted to play the role of providential savior than the revolutionary author of MAN'S HOPE, the romantic Man of Destiny with the pale Napoleonic brow?

So thought the enthusiasts when Malraux took the job three years ago. Malraux, the orientalist who set out for the Far East when he was 22 and worked his way through the Cambodian jungle to uncover the half-buried temple ruins of Bantai Frey; Malraux, the precocious author of half a dozen novels who won France's highest literary award, the Prix Goncourt, when he was barely 32 (for MAN'S FATE, published in 1933); Malraux, the impassioned archaeologist who ...

QUESTIONS

1. Gide probably did NOT supply Malraux with the requested definition because

    A. he did not believe Malraux wanted an answer
    B. he did not expect Malraux would agree
    C. the question was of too personal a nature
    D. he felt somewhat intimidated by Malraux's discourse
    E. he felt Malraux was far more brilliant than he

2. As Minister of Cultural Affairs, Malraux

    A. fulfilled the expectations of the people of France
    B. is second only to De Gaulle in popularity and success
    C. might be considered a near-failure
    D. has worked a small miracle
    E. is an abysmal failure

3. The author of MAN'S HOPE was

    A. De Gaulle
    B. Andre Gide
    C. Bantai Frey
    D. Joan of Arc
    E. Andre Malraux

4. After listing Malraux's accomplishments, the author is apparently about to go on to say that   4.____

   A. this man had to be successful in any undertaking
   B. Malraux was probably over-qualified for the job of Minister of Cultural Affairs
   C. his greatest achievement was in politically serving France
   D. a man with so many interests and accomplishments could not possibly excel in politics
   E. Malraux, unexpectedly, failed to do well as Minister of Cultural Affairs

5. Two well-known works of Malraux are _____ and _____.   5.____

   A. ARIEL, a biography of Shelley; THE SILENCE OF COLONEL BRAMBLE
   B. THE ROYAL WAY; MAN'S FATE
   C. OEDIPE; LA PUCELLE D'ORLEANS
   D. GARGANTUA; PANTAGUEL
   E. THE MAIDS; THE BLACKS

6. A famous work of Andre Gide's is   6.____

   A. SYMPHONY PASTORAL
   B. OUR LADY OF THE FLOWERS
   C. WAITING FOR GODOT
   D. THE TIME OF YOUR LIFE
   E. CALIGULA

3 (#2)

KEY (CORRECT ANSWERS)

1. D 4. E
2. C 5. B
3. E 6. A

EXPLANATION OF ANSWERS

1. There is no basis for answers A and B. Answer E is not implied in the passage. C is, of course, false. D, however, while not directly stated, is indicated in sentence 3 of paragraph 1 and in the last sentence of paragraph 1.

2. According to the passage, the people of France did expect much from Malraux; therefore, answers A, B, and D are incorrect. The correct answer, C, is indicated in sentence 2, paragraph 2. Answer E is incorrect because it expresses too harsh a judgment.

3. At the end of the passage, it is mentioned that Malraux won the Prix Goncourt for MAN'S HOPE. Therefore, the proper answer is E.

4. From the opening sentence of paragraph 4, one gathers that the author is about to go on to prove the *enthusiasts* wrong. Therefore, E is the correct answer. D is incorrect because it is in no way to be inferred that Malraux's previous accomplishments and a political career would be incompatible; in fact, the opposite is to be deduced.

5. Of the listed items, A lists two works of Andre Maurois; B, Andre Malraux; C, Voltaire; D, Rabelais; and E, Jean Genet. Therefore, B is the correct answer.

6. A is the work of Andre Gide, the correct answer; B of Genet; C of Beckett; D of Saroyan; E of Camus.

TEST 3

PASSAGE

In deciding to send the heir to the throne to Gordonstoun, about the least conventional public school in Britain, the Queen has initiated a new pattern of princely education. For Gordonstoun is significantly different from the socially exclusive kind of public school, like Eton or Harrow, which English princes might naturally be expected to attend.

Oddly enough, this has very little to do with its educational system, or with the fact that it was founded by a German, Kurt Hahn, who was expelled by the Nazis. Indeed, as far as education goes, Gordonstoun is probably far more like the Rugby of Tom Brown's school days than Rugby itself is now, and Dr. Hahn, who even in Germany was fascinated by British public school methods and by the ideals which inspired them, has probably much more in common with the nineteenth century Dr. Arnold than have most British headmasters of today.

Why, then, is the decision to send 13-year-old Prince Charles to Gordonstoun, starting with the summer term May 1, so remarkable? The answer, of course, is that what really distinguishes the top-rank British public school is not its type of education but the class of boy who goes there. What is unique about Eton is not the way it teaches Latin or math, but the fact that virtually all its pupils come either from the upper class or upper middle class.

In other words, the essence of Eton is not educational but social. Thus the significance of the decision not to send Prince Charles there, and not to have him educated by private tutors, but to send him instead to Gordonstoun, is not that he will get an education radically different from that of his predecessors, but that he will be the first monarch to be educated in an institution which is fundamentally classless.

QUESTIONS

1. In the passage, the *heir to the throne* is referred to. This specifically means

    A. the children of the Royal Family
    B. the son of the Queen
    C. the children of Queen Elizabeth
    D. Prince Andrew
    E. Prince Charles

2. Gordonstoun is a significantly different school because

    A. it is progressive
    B. one might expect an English prince to attend it
    C. it is essentially social rather than educational
    D. it is fundamentally classless
    E. it was founded by a German

3. It would seem to be the Queen's wish that

    A. her son receive a progressive education
    B. Prince Charles be educated by private tutors
    C. her son follow in his predecessors' footsteps
    D. England shall become a classless society

E. the Prince shall be educated quite differently than his predecessors

4. Dr. Hahn, the passage implies, had something in common with   4.____

    A. German education   B. the Nazis
    C. Dr. Arnold   D. British headmasters
    E. the 19th century

5. The relationship of Prince Charles to the late King George is that of   5.____

    A. grandfather   B. nephew   C. son
    D. grandson   E. father

6. The Duke of Edinburgh is   6.____

    A. the husband of Princess Margaret
    B. the husband of Queen Elizabeth
    C. a cousin of Prince Charles
    D. the King of England
    E. the brother of Queen Elizabeth

KEY (CORRECT ANSWERS)

1. E   4. C
2. D   5. D
3. E   6. B

EXPLANATION OF ANSWERS

1. The passage is about the older son of Queen Elizabeth, Prince Charles, who is heir to the throne. He is mentioned in sentence 1, paragraph 3. E is the correct answer.

2. The last sentence of the passage states that the school is fundamentally classless. E is the only other true statement about the school but it is not a significant difference. D is the correct answer.

3. One may surmise from the passage that the Queen's wish is E. It is stated that the school does not provide a progressive education, which discounts A. B and C, it is stated, are what the Queen does not want. D is neither mentioned nor implied. The correct answer is E.

4. The correct answer is C. He had, as stated in the passage, nothing in common with A and B; little, it is implied, with D. And his name was linked with *nineteenth century Dr. Arnold's,* not with the nineteenth century.

5. Prince Charles is the son of Queen Elizabeth. She is the daughter of the late King George. Therefore, D is the correct answer.

6. The Duke of Edinburgh is the husband of Queen Elizabeth and the father of Prince Charles. B is the correct answer.

TEST 4

PASSAGE

But how can I say if we'll get by again? I don't know enough of the details of how the bombs work, how things are going. It's a three-way race. There's the long race to develop our culture. The whole story of thousands of years, Greece, Palestine, Magna Charta, the French Revolution, it's the story of a boy growing up, learning to straighten his shoulders. But we haven't learned enough yet to live side by side. Then there is technology, the excesses of scientists who learn how to make things much faster than we can learn what to do with them. The third runner is the strain between two parts of the world that grew up unevenly.

You know, the Russians have banned my work. They banned OUR TOWN (a drama of the beauty of everyday joys and cares) because they were campaigning against the family at the time and it is a family story. And they banned THE SKIN OF OUR TEETH because they said it equated war with flood and the ice age as natural catastrophes, when every good Marxist knows war is only the work of capitalists. Wars and human disasters come from the ugly unresolved things in us, just as earthquakes come from ugly unresolved things in nature, the cooling of the earth's crust.

I have no patience with people who say they love nature and go out to look at a field on Sunday afternoon. Our families, the way we live with our fellowmen, are a part of nature, too.

QUESTIONS

1. The speaker in the passage makes a comparison between

    A. the development of the culture of the human race and a boy growing up
    B. two parts of the world
    C. technology and the scientists
    D. Russia and the U.S.
    E. the Magna Charta and the French Revolution

2. The Russians banned THE SKIN OF OUR TEETH because they felt

    A. wars come from the unresolved things in human beings
    B. it contained the same sort of message as OUR TOWN
    C. it spoke of floods and the ice age as natural catastrophes
    D. it considered war a natural catastrophe
    E. the playwright was a capitalist

3. The speaker has no patience with those who

    A. think of nature as something to look at
    B. believe that wars are inevitable
    C. profess to love people and nature
    D. think nature is more important than how we live with our fellowmen
    E. say they love nature and do nothing about it

4. The speaker feels that wars

A. are the work of Marxists
B. are the work of unresolved inner human conflict
C. are the work of capitalists
D. will continue as long as the scientists continue to learn how to make things faster than we can learn what to do with them
E. though bound to reoccur, will always be survived

5. The man who is speaking his thoughts in the passage is

   A. Maxwell Anderson   B. Elmer Rice
   C. William Saroyan   D. Thornton Wilder
   E. Tennessee Williams

6. Aside from being a playwright, he is also a novelist. One of his novels is

   A. THE BRIDGE OF SAN LUIS REY
   B. THE GRAPES OF WRATH
   C. MISS LONELYHEARTS
   D. THE DAY OF THE LOCUST
   E. THE LOVED ONE

3 (#4)

KEY (CORRECT ANSWERS)

1. A 4. B
2. D 5. D
3. A 6. A

EXPLANATIONS OF ANSWERS

1. In paragraph 1, the speaker states, *There's the long race to develop our culture.... it 's the story of a boy growing up....* The correct answer, then, is A. Though the other answers are mentioned in the passage, no comparisons are drawn.

2. The answer is contained in paragraph 2, where the speaker states, *they said it equated war with flood and the ice age as natural catastrophes.* D is the correct answer. C and E are irrelevant. B is false; and A is the sentiment of the playwright, not the Russians.

3. The speaker thinks that how we live with our fellowmen is nature too. This is explained in paragraph 3. The correct answer is A and can be found in the first sentence of the last paragraph.

4. *Wars...come from the ugly, unresolved things in us,* the speaker says in paragraph 2. Therefore, B is the correct answer. A and D are neither stated nor implied. C is said sarcastically. E is refuted in the first sentence of the passage.

5. The author of THE SKIN OF OUR TEETH, and winner of the Pulitzer Prize for OUR TOWN, is Thornton Wilder. Therefore, D is correct.

6. Of the listed items, A is correct since it is the work of Thornton Wilder; B is the work of John Steinbeck; C, of Nathaniel West; D, of Nathaniel West; E, of Evelyn Waugh.

TEST 5

PASSAGE

Improvisation of sketches, whether topical or not, is a chancy affair. It goes best when practiced, like a parlor game, among friends. There is more risk in a cafe or night club, but with relaxed, imbibing customers around the performers, it takes on the atmosphere of communal sport. In a theater with a sober, paying audience waiting in expectant rows to be entertained swiftly and efficiently, improvisation is all but impossible.

Indeed, sketches that bear the birthmarks of improvisatory genesis seldom hold up in the formal procedures of a theater revue. They have a tendency to stammer and dawdle, to seem coy and amateurish. They make an audience restless, for they spread a sense of indecision and ineffectualness, and there is little that is more disaffecting in the theater than a lack of authority and control on the stage.

All the revues bred in improvisation that have tackled Broadway in recent years have had moments when they fell into doldrums, as if the performers were praying for any kind of a wind. One does not speak of a passing lapse of memory or a miscue, which could happen on any stage in any performance, but of doubts and hesitant attacks left over from the improvisatory embryo.

QUESTIONS

1. The writer seems to feel that improvisations

    A. are a vital embryo from which spontaneous ideas evolve
    B. hold up well under the formal procedures of a revue
    C. do not really belong in the theatre
    D. are a swift and efficient entertainment
    E. are best executed in the nightclub or cafe

2. An improvisation is a risky thing because

    A. performers often miss their cue
    B. it leads to a sense of indecision and ineffectualness
    C. performers are fraught with lapses of memory
    D. it can unsettle an audience by the lack of authority and control on the stage
    E. since much is not committed to memory, there can occur silences where the performers lose their direction

3. The theme of the passage seems to be that

    A. improvisation should be stricken and abolished from the theatre
    B. improvisation is a vital tool but should be reserved for the actors' schools
    C. improvisations are a frail reed on which to depend in the theatre
    D. only the most skilled can successfully employ improvisation to the point where it becomes theatre
    E. only the most successful improvisation can affect the audience as would the well-written speech of a good playwright

4. The writer of *sketches that bear the birthmarks of improvisatory genesis.* By this, he means

1.____

2.____

3.____

4.____

A. otherwise well-prepared sketches that seem to flounder midway
B. sketches that have been badly written by a lesser playwright
C. sketches that obviously began as improvisations
D. an improvisation that is all too obviously made up as the actor proceeds
E. a rich nature will improvise more rewardingly than an indigent one

5. An example of improvisation in the theatre would be

    A. the presentations of the ACTORS' STUDIO
    B. any ad lib or aside supplied by the actor rather than the playwright
    C. the sketches of Nichols and May
    D. the sketches of a Noel Coward revue
    E. any dialogue where performers do not adhere faithfully to their words as written

6. The remarks might appear as or in

    A. a book review
    B. a drama review
    C. WHO'S WHO IN THE THEATRE
    D. the preface to a play
    E. the news section of any newspaper

KEY (CORRECT ANSWERS)

1. C   4. C
2. D   5. C
3. C   6. B

EXPLANATION OF ANSWERS

1. Answers B and D, the author most definitely does not believe. A is not stated. And the author feels they go best when ...*practiced among friends,* which discounts E. Though he uses other words, the author does seem to be of the opinion of item C, which is the correct answer.

2. The correct answer is D. E does occur in improvisation, but that is not what makes it risky. B is often the result but not the aim. C and E are invalid for the same reason. A is false because there are no cues in improvisation.

3. The author's ever-recurring theme would be item C. Nowhere are answers B, D, or E stated or implied. Answer A is a harsher statement than the author makes, and so is false.

4. The correct answer is C. By the term *improvisitory genesis,* the author is referring to that which begins as improvisation. None of the other items is mentioned in the passage.

5. C is the correct answer. Noel Coward as a playwright does not use improvisational techniques; this discounts item D. The Actors' Studio do not use improvisation in their presentation of plays, but only in their classrooms. This discounts answer A. B and E do not constitute a definition of improvisation.

6. The correct answer is B. None of the other answers is suited to the material or the type of presentation used in the passage.

TEST 6

PASSAGE

BURNT NORTON

Time present and time past
Are both perhaps present in time future,
And time future contained in time past.
If all time is eternally present
All time is unredeemable.
What might have been is an abstraction
Remaining a perpetual possibility
Only in a world of speculation.
What might have been and what has been
Point to one end, which is always present.
Footfalls echo in the memory
Down the passage which we did not take
Towards the door we never opened
Into the rose-garden. My words echo
Thus, in your mind.
                    But to what purpose
Disturbing the dust on a bowl of rose-leaves
I do not know.

QUESTIONS

1. The essential point concerning time that the poet is trying to make is:

    A. Time is an abstraction
    B. Past time is contained in future time
    C. It is eternally present
    D. Present time is contained in past time
    E. That it exists in a world of speculation

2. There is a relationship in the poem between *What might have been* and

    A. ... one end, which is always present
    B. ... memory
    C. ... The passage which we took
    D. ... the door we never opened
    E. ... a bowl of rose-leaves

3. The rose-garden is meant to symbolize

    A. past happiness experiences
    B. Nirvana
    C. Heaven
    D. life after death
    E. something unattained

4. The poem was written by the author of THE WASTE LAND, an expatriate American; he is

2 (#6)

- A. Lawrence Durrell
- B. Thomas Stearns Eliot
- C. Ezra Pound
- D. Allen Ginsberg
- E. Robert Frost

5. Of the following, this poet did NOT write

    A. THE FAMILY REUNION
    B. THE UNVANQUISHED
    C. FOUR QUARTETTES
    D. OLD POSSUM'S BOOK OF PRACTICAL CATS
    E. MURDER IN THE CATHEDRAL

5.____

6. Probably his MOST famous character is

    A. Miniver Cheevy
    B. Ichabod Crane
    C. Thomas a Becket
    D. Alfred J. Prufrock
    E. Mrs. Erlynne

6.____

3 (#6)

KEY (CORRECT ANSWERS)

1. C 4. B
2. D 5. B
3. E 6. D

EXPLANATION OF ANSWERS

1. In reading the poem, the reader is presented with the hypothesis in line 4 from which all the other conclusions about time are formed. Item C, then, is the correct answer.

2. The closest in meaning would be D. There is no other choice presented that relates to the line, *What might have been....*

3. The poet says, *Footfalls echo in the memory... towards the door we never opened into the rose-garden.* He is speaking of a human condition. E, then, is the correct answer. B, C, and D have nothing to do with memory.

4. Eliot, item B, is the correct answer, and THE WASTE LAND is his most famous work.

5. The only work not written by Eliot is item B, which was written by William Faulkner.

6. Prufrock, item D, is distinctly Eliot's. He exists in THE LOVE SONG OF ALFRED J. PRUFROCK, as the passive New Englander who lives a life without meaning.

TEST 7

PASSAGE

I want to make a few admissions and disclosures. My poems on Hawthorne and Edwards draw heavily on prose sentences by their subjects. THE SCREAM owes everything to Elizabeth Bishop's beautiful, calm story, IN THE VILLAGE. THE LESSON picks up a phrase or two from Rafael Alberti. RETURNING was suggested by Giuseppe Ungaretti's CANZONE. THE PUBLIC GARDEN is a recasting and clarification of an old confusing poem of mine called DAVID AND BATHSHEBA IN THE PUBLIC GARDEN. BEYOND THE ALPS is the poem I published in LIFE STUDIES, but with a stanza restored at the suggestion of John Berryman.

He has a great gift for friendship. No one is more generous than Robert Lowell in acknowledging his indebtedness to anybody who has ever helped him with a problem or with a poem.

The poets who most directly influenced me, he says, were Allen Tate, Elizabeth Bishop, and William Carlos Williams. An unlikely combination! ... but you can see that Bishop is a sort of bridge between Tate's formalism and Williams' informal art. For sheer language, Williams beats anybody. And who compares with him for aliveness and keenness of observation? I admire Pound but find it impossible to imitate him. Nor do I know how to use Eliot or Auden-their voice is so personal. Williams can be used, partly because he is somewhat anonymous. His poems are as perfect as anybody's, but they lead one to think of the possibility of writing them in different ways-for example, putting them into rhyme.

QUESTIONS

1. The poem DAVID AND BATHSHEBA IN THE PUBLIC GARDEN referred to in the passage was written by

   A. Elizabeth Bishop
   B. Nathaniel Hawthorne
   C. Rafael Alberti
   D. Robert Lowell
   E. Giuseppe Ungaretti

2. In the passage, Elizabeth Bishop is referred to as

   A. the poetess who wrote THE SCREAM
   B. a person with a great gift for friendships
   C. the poet who most greatly influenced Lowell
   D. incomparable for aliveness and keenness of observation
   E. a bridge between Tate and Williams

3. One gets the impression from the passage that Lowell

   A. can hardly be considered an original poet because he borrowed so liberally from so many sources
   B. feels a great debt to such poets as Pound and Eliot
   C. is indebted to many poets and readily acknowledges this debt
   D. though he speaks highly of certain other poets, considers himself superior as a poet
   E. considers Williams lacking as a poet because his poems do not rhyme

4. The three poets mentioned in the passage by last name only refer to

A. George Eliot, Tennessee Williams, and W.H. Auden
B. Allen Tate, William Carlos Williams, and Elizabeth Bishop
C. Ezra Pound, W.H. Auden, and T.S. Eliot
D. John Berryman, T.S. Eliot, and Nathaniel Hawthorne
E. Rafael Alberti, Ezra Pound, and T.S. Eliot

5. Some of the works written by William Carlos Williams, though not mentioned in the passage, are

   A. ADAM AND EVE AND THE CITY, AN EARLY MARTYR, and SPRING AND ALL
   B. THE HOLLOW MEN, OLD POSSUM'S BOOK OF PRACTICAL CATS, and FOUR QUARTETS
   C. CANTOS, EXULTATIONS, and RIPOSTES
   D. THE ORATORS, THE DANCE OF DEATH, and THE DOG BENEATH THE SKIN
   E. THE CRITIQUE OF HUMANISM, MR. POPE, and THE MEDITERRANEAN

6. The passage might be considered illustrative of a part of the kind of article that might be found in

   A. an Art news periodical
   B. THE READER'S ENCYCLOPEDIA
   C. THE WORLD ALMANAC
   D. THE TIMES BOOK REVIEW (or A WRITERS' DIGEST)
   E. TIME magazine's literary section

KEY (CORRECT ANSWERS)

1. D   4. C
2. E   5. A
3. C   6. D

EXPLANATION OF ANSWERS

1. Toward the end of paragraph 1, the title is mentioned as *an old ....poem of mine*. In paragraph 2, the speaker is revealed to be Robert Lowell. All the poets mentioned in paragraph 1 are listed in relation to the poems they wrote; however, the above poem was written by Lowell himself. Therefore, the correct answer is D.

2. Only items C and E refer to Elizabeth Bishop. C, however, is inaccurate because she is referred to as one of three poets who most greatly influenced Lowell, all of seemingly equal importance. E, then, is the correct answer.

3. The correct answer is C. one does not get the feeling from the passage that borrowing and originality are incompatible, as suggested in A. Pound and Eliot had no direct influence on him, which discounts B. Nowhere does the reader get the feeling that he considers himself superior, nor that Williams should have made his poems rhyme.

4. C is the only possible correct answer. Toward the end of paragraph 3, Lowell states, *I admire Pound....Nor do I know how to use Eliot or Auden. . . .* George Eliot is known as a novelist, not as a poet; and, though Hawthorne is only mentioned by last name, he too was a novelist.

5. Of the above works, B lists the works of T.S. Eliot; C, the works of Pound; D, the works of Auden; and E, the works of Tate. All of them are poets mentioned in the passage. Only item A lists the works of Williams, and is the correct answer.

6. Items B and C would contain nothing so lengthy as the passage, but would offer a brief biographical sketch. Item E would be a review of a work only. Item D, however, could present a conversation with an author such as the above passage and is the correct answer.

TEST 8

PASSAGE

Intended primarily as a showcase for the artists who have been or are associated with Mr. Maeght's art gallery-Braque, Chagall, Miro, Giacometti-the museum has a separate room for the works of each, and there are additional rooms for other members of Mr. Maeght's stable - among them, Leger, Bazaine, Ubac, Tal Coat.

These rooms are a painter's dream for showing off art. The walls are white, and the paintings are hung not by nails but by suction. The light is ideal-cool and even, illuminating the canvases at the perfect angle of 45 degrees on every day of the year but four. The architect, Mr. Sert, has exiled reflections, the bane of all painting, by banning windows and lighting the rooms by what he calls "light traps." The blazing rays of the Riviera sun strike the roof and are refracted along the curved surfaces of the concrete veils that compose the ceiling according to angles Sert worked out in a specially built laboratory at Harvard.

The artists themselves have played a major role in the construction and decoration of the museum. Miro designed a series of fantastic creatures of ceramic and cement which wind around the foundation like ivy around a tree trunk. There are mosaics by Chagall, Braque, and Tal Coat, and sculpture in the central courtyard and among the surrounding pines.

QUESTIONS

1. A GOOD title for this passage might be

    A. MR. MAEGHT'S ART GALLERY
    B. THE MUSEUM ON THE RIVIERA
    C. FRENCH ART AND ARCHITECTURE
    D. THE SCIENCE OF LIGHT
    E. THE IMPRESSIONIST PAINTERS

2. Why did Mr. Sert ban windows from the rooms of the museum?

    A. This is not an accurate statement. He did not ban windows, but, rather, exiled reflections.
    B. He wished to light the rooms with *light traps* and exile reflections.
    C. Exiled reflections are the bane of all painting.
    D. Refracted natural light and windows cannot satisfactorily exist in the same enclosure.
    E. He preferred natural light to artificial light.

3. An unusual feature of the museum is the part played by the artists in its decorations; for example, there are

    A. ceramics by Braque
    B. mosaics of fantastic creatures
    C. sculpture by Chagall
    D. mosaics by Giacometti
    E. ceramics by Miro

4. The light is considered ideal because

A. of the angle of illumination
B. the canvases are illuminated at the perfect angle of 45 degrees on every day of the year
C. the walls are white
D. the walls have curved surfaces
E. Sert worked out the angles in a specially built laboratory at Harvard

5. Two very prominent painters who lived and worked in the vicinity of the museum, but who are not mentioned in the passage, are

    A. Juan Gris and Corot
    B. Manet and Utrillo
    C. Delacroix and Matisse
    D. Picasso and Dubuffet
    E. Seurat and Cezanne

6. The Riviera is

    A. a coastal area bordered by Rapallo and San Remo, on Italy's northern coast
    B. a coastal area extending from Le Havre to Brittany, in the north of France
    C. an island in the Mediterranean, off the coast of Monte Carlo
    D. an area of beaches and small provinces extending from Costa Brava, Spain, to Nice, France
    E. the southern coast of France

KEY (CORRECT ANSWERS)

1. B   4. A
2. B   5. D
3. E   6. E

EXPLANATION OF ANSWERS

1. This passage describes in detail the interior of a museum. Toward the end of paragraph 2, the author mentions ....*the Riviera sun*...., thereby placing it geographically. Items C, D, and E are inappropriate and incorrect. A is directly mentioned in the passage and might be considered were it not for the more inclusive item B, which is the correct answer.

2. B is the correct answer. C and D are false statements. E is not referred to in the passage, and A is incorrect because, in order to exile reflections, he had to ban windows.

3. E is the only possible correct answer. The mosaics are by Chagall and Braque. There is no mention of who did the sculpture. Miro, however, did design ceramic creatures as decoration.

4. Though all the answers, except B (the passage mentions *every day of the year but four*) are factually true, only A directly states why the light is ideal (sentence 3, paragraph 2).

5. Picasso and Dubuffet lived and worked near the museum.

6. The correct answer is E. The Riviera, or Blue Coast, is situated along the southern coast of France.

TEST 9

PASSAGE

JULES RENARD was a minor writer in a time of extraordinary French flowering. As one of the founders of the powerful periodical, MERCURE DE FRANCE, and an early member of the Goncourt Academy, he had a foot in both the Symbolist and the Naturalist camps, generally considered antithetical. Yet, he was a maverick in his journalism, his plays, his famous tale POIL DE CAROTTE (RED HEAD), and in such novels as L'ECORNIFLEUR (THE SCROUNGER). Perhaps this is why, somewhat eclipsed by younger men like Claudel, Gide, Proust, and Valery, he will live chiefly for his comments on his contemporaries.

Having won a reputation in France in the Nineties for his embittered, rather sour pictures of family life (chiefly drawn from his own bickering parents), Renard enjoyed a revival of interest in 1925, when his JOURNAL was posthumously published. With its thumbnail sketches of such friends and acquaintances as Goncourt, Wilde, Claudel, Toulouse-Lautrec, Sarah Bernhardt, and Pierre Loti, and its acerbic comments on the events and follies of his times, the JOURNAL became a source reference for many literary historians who were now far more interested in his contemporaries than in Renard himself.

QUESTIONS

1. Renard is remembered CHIEFLY for the kind of writing that appeared in

    A. POIL DE GAROTTE
    B. L'ECORNIFLEUR
    C. JOURNAL
    D. his plays
    E. his journalism

2. Renard's writing is considered

    A. a part of the Symbolist group
    B. a part of the Naturalist group
    C. influenced by the MERCURE DE FRANCE
    D. a part of both groups
    E. more important than most of his contemporaries

3. The author seems to consider Claudel

    A. the same sort of writer as was Jules Renard
    B. more in a class with Valery than Proust
    C. a better writer than Renard
    D. a minor writer of his period
    E. as having won his reputation with rather sour pictures of his family life

4. Renard enjoyed a revival of interest

    A. as one of the founders of the MERCURE DE FRANCE
    B. after his death
    C. as an early member of the Goncourt Academy
    D. when he was considered a *maverick* in journalism
    E. with the writing of the notes on his family life

5. The period of French writing of which the author is writing is the _____ century.

A. late 19th   B. early 19th
C. early 20th   D. 18th
E. turn of the

6. A work written by Marcel Proust is   6.____

   A. THE NABOB
   B. KINGS IN EXILE
   C. REMEMBRANCE OF THINGS PAST
   D. SAPHO
   E. MADAME BOVARY

3 (#9)

KEY (CORRECT ANSWERS)

1. C 4. B
2. D 5. A
3. C 6. C

EXPLANATION OF ANSWERS

1. The passage states (end of first paragraph) that he ...*will live chiefly for his comments on his contemporaries.* Later, in paragraph 2, the reader is told that his JOURNAL contained thumbnail sketches of his friends and acquaintances. Therefore, C is the correct answer. Items A and B are referred to merely as a famous play and novel. Items D and E are mentioned but not elaborated upon.

2. The correct answer here is D and is to be found in the first paragraph of the passage. Regarding item E, most of his contemporaries came to be more famous than Renard (end of second paragraph). Since, as the passage states in paragraph 1, ... *he had a foot in both the Symbolist and Naturalist camps* ... , items A and B must be disregarded as incorrect. Item C is not mentioned as exerting any literary influence.

3. The author states (paragraph 1) that Renard was ...*somewhat eclipsed by younger men like Claudel.* This would indicate that C is the correct answer. Item D actually refers to Renard. The author puts Valery and Proust in the same class, thus discounting B. Item E refers, again, to Renard.

4. Item E won him his reputation, but the revival of interest in him came with the publication of his JOURNAL. It was published posthumously, so the correct answer is B. Since the revival of interest mentioned in the question-stem and item B (the answer) are directly linked in the passage, items A, C, and D must be discarded.

5. The time of which the author is writing is the time of Proust, Toulouse-Lautrec, and Oscar Wilde. It was the late 19th century. Therefore, the correct answer is A. All the other items listed, B, C, D, and E, are false.

6. Items A, B, and D were written by Daudet. Item E was written by Flaubert. The correct answer is C.

265

TEST 10

PASSAGE

When he died, Thoreau was not quite 45 years old. His claims to fame were slim. He was well-known, of course, in his hometown as sometime pencil manufacturer, surveyor, handyman- an obviously not unbeloved odd stick who had preferred to put in much of his days, no matter what the wind or weather, walking the woods and fields and who had once even lived alone for a couple of years in a shack over by walden Pond.

Even so admiring - however ambivalent - a friend as Emerson felt that Thoreau had failed of some great promise and had ended up as a mere "captain of a huckleberry party. "

Nevertheless, there it was: WALDEN, the masterwork; it was out in the world, and so was the fiery essay on CIVIL DISOBEDIENCE. Thoreau died, and the work began to grow as did the legend of the man.

The growth was slow and partial. Except for the journal, as Henry Seidel Canby noted, all Thoreau's important writings were in print within three years after his death. Nevertheless, he was antipathetic to both the gilded and the genteel age; his continuing survival for most readers was as a nature writer; only in the less sanguine decades of our time-and with books and essays about him from abroad and many studies here at home - has the whole Thoreau emerged.

Thoreau said he required "of every writer, first or last, a simple and sincere account of his own life." That was the requirement he himself strove to meet. yet one must say Thoreau was not a simple man-or better, he was of a simplicity so colossal as to baffle the usual run of hectic mankind.

When he said, famously, that most men "lead lives of quiet desperation," one has no feeling that he included himself. On the contrary, one feels that this eccentric achieved in living a deep sanity and a deep joy. " I wish to know," he beautifully declared, an entire heaven and an entire earth. And did he not?

QUESTIONS

1. The peak of Thoreau's popularity was reached

    A. when he was 45 years of age
    B. directly after the writing of WALDEN
    C. with his essay CIVIL DISOBEDIENCE
    D. three years after his death
    E. in recent generations

2. His hometown, during his lifetime, revered him as

    A. a famous man
    B. a writer
    C. a man of practical, workaday talents
    D. an unbeloved odd stick
    E. the man who lived in a shack near Walden Pond

3. How do we know that Thoreau was *antipathetic to both the gilded and the genteel age*? Because he

   A. did think much of civility and manners
   B. obviously preferred the life of the woods and fields
   C. also liked the towns and cities of America
   D. distrusted all forms of animal life
   E. disliked people

4. Thoreau was, really,

   A. no more unusual than his fellow townsmen
   B. a respected member of the community
   C. much emulated in his hometown
   D. looked upon as a genius
   E. a man, simple in the extreme

5. His famous remark that men *lead lives of quiet desperation* means that they

   A. live in both *heaven and hell*
   B. live as outcasts of society
   C. are victims of conformity
   D. live in a kind of miserable human condition to which they give little or no voice
   E. live as uncomplaining people; as stoics

6. Another work by Thoreau is

   A. REPRESENTATIVE MEN
   B. ESSAYS ON FRIENDSHIP
   C. ENGLISH TRAITS
   D. SOCIETY AND SOLITUDE
   E. A YANKEE IN CANADA

7. A work by Emerson is

   A. THE CONDUCT OF LIFE
   B. THE GATHERING OF THE FORCES
   C. LEAVES OF GRASS
   D. THE HALF-BREED
   E. DRUM-TAPS

KEY (CORRECT ANSWERS)

1. E   5. D
2. C   6. E
3. B   7. A
4. E

EXPLANATION OF ANSWERS

1. E is the desired answer. He died at 45, discounting item A. WALDEN had to wait quite a time to become famous, discounting B. Item D relates to the printing of his writings. And WALDEN is a far more famous work than CIVIL DISOBEDIENCE, discounting item C.

2. He was considered neither a famous man nor a writer during his lifetime; this discounts items A and B. The answer is given in C (see paragraph one). Item D subtly twists the facts and is incorrect; he was NOT unbeloved. Item E is correct, but this is not that for which he was admired by his town.

3. Immediately following the quotation in paragraph 3, the explanation is given that *his continuing survival for most readers was as a nature writer.* B, then, is the correct answer. Items A and C do not relate to the idea of *antipathetic*. D and E are patently false.

4. He is spoken of (in paragraph 5) as possessing a *simplicity so colossal....,* thereby indicating E as the correct completion of the statement. Items A, B, and C are false. And if he were a genius, his townspeople did not look upon him as such (paragraph 1). Thus, item D may be discounted.

5. Item D is the correct answer. *Quiet desperation* is a term given to a kind of unhappiness which cannot be named or talked about. But this does not mean that item E would do as well: most people are NOT stoics. Whether or not items B and C might produce quiet desperation, that is not the kind of basic, inner unhappiness Thoreau had reference to. And the phrase *quiet desperation* leaves no room for any glimpse of heaven, also discounting item A.

6. Item E is the correct answer. All the other works (items A, B, C, and D) were written by Emerson, who was Thoreau!s greatest literary influence.

7. A was written by Emerson. The others (items B, C, D, and E) were written by Whitman, who was also greatly influenced by Emerson.

TEST 11

PASSAGE

Existentialism, as developed in the past 25 years by the French writer-philosopher Jean-Paul Sartre, holds that a man's life acquires meaning only when he makes his choice on an issue that significantly affects his fellow-men - and acts accordingly.

Last week, Mr. Sartre, now 59, chose not to accept the Nobel Prize for literature. He made his stand clear through, his publishers when unofficial reports that he had been selected by the Swedish Academy of Letters reached Paris Tuesday. And he stuck, by his decision when the Academy announced Thursday that it was awarding him the prize for 1964 in recognition of the " vast influence" of his novels, short stories, and plays, with their " spirit of liberty and quest for truth."

To have accepted this honor and the $53,000 that goes with it, Mr. Sartre explained, would have diminished his life's meaning. "A writer, " he said, "must act only with the means that are his ... the written word"; to add to his pen the influence of an institution "is not fair to the reader.... It is not the same if I sign myself jean-paul Sartre or if I sign Jean-Paul Sartre, Nobel Prize winner."

Or, as he had put it in his latest book, THE WORDS: " ... With empty hands and empty pockets...I have set myself to work to save my whole self..."

The owlish, stocky "pope of existentialism" was the first recipient of the Nobel Prize for literature to turn it down fully and freely. (George Bernard Shaw rejected it in 1925 but reconsidered, donating the money toward the translation of Swedish literature, and Boris Pasternak refused to accept it in 1958, but under obvious Soviet pressure.) A Swedish Academy spokesman commented that if Mr. Sartre does not collect the money, it will go back into the Nobel Prize funds, but the award would stand: "The Academy is guided not by a possible winner's wishes but by the decision of its members."

QUESTIONS

1. Sartre feels that choice necessarily must NOT preclude

    A. free will
    B. Existentialism
    C. liberty
    D. truth
    E. action

2. How would the acceptance of the prize have *diminished his life's meaning?* He

    A. would lose the approval he has gained on his own
    B. would cease to write existentially
    C. would come under the influence of the Academy
    D. would cease to act with and within his work
    E. felt the influence of an institution would redound unfavorably upon his readers

3. Sartre, in turning down the award fully and freely,

    A. is the first to do so
    B. may yet accept the money
    C. incurred the wrath of the Academy

269

D. joins Pasternak and Shaw
E. was acting under Soviet pressure

4. The Nobel Prize is awarded by a(n) _____ Academy.

   A. French   B. Swedish   C. American
   D. international   E. Swiss

5. Why does Sartre feel that to sign himself Jean-Paul Sartre, Nobel Prize winner, would not be fair to the reader?

   A. He feels the award is a political maneuver.
   B. It would hurt the sales of his works in certain countries.
   C. Because he did not actually accept the prize.
   D. It would influence him (the reader) in a way he does not wish to.
   E. He wishes to remain anonymous for the sake of his work.

6. Existentialism has as its basis the teachings of

   A. Locke   B. Bentham   C. Russell
   D. Heidegger   E. Nietzsche

7. A work of Sartre's is

   A. L'HOMME REVOLTE   B. LE MYTHE DE SISYPHE
   C. UN CHANT D'AMOUR   D. NAUSEA
   E. L'ETRANGIER

3 (#11)

KEY (CORRECT ANSWERS)

1. E   5. D
2. D   6. D
3. A   7. D
4. B

EXPLANATION OF ANSWERS

1. In the opening paragraph of the passage, Sartre is stated to hold that *a man's life acquires meaning only when he makes his choice...and acts accordingly.* Therefore, E is the correct answer. Item A is not mentioned in the passage, nor is Sartre's Existentialism (item B) mentioned in this connection. Items C and D are not referred to

2. In paragraph 3, Sartre states that a writer must act only with the means that are his ...*the written word.* This indicates that D is the correct answer. There is no mention of the ideas contained in items A, B, or C. While he felt that the influence of an institution would not be *fair* to readers, he made no evaluation of *unfavorable*. This discounts item E.

3. The final paragraph states that he ....*was the first recipient of the Nobel Prise for literature to turn it down fully and freely.* Therefore, the correct answer is A. This also serves to eliminate item E from further consideration. Pasternak was put under pressure to reject the prize; and Shaw, after rejecting it, reconsidered; this results in discarding item D. Item B is not considered in the passage. Item C is not so: the Academy was not angered by his refusal.

4. The second paragraph of the passage states that ...*he had been selected by the Swedish Academy of Letters.* Therefore, the correct answer is B. Items A, C, D, and E are incorrect.

5. ...*To add to his pen the influence of an institution is not fair to the reader,* we are told in paragraph 3. Thus, D is the correct answer. This has nothing to do with anonymity, discounting item E. Item C is incorrect since the question itself is based on the fact that he did not accept the prize. There are no grounds for item B, and item A is neither mentioned nor implied.

6. The teachings that form the basis of Sartre's Existentialism were those of Heidegger. Therefore, D is the correct answer. Items A, B, C, and E are incorrect.

7. Items A, B, and E were works of Albert Camus. Item C refers to a film by Jean Genet. D is the correct answer.

TEST 12

PASSAGE

THE RUBAIYAT

Myself when young did eagerly frequent
Doctor and saint, and heard great argument
    About it and about; but evermore
Came out by the same door wherein I went.

QUESTIONS

1. In his youth, the poet

   A. wished to achieve knowledge
   B. wanted to learn about medicine and religion
   C. liked arguments
   D. felt he had nothing to learn from doctor or saint
   E. was not religious

2. The *same door* of the stanza refers to the

   A. door of the temple visited
   B. way of doctor and saint
   C. poet's return to himself
   D. poet emerging with greater knowledge
   E. poet emerging with less knowledge

3. These four lines are an example of what is known as

   A. Rococo
   B. Scansion
   C. the Spenserian stanza
   D. the Rubaiyat stanza
   E. slant rhyme

4. The meter of this stanza is

   A. trochaic
   B. pyrrhic
   C. amphibrachic
   D. iambic
   E. anapestic

5. THE RUBAIYAT was written by

   A. Saki
   B. Omar Khayyam
   C. Rudyard Kipling
   D. Mor Jokai
   E. Boccaccio

6. The famous and excellent poetic translation of this work was done by

   A. Edward Taylor
   B. John Bannister Tabb
   C. Walter Pater
   D. Gerard Hopkins
   E. Edward Fitzgerald

2 (#12)

KEY (CORRECT ANSWER)

1. A 4. D
2. C 5. B
3. D 6. E

EXPLANATION OF ANSWERS

1. The poet was, in his youth, in search of knowledge. Therefore, Item A is correct. Items B and C are too narrow in scope. Item D is false because he did *eagerly frequent.* Item E is irrelevant and not mentioned or implied in the stanza.

2. In this phrase, the poet means he left them (doctor and saint) as he found them. He was neither improved nor diminished by their argument. This discounts items B, D, and E. Item C is, therefore, correct. The door mentioned is an intellectual one (item C) rather than a physical one, discounting item A.

3. These lines constitute what is poetically known as the Rubaiyat stanza, so named because the title of this poem is the RUBAIYAT. Therefore, item D is correct. Item A refers to an elaborate 18th century style. Item B is the system of marking lines off into feet. Item C is so named because of Spenser's use of meter. Item E refers to a loose or approximate rhyme.

4. The iamb refers to two syllables: the first unaccented, the second accented. Therefore, item D is correct. Items A, B, C, and E are false. Specifically, item A (trochee) refers to two syllables, the first accented followed by the second unaccented. Item B (pyrrhic) refers to two unaccented syllables. Item C (amphibrach) refers to three syllables, the accented between the two unaccented. Item E (anapest) refers to two unaccented syllables followed by one accented.

5. Item B is correct. The RUBAIYAT was written by Omar Khayyam, a famous Persian poet-astronomer (died 1123?). Items A, C, D, and E are incorrect.

6. Edward Fitzgerald (1809-83) was a British poet and scholar of the Victorian Period in literature. He became famous for what is universally acknowledged as far more than a mere translation of THE RUBAIYAT. Therefore, item E is correct. Items A, B, C, and D are incorrect.

TEST 13

PASSAGE

AND DEATH shall have no dominion.
Dead men naked they shall be one
With the man in the wind and the west moon;
When their bones are picked clean and the clean bones gone,
They shall have stars at elbow and foot;
Though they go mad they shall be sane,
Though they sink through the sea they shall rise again;
Though lovers be lost love shall not;
And death shall have no dominion.

Dylan Thomas

QUESTIONS

1. The poet denies

   A. the existence of death
   B. the authority of death
   C. the inevitability of death
   D. the immortality of man as opposed to the elements of nature
   E. man's immortality

2. Lines _____ and _____ are a part of the same image.

   A. one; two   B. one; three   C. three; five
   D. two; three   E. four; six

3. The poet invests the moon and the wind with

   A. omniscience   B. humanity
   C. the bones of dead men   D. godliness
   E. the sea and the stars

4. The theme of the poem is that

   A. the living do not forget the dead
   B. the work of the dead becomes a part of eternity
   C. the dead rule over the living in the moon, stars, and seas
   D. love cannot die
   E. death is unimportant

5. Another poem by Dylan Thomas was

   A. THUS THE CITY WAS FOUNDED
   B. DO NOT GO GENTLY INTO THAT GOOD NIGHT
   C. LET US NOW PRAISE FAMOUS MEN
   D. HOW MANY ACTS ARE THERE IN IT
   E. MR. APOLLINAX

6. Thomas died in the decade of the

   A. 1900's   B. 1910's   C. 1920's   D. 1930's   E. 1950's

2 (#13)

KEY (CORRECT ANSWER)

1. B 4. B
2. C 5. B
3. B 6. E

EXPLANATION OF ANSWERS

1. The poet does not deny the existence, actuality, or prospect of death (items A and C) but, rather, its dominion or hegemony. Therefore, item B is correct. Item D is false because the poet unites these two phases or aspects. Item E is affirmed, not denied.

2. The only combination of lines listed above which creates the same image (a celestial one) is that of lines 3 and 5, which constitute item C. Items A, B, D, and E do not produce a similar effect.

3. The poet speaks of ...*the man in the wind and the west moon,* thereby investing them with a kind of humanity. Therefore, item B is correct. Items A and D are not mentioned in the poem. And items C and E are not mentioned in connection with the wind and the moon.

4. Item B is correct. This is distinctly the genius or pith of the poem. There is no mention made of forgetting or ruling, thus discounting items A and C. Item D constitutes merely an element, not the whole of the contribution of those who have gone before us. Were item E correct, it is doubtful that the poem would have been written at all.

5. The poems are ascribed as follows: item A by St. John Perse; item C by James Agee; item D by Gertrude Stein; item E by T.S. Eliot. Item B is the correct answer-it was written by Thomas.

6. Dylan Marlais was born in Wales in 1914 and Thomas died in 1953. Therefore, item E is correct. Items A, B, C, and D are, accordingly, incorrect.

TEST 14

PASSAGE

The wind that rolls a heart on the pavestones of courtyards
An angel that sobs caught in a tree
The column of azure round which twines the marble
Unlock in my darkness emergency exits.

Jean Genet

QUESTIONS

1. Were the first line to read *And the wind that rolls a heart on the pavestones of courtyards*, the poet would

    A. have improved the poem
    B. have created a stronger image
    C. reduced poetry to prose
    D. made the line more mysterious
    E. made the line more abstract

2. The first three lines of the poem

    A. are symbolically in opposition to one another
    B. contain euphemisms
    C. are independent images
    D. are meaningfully united
    E. do not smoothly lead one to the fourth line

3. In the poem, the sky is represented by

    A. the wind   B. an angel
    C. the column   D. emergency exits
    E. marble

4. The poem suggests a condition of

    A. freedom   B. happiness   C. confinement
    D. strife   E. disillusionment

5. While Jean Genet has written many poems, he is better known as a playwright. One of his MOST famous plays is

    A. ENDGAME
    B. THE BALD SOPRANO
    C. CALIGULA
    D. THE BALCONY
    E. WHO'S AFRAID OF VIRGINIA WOOLF?

6. Since the recurrent theme of his works is the condition of man in relation to evil, Genet has often been directly compared with

    A. Cocteau   B. Mallarme
    C. Verlaine   D. St. John Perse
    E. Baudelaire

2 (#14)

KEY (CORRECT ANSWER)

1. C   4. C
2. D   5. D
3. C   6. E

EXPLANATION OF ANSWERS

1. Had Genet written this version of the line, he would have been composing prose. The sentence would become a fact, an event precise and dated, rather than a strong, mysterious, poetic image. Therefore, item C is correct. Items A, B, D, and E are false for this reason.

2. The objects of which the first three lines speak resemble each other in the mind of the poet. He wishes to make us aware of this resemblance and, then, leads us to the fourth line, which is explanatory, and informs us why these units are united. Therefore, item D is correct. Item A is false. If they are linked, they cannot be in opposition. Item B is false. If anything, the images are exaggerated rather than understated. Item C is false since the lines are interdependent. Item E is false since the lines do lead the reader straight on to the fourth.

3. In the poem, the sky is represented by *the column of azure*. Therefore, item C is correct. Items A, B, D, and E do not present the reader with the image of the sky and are, accordingly, false.

4. The mention of *emergency exits* being *unlocked* suggest strongly a condition of confinement, of some form of escape being sought. Therefore, item C is correct. Items A and B are in no way indicated, neither in words nor in mood. Item D is not suggested. Item E is untrue because the poem seems to contain an element of hope.

5. Item A is the work of Samuel Beckett; item B is by Eugene Ionesco; item C was written by Albert Camus; item E was authored by Edward Albee. Only item D is the work of Jean Genet and is the correct choice.

6. Item E is correct. Charles Pierre Baudelaire, poet (1821-1867), whose most famous work is FLEURS DU MAL, has shared this comparison with Genet. Items A, B, C, and D are incorrect since none of these men have been involved with this theme.

TEST 15

PASSAGE

It was my thirtieth year to heaven
Woke to my hearing from harbour and neighbor wood
And the mussel pooled and the heron priested shore
    The morning beckon
With water praying and call of seagull and rook And the knock of sailing boats on the net webbed wall
    Myself to set foot
      That second
In the still sleeping town and set forth My birthday began with the water-birds and the birds Of the winged trees flying my name Above the farms and the white horses
    And I rose
    In rainy autumn
And walked abroad in a shower of all my days High tide and the heron dived when I took the road
    Over the border
      And the gates
Of the town closed as the town awoke.

                      Dylan Thomas

QUESTIONS

1. The poet was looking at his surroundings

    A. late at night
    B. at a time of day (or night) not stated in the poem
    C. before the people awakened
    D. when everyone was arising
    E. after everyone had gone to sleep

2. The poet speaks mostly of the sights and sounds of the

    A. sea and woods
    B. city and the town
    C. border
    D. people in the town
    E. sea shore

3. In which, if any, season of the year does the poem take place?

    A. Winter
    B. Summer
    C. Autumn
    D. Spring
    E. No season is mentioned

4. When the poet says, *And walked abroad in a shower of all my days*, he means he

    A. is walking in the rain
    B. remembers his past
    C. is thinking of his birthday
    D. is walking by the ocean
    E. is thinking of past birthdays

5. The poet, Dylan Thomas, is writing of his native

2 (#15)

A. Scotland   B. France   C. England
D. Ireland   E. Wales

6. Another famous poem by Dylan Thomas is   6._____
   A. THE CLOUD IN TROUSERS
   B. EAST CORKER
   C. A SEASON IN HELL
   D. IN MY CRAFT OR SULLEN ART
   E. I, MYSELF

3 (#15)

KEY (CORRECT ANSWERS)

1. C   4. B
2. A   5. E
3. C   6. D

EXPLANATION OF ANSWERS

1. The poet uses the words *the still sleeping town* and also the words *And I rose*. These indicate that he awoke before the people of the town, sometime in early morning. Therefore, item C is correct. Items A, B, D, and E are not mentioned or indicated in the poem and are incorrect.

2. The poet speaks of seagulls and sailing boats and of farms and trees. He uses the line *Woke to my hearing from harbour and neighbor wood*. Item A, then, is correct. The town is mentioned only in passing, discounting B and D. Items C and E are both insufficient, and, therefore, unacceptable as correct answers.

3. The poet says, *And I rose in rainy autumn*. Therefore, item C is correct. And the other items, A, B, D, and E, are accordingly false.

4. The *shower of all my days* refers to all his past. Therefore, item B is the correct choice. The poem occurs on the occasion of his birthday (item C) but that is not what the line refers to. Nor is item E correct, because he speaks of ALL his days. Items A and D are obviously not the essence of his thoughts and are incorrect.

5. Thomas lived and wrote in Wales. Item E is correct. Items A, B, C, and D are false.

6. Poems A and E are by Vladimir Mayakovsky. Item B is a poem by T.S. Eliot. Item C is a poem by Rimbaud. Item D is a poem by Dylan Thomas and is the correct answer.

INTERPRETATION OF LITERARY MATERIALS
EXAMINATION SECTION
TEST 1

DIRECTIONS: In the passages that follow, each question or incomplete statement that follows each passage is followed by several suggested answers or completions. Select the one that BEST answers the question or completes the statement. Base your choice in each case on the materials given and on your own understanding of the subject matter.

What things there are to write, if one could only write them! My mind is full of gleaming thoughts; gay moods and mysterious, mothlike meditations hover in my imagination, fanning their painted wings. They would make my fortune if I could catch them; but always the rarest, those freaked with azure and the deepest crimson, flutter away beyond my reach. The ever-baffled chase of these filmy nothings often seems, for one of sober years in a sad world, a trifling occupation. But have I not read of the great Kings of Persia who used to ride out to hawk for butterflies, nor deemed this pastime beneath their royal dignity?

1. The author believes that striving to write well is

    A. inappropriate for a mature person
    B. unappreciated
    C. unnecessary
    D. a trifling occupation
    E. a worthy occupation

2. The author finds that

    A. there are few subjects to write about
    B. he cannot capture the pictures of his imagination
    C. he is too old for writing gay trifles
    D. he cannot keep his mind on his writing
    E. it is easy to write

3. The theme of this paragraph is

    A. thoughts about butterflies
    B. the sport of kings
    C. the pursuit of ideas
    D. fortune out of reach
    E. the joy of writing

KEY (CORRECT ANSWERS)

1. E
2. B
3. C

TEST 2

DIRECTIONS: In the passages that follow, each question or incomplete statement that follows each passage is followed by several suggested answers or completions. Select the one that BEST answers the question or completes the statement. Base your choice in each case on the materials given and on your own understanding of the subject matter.

The single business of Henry Thoreau, during forty-odd years of eager activity, was to discover an economy calculated to provide a satisfying life. His one concern, that gave to his ramblings in Concord fields a value of high adventure, was to explore the true meaning of wealth. As he understood the problem of economics, there were three possible solutions open to him: to exploit himself, to exploit his fellows, or to reduce the problem to its lowest denominator. The first was quite impossible—to imprison oneself in a treadmill when the morning called to great adventure. To exploit one's fellows seemed to Thoreau's sensitive social conscience an even greater infidelity. Freedom with abstinence seemed to him better than serfdom with material well-being, and he was content to move to Walden Pond and to set about the high business of living, "to front only the essential facts of life and to see what it had to teach." He did not advocate that other men should build cabins and live isolated. He had no wish to dogmatize concerning the best mode of living—each must settle that for himself. But that a satisfying life should be lived, he was vitally concerned. The story of his emancipation from the lower economics is the one romance of his life, and WALDEN is his great book. It is a book in praise of life rather than of Nature, a record of calculating economies that studied saving in order to spend more largely. But it is a book of social criticism as well, in spite of its explicit denial of such a purpose. In considering the true nature of economy, he concluded, with Ruskin, that the cost of a thing is the amount of life which is required in exchange for it, immediately or in the long run. In WALDEN, Thoreau elaborated the text: "The only wealth is life."

1. In Thoreau's opinion, the price of a thing should always be measured in terms of

    A. time B. effort C. money
    D. romance E. life

2. According to Thoreau, the wealth of an individual is measured by

    A. the money he makes
    B. the experience he gains
    C. the amount he saves
    D. the books he writes
    E. his social standing

3. Thoreau's solution to the problem of living was to

    A. study Nature
    B. make other men work for him
    C. work in a mill
    D. live in a simple way
    E. write for a living

4. Thoreau was very

    A. active B. lazy C. dissatisfied
    D. unsociable E. stingy

5. Thoreau's CHIEF aim in life was to

   A. discover a satisfactory economy
   B. do as little work as possible
   C. convert others to his way of life
   D. write about Nature
   E. live in isolation

6. The theme of this paragraph is

   A. problems of economics
   B. Thoreau's philosophy of life
   C. WALDEN, Thoreau's greatest work
   D. how Thoreau saved money
   E. life at Walden Pond

KEY (CORRECT ANSWERS)

1.	E	4.	A
2.	B	5.	A
3.	D	6.	B

TEST 3

DIRECTIONS: In the passages that follow, each question or incomplete statement that follows each passage is followed by several suggested answers or completions. Select the one that BEST answers the question or completes the statement. Base your choice in each case on the materials given and on your own understanding of the subject matter.

A moment's reflection will make it clear that one can not live a full, free, influential life in America without argument. No doubt, people often argue on insufficient evidence and for insufficient reasons; no doubt, they often argue on points about which they should rather be thinking and studying; no doubt, they sometimes fancy they are arguing when they are merely wrangling and disputing. But this is only proof that argument is employed badly, that it is misused rather than used skillfully. Argument, at the right moment and for the right purpose and in the right way, is undoubtedly one of the most useful instruments in American life; it is an indispensable means of expressing oneself and impressing others.

1. The theme of this paragraph is

   A. the usefulness of argument
   B. principles of argument
   C. how to win arguments
   D. misuses of argument
   E. need for evidence in argument

2. Argument is an important factor in American life because it gives people a chance to

   A. talk about things of which they know little
   B. influence the ideas of others
   C. develop sufficient evidence
   D. have friendly conversations
   E. use argument at the right time and in the right way

3. Argumentation is being used unwisely when it results in

   A. understanding   B. compromise
   C. deliberation   D. bickering
   E. differences of opinion

KEY (CORRECT ANSWERS)

1. A
2. B
3. D

TEST 4

DIRECTIONS: In the passages that follow, each question or incomplete statement that follows each passage is followed by several suggested answers or completions. Select the one that BEST answers the question or completes the statement. Base your choice in each case on the materials given and on your own understanding of the subject matter.

The characteristic American believes, first, in justice as the foundation of civilized government and society, and, next, in freedom for the individual, so far as that freedom is possible without interference with the equal rights of others. He conceives that both justice and freedom are to be secured through popular respect for the laws enacted by the elected representatives of the people and through the faithful observance of those laws. It should be observed, however, that American justice in general keeps in view the present common good of the vast majority, and the restoration rather than the punishment of the exceptional malignant or defective individual. It is essentially democratic; and especially it finds sufferings inflicted on the innocent unintelligible and abhorrent.

Blind obedience and implicit submission to the will of another do not commend themselves to characteristic Americans. The discipline in which they believe is the voluntary cooperation of many persons in the orderly and effective pursuit of common ends. Thus, they submit willingly to any restrictions on individual liberty which can be shown to be necessary to the preservation of the public health, and they are capable of the most effective cooperation at need in business, sports, and war.

1. The American people believe in

    A. unquestioning obedience to their laws
    B. strict discipline
    C. liberty without restraint
    D. subservience to the President
    E. working together for a necessary purpose

2. American justice emphasizes

    A. the welfare of the minority
    B. retaliation for disobedience
    C. rehabilitation of wrongdoers
    D. the sufferings of the innocent
    E. punishment of criminals

3. The PRIMARY element in the American way of life is

    A. the right to vote
    B. freedom
    C. willingness to follow leaders
    D. justice
    E. popular respect for laws

4. The theme of this selection is 4.____
   A. American justice
   B. a plea for cooperation
   C. the basis of American democracy
   D. the American government
   E. liberty as the foundation of government

KEY (CORRECT ANSWERS)

1. E
2. C
3. D
4. C

TEST 5

DIRECTIONS: In the passages that follow, each question or incomplete statement that follows each passage is followed by several suggested answers or completions. Select the one that BEST answers the question or completes the statement. Base your choice in each case on the materials given and on your own understanding of the subject matter.

The change in the treatment of his characters is a significant index to Shakespeare's growth as a dramatist. In the earlier plays, his men and women are more engaged with external forces than with internal struggles. In as excellent an early tragedy as ROMEO AND JULIET, the hero fights more with outside obstacles than with himself. In the great later tragedies, the internal conflict is more emphasized, as in the cases of HAMLET and MACBETH. He grew to care less for mere incident, for plots based on mistaken identity, as in the COMEDY OF ERRORS; he became more and more interested in the delineation of character, in showing the effect of evil on Macbeth and his wife, of jealousy on OTHELLO, of indecision on Hamlet, as well as in exploring the ineffectual attempts of many of his characters to escape the consequences of their acts.

1. The development of Shakespeare as a dramatist is MOST clearly revealed in his

    A. improved treatment of complications
    B. increased use of involved plots
    C. handling of emotional conflicts
    D. increased variety of plot
    E. decreased dependency on historical characters

2. In his later plays, Shakespeare became interested in

    A. plots based on mistaken identity
    B. great characters from history
    C. the history of his country
    D. the study of human nature
    E. the struggle of the hero with external forces

3. The theme of this paragraph is

    A. comedies and tragedies of Shakespeare
    B. Shakespeare's best plays
    C. Shakespeare's development as a dramatist
    D. the moral aspects of Shakespeare's later plays
    E. Shakespeare's interest in good and evil

KEY (CORRECT ANSWERS)

1. C
2. D
3. C

TEST 6

DIRECTIONS: In the passages that follow, each question or incomplete statement that follows each passage is followed by several suggested answers or completions. Select the one that BEST answers the question or completes the statement. Base your choice in each case on the materials given and on your own understanding of the subject matter.

Solitude is a great chastener when once you accept it. It quietly eliminates all sorts of traits that were a part of you - among others, the desire to pose, to keep your best foot forever in evidence, to impress people as being something you would like to have them think you are even when you aren't. Some men I know are able to pose even in solitude; had they valets they no doubt would be heroes to them. But I find it the hardest kind of work myself; and as I am lazy, I have stopped trying. To act without an audience is so tiresome and profitless that you gradually give it up and at last forget how to act at all. For you become more interested in making the acquaintance of yourself as you really are, which is a meeting that, in the haunts of men, rarely takes place. It is gratifying, for example, to discover that you prefer to be clean rather than dirty even when there is no one but God to care which you are; just as it is amusing to note, however, that for scrupulous cleanliness, you are not inclined to make superhuman sacrifices, although you used to believe you were. Clothes, you learn, with something of a shock, have for you no interest whatsoever....You learn to regard dress merely as covering, a precaution. For its color and its cut you care nothing.

1. The activities of everyday life seldom give us the chance to

    A. learn our own peculiarities
    B. keep our best foot forward
    C. impress people
    D. dress as we would like
    E. be immaculately clean

2. The desire to appear well-dressed USUALLY depends upon

    A. an audience
    B. industriousness
    C. personal pride
    D. the need for cleanliness
    E. a fondness for acting

3. In solitude, clothes

    A. constitute one item that pleases the valet
    B. make one careless
    C. are part of acting
    D. are valued for their utility only
    E. are tiresome

4. A desire to appear at your best is a trait that

    A. goes with laziness
    B. may disappear when you are alone
    C. depends primarily on clothes
    D. is inhuman
    E. is evil

5. The theme of this paragraph is
    A. carelessness in clothes
    B. acting without an audience
    C. discoveries through solitude
    D. showing off to best advantage
    E. being a hero to yourself

KEY (CORRECT ANSWERS)

1. A
2. A
3. D
4. B
5. C

TEST 7

DIRECTIONS: In the passages that follow, each question or incomplete statement that follows each passage is followed by several suggested answers or completions. Select the one that BEST answers the question or completes the statement. Base your choice in each case on the materials given and on your own understanding of the subject matter.

In width of scope, Yeats far exceeds any of his contemporaries. He is the only poet since the 18th century who has been a public man in his own country and the only poet since Milton who has been a public man at a time when his country was involved in a struggle for political liberty. This may not seem an important matter, but it is a question whether the kind of life lived by poets for the last two hundred years or so has not been one great reason for the drift of poetry away from the life of the community as a whole, and the loss of touch with tradition. Once the life of contemplation has been divorced from the life of action, or from real knowledge of men of action, something is lost which it is difficult to define, but which leaves poetry enfeebled and incomplete. Yeats responded with all his heart as a young man to the reality and the romance of Ireland's struggle, but he lived to be completely disillusioned about the value of the Irish rebellion. He saw his dreams of liberty blotted out in horror by "the innumerable clanging wings that have put out the moon." It brought him to the final conclusion of the futility of all discipline that is not of the whole being, and of "how base at moments of excitement are minds without culture"; but he remained a man to whom the life of action always meant something very real.

1. According to the writer of the paragraph, great poetry is MOST often produced by poets who

    A. are involved in the problems of life around them
    B. spend their time in contemplation
    C. drift away from the community
    D. break away from tradition
    E. take part in war

2. The writer implies that, as compared with older poetry, present-day poetry is more

    A. complete   B. romantic   C. alive
    D. ineffectual   E. comprehensive

3. Yeats was PRIMARILY a

    A. soldier   B. man of action
    C. dreamer   D. rigid disciplinarian
    E. politician

4. The theme of this paragraph is

    A. basis of true poetry
    B. the necessity of culture
    C. action versus contemplation
    D. Yeats as a poet and patriot
    E. Yeats' part in the Irish rebellion

KEY (CORRECT ANSWERS)

1. A
2. D
3. B
4. D

TEST 8

DIRECTIONS: In the passages that follow, each question or incomplete statement that follows each passage is followed by several suggested answers or completions. Select the one that BEST answers the question or completes the statement. Base your choice in each case on the materials given and on your own understanding of the subject matter.

Only twice in literary history has there been a great period of tragedy, in the Athens of Pericles and in Elizabethan England. What these two periods had in common, two thousand years and more apart in time, that they expressed themselves in the same fashion, may give us some hint of the nature of tragedy, for far from being periods of darkness and defeat, each was a time when life was seen exalted, a time of thrilling and unfathomable possibilities. They held their heads high, those men who conquered at Marathon and Salamis and those who fought Spain and saw the Great Armada sink. The world was a place of wonder; manking was beauteous; life was lived on the crest of the wave. More than all, the poignant joy of heroism had stirred men's hearts. Not stuff for tragedy, would you say? But on the crest of the wave, one must feel either tragically or joyously; one cannot feel tamely. The temper of mind that sees tragedy in life has not for its opposite the temper that sees joy. The opposite pole to the tragic view of life is the sordid view. When humanity is seen as devoid of dignity and significance, trivial, mean, and sunk in dreary hopelessness, then the spirit of tragedy departs.

1. In an age of glory, one

   A. is not indifferent
   B. usually feels tragic
   C. feels happy
   D. is apathetic
   E. feels mean and hopeless

2. The two periods in which great tragedies were written were periods of

   A. gloom   B. serenity   C. defeat
   D. confusion   E. valor

3. The mental attitude that finds tragedy in life is characterized by

   A. sordidness   B. indifference   C. exaltation
   D. triviality   E. hopelessness

4. The theme of this paragraph is

   A. two thousand years of tragedy
   B. Periclean Athens
   C. the tragedy of war
   D. the psychology of happiness
   E. mainsprings of tragic drama

KEY (CORRECT ANSWERS)

1. A
2. E
3. C
4. E

TEST 9

DIRECTIONS: In the passages that follow, each question or incomplete statement that follows each passage is followed by several suggested answers or completions. Select the one that BEST answers the question or completes the statement. Base your choice in each case on the materials given and on your own understanding of the subject matter.

There are few books which go with midnight, solitude, and a candle. It is much easier to say what does not please us then than what is exactly right. The book must be, anyhow, something benedictory by a sinning fellow man. Cleverness would be repellent at such an hour. Cleverness, anyhow, is the level of mediocrity today, we are all too infernally clever. The first witty and perverse paradox blows out the candle. Only the sick mind craves cleverness, as a morbid body turns to drink. The late candle throws its beams a great distance, and its rays make transparent much that seemed massy and important. The mind at rest beside that light, when the house is asleep, and the consequential affairs of the urgent world have diminished to their right proportions because we seem them distantly from another and a more tranquil place in the heavens, where duty, honor, witty arguments, controversial logic on great questions, appear such as will leave hardly a trace of fossil in the indurated mud which will cover them—the mind then smiles at cleverness. For though at that hour the body may be dog-tired, the mind is white and lucid, like that of a man from whom a fever has abated. It is bare of illusions. It has a sharp focus, small and starlike, as a clear and lonely flame left burning by the altar of a shrine from which all have gone but one. A book which approaches that light in the privacy of that place must come, as it were, with open and honest pages.

1. At midnight in the solitude of one's room, the mind is

   A. tired B. keen C. sick
   D. troubled E. clever

2. The author considers the average book of today

   A. inane B. sinful C. benedictory
   D. restful E. open and honest

3. Naming the qualities of a book suitable for reading when one retires is

   A. logical B. a clever job
   C. difficult D. like lighting a candle
   E. tiresome

4. To make good reading at bedtime, a book must be

   A. light B. witty C. controversial
   D. historical E. straightforward

5. The theme of this paragraph is

   A. reading by candlelight
   B. books for convalescents
   C. not a time to read
   D. books for tired minds
   E. books for midnight reading

KEY (CORRECT ANSWERS)

1. B
2. A
3. C
4. E
5. E

TEST 10

DIRECTIONS: In the passages that follow, each question or incomplete statement that follows each passage is followed by several suggested answers or completions. Select the one that BEST answers the question or completes the statement. Base your choice in each case on the materials given and on your own understanding of the subject matter.

Few things are move stimulating than the sight of the forceful wings of large birds cleaving the vagueness of air and making the piled clouds a mere background for their concentrated life. The peregrine falcon, becalmed in the blue depths, cruises across space without a tremor of his wide wings. Wild geese beat up in the sky in a compact wedge. Primeval force is in their strongly moving wings and their beautiful, outstretched necks, in their power of untiring effort, and the eager search of their wild hearts for the free spaces they love. The good fellowship of swift, united action, the joy of ten thousand that move as one, is in the flight of flocks of birds. When seagulls flash up from the water with every wing at full stretch, there is no deliberation; it is as if each bird saw a sweeping arc before it and followed its individual way faithfully. The unerring judgment of the grand curve when the wings are so near and yet never collide, the speed of the descent, are pure poetry.

1. He admires the ability of seagulls to

   A. coordinate their flight
   B. reach great heights
   C. stretch their wings
   D. rise from the water
   E. dive swiftly

2. The flight of the wild goose, as compared with that of the falcon, is MORE

   A. active
   B. beautiful
   C. poetic
   D. deliberate
   E. graceful

3. The author finds the sight of flying birds

   A. inspiring
   B. awesome
   C. joyful
   D. consoling
   E. primitive

4. The author admires the falcon's

   A. wild freedom
   B. effortless flight
   C. united action
   D. primitive force
   E. unerring judgment

5. The theme of this paragraph is

   A. our wild birds
   B. the superb falcon
   C. the beauty of flight
   D. citizens of the sky
   E. the lure of the wild

KEY (CORRECT ANSWERS)

1. A
2. A
3. A
4. B
5. C

TEST 11

DIRECTIONS: In the passages that follow, each question or incomplete statement that follows each passage is followed by several suggested answers or completions. Select the one that BEST answers the question or completes the statement. Base your choice in each case on the materials given and on your own understanding of the subject matter.

As we know the short story today, it is largely a product of the nineteenth and twentieth centuries and its development parallels the rapid development of industrialism in America. We have been a busy people, busy principally in evolving a production system supremely efficient. Railroads and factories have blossomed almost overnight; mines and oil fields have been discovered and exploited; mechanical inventions by the thousand have been made and perfected. Speed has been an essential element in our endeavors, and it has affected our lives, our very natures. Leisurely reading has been, for most Americans, impossible. As with our meals, we have grabbed bits of reading standing up, cafeteria style, and gulped down cups of sentiment on the run. We have had to read while hanging on to a strap in a swaying trolley car or in a rushing subway or while tending to a clamoring telephone switchboard. Our popular magazine has been our literary automat, and its stories have often been no more substantial than sandwiches.

1. From this selection, one would assume that the author's attitude toward short stories is one of   1._____

   A. approval   B. indifference   C. contempt
   D. impartiality E. regret

2. The short story has developed because of Americans'   2._____

   A. reactions against the classics
   B. need for reassurance
   C. lack of culture
   D. lack of education
   E. taste for speed

3. The short story today owes its popularity to its   3._____

   A. settings   B. plots   C. style
   D. length   E. characters

4. The theme of this paragraph is   4._____

   A. *quick-lunch* literature
   B. life in the machine age
   C. culture in modern life
   D. reading while traveling
   E. the development of industrialism

KEY (CORRECT ANSWERS)

1. E
2. E
3. D
4. A

TEST 12

DIRECTIONS: In the passages that follow, each question or incomplete statement that follows each passage is followed by several suggested answers or completions. Select the one that BEST answers the question or completes the statement. Base your choice in each case on the materials given and on your own understanding of the subject matter.

If Shakespeare needs any excuse for the exuberance of his language (the high key in which he pitched most of his dramatic dialogue), it should be remembered that he was doing on the plastic stage of his own day what on the pictorial stage of our day is not so much required. Shakespeare's dramatic figures stood out on a platform-stage, without background, with the audience on three sides of it. And the whole of his atmosphere and environment had to come from the gestures and language of the actors. When they spoke, they provided their own scenery, which we now provide for them. They had to do a good deal more (when they spoke) than actors have to do today in order to give the setting. They carried the scenery on their backs, as it were, and spoke it in words.

1. The nature of the stage for which Shakespeare wrote made it necessary for him to

    A. employ only highly dramatic situations
    B. depend on scenery owned by the actors themselves
    C. have the actors shift the scenery
    D. create atmosphere through the dialogue
    E. restrict backgrounds to familiar types of scenes

2. In comparison with actors of Shakespeare's time, actors of today

    A. carry the settings in their words
    B. pitch their voices in a lower key
    C. depend more on elaborate settings
    D. have to do more to make the setting clear
    E. use many gestures

3. The theme of this paragraph is

    A. the scenery of the Elizabethan stage
    B. the importance of actors in the Shakespearean drama
    C. the influence of the Elizabethan stage on Shakespeare's style
    D. the importance of words
    E. suitable gestures for the Elizabethan stage

KEY (CORRECT ANSWERS)

1. D
2. C
3. C

TEST 13

DIRECTIONS: In the passages that follow, each question or incomplete statement that follows each passage is followed by several suggested answers or completions. Select the one that BEST answers the question or completes the statement. Base your choice in each case on the materials given and on your own understanding of the subject matter.

It is no secret that I am not one of those naturalists who suffer from cities, or affect to do so, nor do I find a city unnatural or uninteresting, or a rubbish heap of follies. It has always seemed to me that there is something more than mechanically admirable about a train that arrives on time, a fire department that comes when you call it, a light that leaps into the room at a touch, and a clinic that will fight for the health of a penniless man and mass for him the agencies of mercy, the x-ray, the precious radium, the anesthetics and the surgical skill. For, beyond any pay these services receive, stands out the pride in perfect performance. And above all, I admire the noble impersonality of civilization that does not inquire where the recipient stands on religion or politics or race. I call this beauty, and I call it spirit — not some mystical soulfulness that nobody can define, but the spirit of man, that has been a million years a-growing.

1. The author implies that efficient operation of public utilities is

   A. expensive
   B. of no special interest
   C. admired by most naturalists
   D. mechanically commendable
   E. spiritual in quality

2. The aspect of city life MOST commendable to this author is its

   A. punctuality   B. free benefits
   C. impartial service   D. mechanical improvement
   E. health clinics

3. The author makes a defense of

   A. cities   B. prompt trains
   C. rural life   D. nature
   E. free clinics

4. The services rendered by city agencies are given

   A. only for pay
   B. on time
   C. only to people having a certain political allegiance
   D. to everybody
   E. to the spirit of man

5. The theme of this paragraph is

   A. the spirit of the city
   B. advantages of a city home
   C. disagreement among naturalists
   D. admirable characteristics of cities
   E. tolerance in the city

KEY (CORRECT ANSWERS)

1. E
2. C
3. A
4. D
5. D

TEST 14

DIRECTIONS: In the passages that follow, each question or incomplete statement that follows each passage is followed by several suggested answers or completions. Select the one that BEST answers the question or completes the statement. Base your choice in each case on the materials given and on your own understanding of the subject matter.

The annual survey of chemistry published by the American Chemical Society attributes the vast change in warfare to the airplane and, above all, to the motor fuels of today. We never think of gasoline as an explosive, yet it has to some extent taken the place of the artillery propellants of a quarter of a century ago. A bomber is hardly a gun, but it certainly performs the function of one, with a range of many hundred miles.

About fifteen years ago, we began to hear of iso-octane, a fuel used to measure antiknock qualities of high-compression gasoline. It was ideal for airplanes but quantity production was not practical Now we make lakes of it. Its performance is so remarkable that the planes propelled by it can carry loads that would have been inconceivable only ten years ago. As a result, octane numbers and indexes of antiknock properties have lost much of their former significance. It will probably be necessary to adopt some new standard. If we relate size and weight of engine to octane number, a truer picture of what aviation fuels really are is obtained. For each pound of weight, aviation engines of today produce, respectively, 100 percent and 50 percent more power than could those of 1918 and 1930.

1. The writer suggests that gasoline may be considered an explosive because

    A. it produces high compression
    B. modern bombing planes are essentially long-range guns
    C. guns now have greater range
    D. iso-octane is now manufactured in quantity
    E. it has replaced explosives in cannons

2. The proposed standard for measuring the quality of motor fuels is the

    A. ratio of power to weight
    B. antiknock index
    C. iso-octane number
    D. load-carrying ability
    E. relation of engine weight and size to octane number

3. Per pound of weight, the average engine now produces

    A. very much iso-octane
    B. high compression
    C. twice as much power as in 1930
    D. double the power of 1918
    E. 100 percent efficiency

303

4. The theme of this selection is 4.____
   A. the chemist speeds the airplane
   B. mass production of iso-octane
   C. improving the gasoline engine
   D. changing methods in warfare
   E. gasoline as an explosive

KEY (CORRECT ANSWERS)

1. B
2. E
3. D
4. A

TEST 15

DIRECTIONS: In the passages that follow, each question or incomplete statement that follows each passage is followed by several suggested answers or completions. Select the one that BEST answers the question or completes the statement. Base your choice in each case on the materials given and on your own understanding of the subject matter.

Once the rivers of America slid undisturbed between their banks, save when a birch canoe, manned by stolid Indians, sewed a narrow seam in the water. Then came a day when our rivers were broad highways filled with packets, lumber rafts, and houseboats. There were years when the rivers languished, deserted by the great commerce they had carried; years, too, of floods and devastation. Today, there is a difference. Efforts are being made to tame the untamed, to yoke the slow-sliding rivers to useful purpose. Dams are being built that will end the tragic flooding of the lowlands. Wasteful torrents are being taught economy, taught to irrigate the lands that lie fallow, needing only water to bring them to fruitfulness. The life-giving fluid to renewed utility is being fed into these rivers of ours, and they are again becoming a vital and integral part of our economy.

1. A MAJOR reason for flood control is

   A. provision of suitable streams for the Indians
   B. profits for the public utilities
   C. conservation of farming areas
   D. relief of unemployment
   E. restoring river commerce

2. America's rivers have

   A. been a steady commercial asset
   B. helped protect us against invasion
   C. brought serious destruction through floods
   D. alternated frequently between periods of usefulness and of destruction or neglect
   E. suffered complete neglect as railroads developed

3. Failing to utilize a country's rivers

   A. is economically wasteful
   B. makes the rivers sluggish
   C. restores their scenic beauty
   D. renews their picturesque traffic
   E. causes wasteful torrents

4. For the safety of property and people, rivers must be

   A. made into highways
   B. used for irrigation
   C. allowed to lie fallow
   D. utilized for commerce
   E. brought under control

5. The theme of this paragraph is 5.____
   A. from Indian canoe to modern boat
   B. conservation and our rivers
   C. the utility of water
   D. changing river traffic
   E. rivers, dams, and the public utilities

KEY (CORRECT ANSWERS)

1. C
2. C
3. A
4. E
5. B

ARITHMETICAL REASONING
EXAMINATION SECTION
TEST 1

DIRECTIONS: Briefly and concisely, solve each of the following problems, using the processes of arithmetic ONLY.

1. It is believed that every even number is the sum of two prime numbers. Two prime numbers whose sum is 32 are

    A. 7, 25   B. 11, 21   C. 13, 19   D. 17, 15

2. To divide a number by 3000, we should move the decimal point 3 places to the _____ by 3.

    A. right and divide   B. left and divide
    C. right and multiply D. left and multiply

3. The difference between the area of a rectangle 6 ft. by 4 ft. and the area of a square having the same perimeter is

    A. 1 sq. ft.   B. 2 sq. ft.
    C. 4 sq. ft.   D. none of the above

4. The ratio of 1/4 to 3/8 is the same as the ratio of

    A. 1 to 3   B. 2 to 3   C. 3 to 2   D. 3 to 4

5. If 7 1/2 is divided by 1 1/5, the quotient is

    A. 6 1/4   B. 9   C. 7 1/10   D. 6 3/5

6. A farmer has a cylindrical metal tank for watering his stock. It is 10 ft. in diameter and 3 ft. deep.
   If one cubic foot contains about 7.5 gallons, the APPROXIMATE capacity of the tank, in gallons, is

    A. 12   B. 225   C. 4   D. 1707

7. The fraction which fits in the following series, 1/2, 1/10, _____ , 1/250 is

    A. 1/20   B. 1/100   C. 1/10   D. 1/50

8. In two years $200 with interest compounded semi-annually at 4% will amount to

    A. $216.48   B. $233.92   C. $208   D. $216

9. With a tax rate of .0200, a tax bill of $1050 corresponds to an assessed valuation of

    A. $21,000   B. $52,500   C. $21   D. $1029

10. A sales agent, after deducting his commission of 6%, remits $2491 to his principal. The sale amounted to

    A. $2809   B. $2640   C. $2650   D. $2341.54

11. The percent equivalent of .0295 is

    A. 2.95%   B. 29.5%   C. .295%   D. 295%

12. An angle of 105° is a(n) _____ angle.

    A. straight   B. acute   C. obtuse   D. reflex

13. A quart is approximately sixty cubic inches. A cubic foot of water weighs approximately sixty pounds.
    Therefore, a quart of water weighs APPROXIMATELY _____ lbs.

    A. 2   B. 3   C. 4   D. 5

14. If the same number is added to both the numerator and the denominator of a proper fraction, the

    A. value of the fraction is decreased
    B. value of the fraction is increased
    C. value of the fraction is unchanged
    D. effect of the operation depends on the original fraction

15. The LEAST common multiple of 3, 8, 9, 12 is

    A. 36   B. 72   C. 108   D. 144

16. On a bill of $100, the difference between a discount of 30% and 20% and a discount of 40% and 10% is

    A. nothing   B. $2   C. $20   D. 20%

17. 1/3 percent of a number is 24.
    The number is

    A. 8   B. 72   C. 800   D. 7200

18. The cost of importing five dozen china dinner sets, billed at $32 per set and paying a duty of 40%, is

    A. $224   B. $2688   C. $768   D. $1344

19. The net price of a television set is $756.
    If bought with a trade discount of 20%, and 10% for cash, the list price is

    A. $925.00   B. $957.80   C. $982.80   D. $1050.00

20. If Bob can complete a job in 6 hours and Steven can finish it in 8 hours, together they can complete the job in _____ hrs. _____ min.

    A. 2; 45   B. 3; 10   C. 3; 25   D. 4; 5

21. If the diameter is 80', the APPROXIMATE area of a skating rink is _____ square feet.

    A. 251.33   B. 1281.74   C. 2538.77   D. 5026.56

22. If an employer is subject to the Unemployment Insurance Fund and his quarterly payroll totals to $18,000, the quarterly tax payable to the Fund would be _____ (assuming the tax to be 2.7%).

    A. $233   B. $486   C. $977   D. $1,944

    22.____

23. During a certain year, the weekly pay of John Smith was $900, his withholding tax 15%, and his Social Security tax was 4.4%.
    Then, Mr. Smith's take-home pay amounted to

    A. $685.85   B. $711.00   C. $725.40   D. $755.65

    23.____

24. A 5% mortgage of $90,000 is for sale.
    What will the buyer have to pay for it to net 9%?

    A. $50,000   B. $85,500   C. $65,000   D. $81,900

    24.____

25. If the passenger rate is $54, the operating cost per passenger to the railroad on the basis of 12 1/2% profit on fares is

    A. $6.75   B. $38.95   C. $47.25   D. $49.68

    25.____

26. What is the amount of premium refunded to the insured if the insurance company cancels a 3-year policy at the end of 15 months?
    The rate is $30 per year.

    A. $37.50   B. $41.50   C. $43.00   D. $43.75

    26.____

27. Suits originally selling for $200 were marked down to yield 20% on cost.
    If the original profit was 33 1/3% on cost, the new sales price will be

    A. $134   B. $160   C. $171   D. $180

    27.____

28. If he works 10 hours on Tuesday and 12 hours on Friday, and regular hours on the other days, for an 8-hour day, 5 days per week, daily pay $120, Samuels will earn _____ (time and a half for overtime).

    A. $600   B. $735   C. $750   D. $785

    28.____

29. To provide 10,000 typewriting sheets (8 1/2 x 11), the mill will have to cut how many reams of folio stock which measures 17 x 22?

    A. 5   B. 6 1/2   C. 8   D. 10

    29.____

30. Property worth $1.6 million was insured for $1 million under a policy containing the 80% co-insurance clause. The damage amounted to $960,000.
    The insured will collect

    A. $480,000   B. $650,000   C. $750,000   D. $780,000

    30.____

31. At the rate of $1.68 for the Sterling, what will the traveler require in American currency to meet expenses and purchases of goods calling for £20 6s. 6d?

    A. $21.34   B. $34.15   C. $38.21   D. $57.12

    31.____

32. The proceeds of a 6% interest-bearing note for $800 due in 45 days and discounted 15 days after it was dated, at the rate of 5%, will be

    A. $796.25   B. $802.64   C. $804.93   D. $805.92

    32.____

33. $4.80 is .08% of

   A. $600   B. $6000   C. $6500   D. $60,000

34. If 25% of a classroom register consists of boys, the ratio of girls to boys is

   A. 4:1   B. 3:1   C. 1:4   D. 1:3

35. If a wage earner who is over 65 years of age, married (wife's age 55) and 2 other dependents whose earnings are below $2,300, pays his Federal income tax, what will his TOTAL exemptions add up to?

   A. 2   B. 3   C. 4   D. 5

36. An equality of ratios is another term for

   A. proportion   B. equilibrium
   C. summation   D. inversion

37. A kilometer is APPROXIMATELY what part of a mile?

   A. 0.059   B. 0.062   C. 0.064   D. 0.067

38. Two liters is a_____ quantity than two quarts.

   A. smaller dry quart/larger liquid quart
   B. larger dry quart/smaller liquid quart
   C. smaller dry quart/smaller liquid quart
   D. larger dry quart/larger liquid quart

39. The square root of 46.24 is

   A. 6.793   B. 6.800   C. 7.984   D. 9.248

40. Ordinary interest is _____ than exact interest for the same time and at the same rate.

   A. less   B. more   C. equal   D. variable

41. After all taxes have been added on, what will the coat cost the purchaser if the advertised price of a natural mink coat is $8,000? (Assume Federal Sales Tax is 10% and the Local Sales Tax is 8 1/4%.)

   A. $8660   B. $9460   C. $9526   D. $9548

42. A ring bearing the mark 12K on the inside contains _____ parts gold and 12 parts alloy.

   A. 2   B. 12   C. 6   D. 14

43. The sounding line recorded a depth of 20 fathoms or _____ feet.

   A. 110   B. 120   C. 130   D. 140

44. If a pound of green peanuts costs $1.25 and peanuts lose 1/6 of its weight in the roasting process, what is the cost of the roasted peanuts?

   A. $1.00   B. $1.20   C. $1.25   D. $1.50

45. A cubic foot (liquid measure) is APPROXIMATELY how many gallons?

   A. 7.48   B. 7.55   C. 7.65   D. 7.80

46. If the closing price of USX Corp. reads 76 1/2 followed by -1/4, it indicates that the previous day's closing price was

    A. 76 3/4   B. 76 1/2   C. 76 5/8   D. 76 3/8

47. An inscription on the cornerstone of a building reads MDCXCIV. This means that the cornerstone was placed there in the year

    A. 1484   B. 1594   C. 1694   D. 1794

48. 12 plus 6 x 6 less 24 ÷ 6 plus 10 equals

    A. 44   B. 64   C. 54   D. 14

49. A motorist travels 120 miles to his destination at the average speed of 60 miles per hour and returns to the starting point at the average speed of 40 miles per hour. His AVERAGE speed for the entire trip is _____ miles per hour.

    A. 53   B. 50   C. 48   D. 45

50. A snapshot measures 2 1/2 inches by 1 7/8 inches. It is to be enlarged so that the longer dimension will be 4 inches. The length of the enlarged shorter dimension will be _____ inches.

    A. 2 1/2
    B. 3 3/8
    C. 3
    D. none of the above

KEY (CORRECT ANSWERS)

1. C	11. A	21. D	31. B	41. B
2. B	12. C	22. D	32. B	42. B
3. A	13. A	23. C	33. B	43. B
4. B	14. B	24. A	34. B	44. D
5. A	15. B	25. C	35. C	45. A
6. B	16. B	26. D	36. A	46. A
7. D	17. D	27. D	37. B	47. C
8. A	18. B	28. B	38. A	48. C
9. B	19. D	29. A	39. B	49. C
10. C	20. C	30. C	40. B	50. C

SOLUTIONS TO PROBLEMS

1. **CORRECT ANSWER: C**
   A prime number is an integer which cannot be divided except by itself and one integer; a whole number as opposed to a fraction or a decimal.

2. **CORRECT ANSWER: B**

   $$3\overline{)6.000}^{2}$$ Example: Divide 6000 by 3000

3. **CORRECT ANSWER: A**

   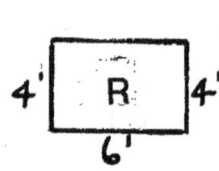   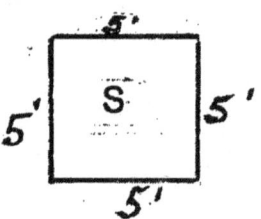

   P = 20 ft.   P = 20 ft.
   A = 24 sq. ft.   A = 25 sq. ft.

   $$25$$
   $$\underline{-24}$$
   $$1$$

4. **CORRECT ANSWER: B**

   $$\frac{1/4}{3/8} = 1/4 \div 3/8 = 1/4 \times 8/3 = 2/3$$

5. **CORRECT ANSWER: A**

   $$\frac{7\frac{1}{2}}{1\ 1/5} = \frac{15}{2} \div \frac{6}{5} = \frac{15}{2} \times \frac{5}{6} = \frac{25}{4} = 6\frac{1}{4}$$

   OR

   $$1.2\overline{)7.5}^{6\frac{\cancel{3}}{\cancel{12}}\frac{1}{4}}$$

6. CORRECT ANSWER: B

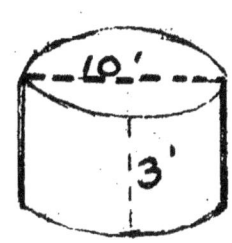

$A = \pi R^2$
$= 3(5)^2$
$= 75$ sq. ft.

$\pi = \dfrac{22}{7} = 3$ (approx.)

Volume of tank $= 75 \times 3 = 225$ cu. ft.
(approximate capacity of tank in gallons)

```
  225
 ×7.5
 ────
 1125
 1575
 ──────
 1687.5 gal.
```

7. CORRECT ANSWER: D
A geometric series: each number is multiplied by the same number to get the succeeding number. (Multiply each number by 1/5.)

1/2, 1/10, 1/50, 1/250

8. CORRECT ANSWER: A
<u>Compound Interest</u>
4% a year compounded semi-annually is the same as 2% for a half year.

(a) $200 $200
    × .02   +   4
    ─────   ─────
    $4.00 Interest for 1st half year $204 Principal for 1st half year

(b) $204 $204.00
    × .02   +   4.08
    ─────   ───────
    $4.08 Interest for 2nd half year $208.08 Principal for 1st half
                                              of 2nd year

(c) $208.08 $208.08
    ×   .02   +   4.16
    ───────   ───────
    $4.1616 Interest for 1st half $212.24 Principal for 2nd
          of 2nd year   half of 2nd year

(d) $212.24 $212.24
    ×   .02   +   4.24
    ───────   ───────
    $4.2448 Interest for 2nd half $216.48 Principal at end of
          of 2nd year   2nd half of 2nd year

9. CORRECT ANSWER: B
```
 .0200x = $1050
  200x  = $10,500,000
    2x  = $105,000
     x  = $52,500 (assessed valuation)
```

10. CORRECT ANSWER: C

$2491 + .06x = x   Proof
x = 2491 + .06x $2650 $2491
1.00x - .06x = 2491   × .06   + 159
.94x = 2491 $159.00 $2650
94x = 249,100

$$94\overline{)249{,}100} = \$2{,}650$$

11. CORRECT ANSWER: A
.0295 = 2.95%

12. CORRECT ANSWER: C
An obtuse angle is an angle greater than 90°.

13. CORRECT ANSWER: A
A quart = 60 cu. in.
80 lbs. = 1 cu. ft. (or 1728 cu.in.)(12x12x12)
(Keep like units of measure together)
60 lbs. = 1728 cu.in.

1 lb. = $\frac{1728}{60}$ = approximately .29 cu. in.

If 29 cu.in. weigh 1 lb., then 60 cu.in. weighs 2 lbs. (approx). Therefore, a quart weighs 2 lbs. (approx.).

14. CORRECT ANSWER: B
(1) Start with the fraction 2/3

(2) $\frac{2+2}{3+2} = \frac{4}{5}$ (Adding 2 to the numerator and the denominator)

(3) $\frac{2}{3} = \frac{10}{15}$

(4) $\frac{4}{5} = \frac{12}{15}$

15. CORRECT ANSWER: B
Common multiple: can be evenly divided by all the numbers. Least common multiple: the lowest of these numbers (72).

16. CORRECT ANSWER: B
Formula
   Step 1. Express percentages as decimals
   Step 2. Subtract each discount from one
   Step 3. Multiply all the results
   Step 4. Subtract the product from one

   Step 1.   .3, .2, and .4, .1

Step 2. .7, .8, and .6, .9
Step 3. .7 x .8 = .56 (represents percent remaining after the .6 x .9 = .54 discounts are taken)
Step 4.   1.00   1.00
         -.56   -.54
         ─────   ─────
          .44   .46

The difference is 2%
Then, $100 x .02 = $2.00.

17. CORRECT ANSWER: D

$\frac{1}{300}x = 24$

x = 24 x 300
x = 7200

18. CORRECT ANSWER: B

   $32
 x 60
 ─────
 $1920 (Cost of dinner sets before paying duty)

 $1920
 x .40
 ──────
 $768.00 (Duty)

 $1920
 + 768
 ─────
 $2688

19. CORRECT ANSWER: D

Single discount for 20% and 10% = 28%
    20 + 10   = 30
    20 x 10%   = 2.0
                ─────
                 28.0

List Price - Discount = Net Price
    100% - 28% = 72%
    $756 = 72% of List Price

        1050
    72)$75600
       72
       ───
        360
        360

20. CORRECT ANSWER: C

$\frac{1}{6} + \frac{1}{8} = \frac{7}{24}$ (job done in 1 hour by both)

$\therefore 24 \div 7 = 3\frac{3}{7}$ (hours together)

= 3 hours, 25 minutes

21. CORRECT ANSWER: D

Area = πr^2

= 3.1416 x (40')^2 = 3.1416 x 1600 = 5026.56 sq. ft.

22. CORRECT ANSWER: B
18,000 x 2.7% = $486 (quarterly) or $1,944 (annually)

23. CORRECT ANSWER: C
1) $900 x 15% = $135 (Withholding Tax)
2) $900 x 4.4% = $39.60 (Social Security Tax)
   $174.60 (Total Tax Deduction)
$900 - $174.60 = $725.40 (Take-home Pay)

24. CORRECT ANSWER: A
5% of $90,000 = $4,500 (income for one year)
To obtain 9%, the cost of the mortgage must be:

$4,500 = \frac{9}{100}$ of the mortgage

$4,500 \times \frac{100}{9} = \$50,000$ (cost of mortgage)

25. CORRECT ANSWER: C

Passenger rate = $54
Profit   =   6.75 (1/8 of 54)
Operating Cost = $47.25

26. CORRECT ANSWER: D
30 x 2 1/2 = $75 (premium for 3 years)
36 months - 15 months = 21 months unexpired time

$\frac{21}{36} \times 75 = \$43.75$ (amount to be refunded)

27. CORRECT ANSWER: D
L.P.   = $200 = 133 1/3% of cost
Cost   = 100%
Profit = 33 1/3%

11 (#1)

$$200 = 1\ 1/3 \text{ of the cost}$$
$$200 \times 3/4 = \$150 \text{ cost}$$
$$\$150 \times 1/5 = \$30 \text{ new profit}$$
$$\$150 + \$30 = \$180 \text{ new marked price}$$

28. CORRECT ANSWER: B

	Regular Time	Overtime
Monday	8	
Tuesday	8	2
Wednesday	8	
Thursday	8	
Friday	8	4
	40 hours	6 hours

Rate per hour = $120 / 8 hours = $15 per hour
Overtime = 6 hours x 1 1/2 x $15 = $22.50 overtime pay x 6 hrs. = $135
Payment for regular time worked = 40 hours x $15 = $600
Samuels earned $135 + $600 = $735

29. CORRECT ANSWER: A
500 sheets = 1 ream of paper
1 ream 17x22 = 4 sheets 8 1/2 x 11
500 sheets x 4 = 2000 sheets from 1 ream (17x22)
∴ 10,000 sheets may be obtained from 5 reams (17x22)

30. CORRECT ANSWER: C

$$\frac{1 \text{ million}}{4/5 \times 1.6 \text{ mil.}} \times 960{,}000 = \$750{,}000$$

31. CORRECT ANSWER: B (12 pence (d) = 1 shilling(s);

6s = .3£   20 s = 1 pound (£);
.5s = .025£   6d = .5s)
  .325£

∴ $1.68 x 20.325 = $34.15

32. CORRECT ANSWER: B
Maturation value of $800 note at 6% interest for 45 days may be computed as follows:
$800 + (1/8 x .06 x 800) = 800 + 6 = $806 (maturation value)

Interest is $8.06 for 72 days at 5%
Interest is $4.03 for 36 days at 5%
Interest is   .67 for   6 days at 5%
Interest is $3.36 for 30 days at 5%
Finally, maturation value = $806.00
              discount =   3.36
              proceeds = $802.64

12 (#1)

33. CORRECT ANSWER: B
$4.80 ÷ .0008 = $6000

34. CORRECT ANSWER: B
Boys = 1/4 of class
∴ Girls = 3/4 of class
Ratio is 3 to 1 (girls to boys)

35. CORRECT ANSWER: C
Exemptions: 1 + 1 + 2 = 4

36. CORRECT ANSWER: A
Proportion

37. CORRECT ANSWER: B
39.37 inches = 1 meter
3937 inches = 1 kilometer
1 kilometer = 3937 ÷ 12 = 328.08 ft.
∴ 328.08 ÷ 5280 = .0621

38. CORRECT ANSWER: A
1 liter = 0.9081 U.S. dry quart ANSWER: Smaller (U.S. dry quart)
1 liter = 1.0567 U.S. liquid quarts ANSWER: Larger (U.S. liquid quart)

39. CORRECT ANSWER: B

$$\begin{array}{r} 6.8 \\ 22\overline{)46.24} \\ \underline{36} \\ 128\overline{)1024} \\ \underline{1024} \end{array}$$

40. CORRECT ANSWER: B
More

41. CORRECT ANSWER: B
$8000 + $800 (Federal Tax 10%) + $660 (Local Sales Tax 3%) = $9460

42. CORRECT ANSWER: B
Gold marked 12K is 12/24 pure and 12/24 alloy.

43. CORRECT ANSWER: B
1 fathom = 6 feet

44. CORRECT ANSWER: D
Cost = $1.25, which is 5/6 of the cost of the roasted peanuts
∴ $1.25 x 6/5 = $1.50, the cost of 1 lb. of roasted peanuts.

45. CORRECT ANSWER: A
    231 cu.in. = 1 gallon
    1 cu.ft. = 12" x 12" x 12" = 1728 cu.in.
    1728 ÷ 231 = 7.48 gallons

46. CORRECT ANSWER: A
    76 1/2 + 1/4 = 76 3/4 (previous day's closing)

47. CORRECT ANSWER: C
    M = 1000
    DC = 600
    XC =   90
    IV =   4

        1694

48. CORRECT ANSWER: C
    12 + 36 - 4 + 10 = 54
    Order of Operations:
    In order to find the value of a number expression:
    1. First, do all the multiplications
    2. Second, do the divisions, taking them in order from left to right
    3. Finally, do the additions and subtractions, taking them in any order

49. CORRECT ANSWER: C
    120 miles = 2 hours (60 mph)
    120 miles = 3 hours (40 mph)
    240 miles = 5 hours = average of 48 mph

50. CORRECT ANSWER: C
    Change 2 1/2 to 20/8

    Change 1 7/8 to 15/8
    Ratio is 20 to 15 or 4 to 3
    If the longer dimension is 4 inches, then the shorter is 3 inches.

EXAMINATION SECTION
TEST 1

DIRECTIONS: Each question or incomplete statement is followed by several suggested answers or completions. Select the one that BEST answers the question or completes the statement. *PRINT THE LETTER OF THE CORRECT ANSWER IN THE SPACE AT THE RIGHT.*

1. Butter is quoted at $ 2 a pound or 54 cents a quarter pound.
   The percent increase over the pound rate is

   A. 2   B. 4   C. 6   D. 8

2. A square has the same area as an oblong 16 inches long and 4 inches wide.
   The perimeter of the oblong

   A. exceeds the perimeter of the square by 100 percent
   B. equals the perimeter of the square
   C. is less than the perimeter of the square by 8 inches
   D. exceeds the perimeter of the square by 8 inches

3. A jet plane made the trip from Albany to New York, a distance of 150 miles, in 15 minutes. The speed of sound is approximately 700 miles per hour.
   This exceeds the speed of the plane, in miles per hour, by

   A. 50   B. 100   C. 150   D. 650

4. The scale on a certain map is given as 1 1/2 inches to 500 miles.
   The distance represented by 5 inches is approximately _____ miles.

   A. 1150   B. 1300   C. 1650   D. 3000

5. If money is invested at 4 percent compounded semi-annually, it will double in 17 1/2 years.
   If interest is compounded at the same rate annually, the number of years in which it will be doubled is

   A. 17 1/2
   B. more than 17 1/2
   C. less than 17 1/2
   D. not determinable without additional data

6. Given: 1 inch = 2.54 centimeters; the number of centimeters by which one meter exceeds one yard is approximately

   A. 3   B. 10   C. 15   D. 90

7. If a baseball team has won ten games and has lost five games, its standing is given by the fraction

   A. .667   B. .500   C. .339   D. .200

8. Two persons start out driving from a given point, one driving north at the rate of thirty miles an hour, and the other driving east at the rate of forty miles an hour. At the end of two hours of continuous driving, they will have reached points the distance between which, in miles, is

   A. 140 B. 50 C. 100 D. 70

9. Three-eighths of a percent of 1600 is

   A. 600 B. 60 C. 6 D. 0.6

10. For which of the following is the answer 1/3 NOT correct?

    A. 18 ÷ ? = 54   B. 16 x ? = 5 2/3
    C. 4 - ? = 3 2/3   D. ? ÷ 2/3 = 1/2

11. A quart is approximately 60 cu. in. A cubic foot of water weighs approximately 60 lbs. Therefore, a quart of water weighs APPROXIMATELY _____ lbs.

    A. 2 B. 3 C. 4 D. 5

12. A dealer purchases a gross of pads for $4.00 and sells all of them at the rate of three pads for 25 cents.
    His rate of profit, based on the cost, is

    A. 66 2/3¢ B. 150% C. 200% D. 300%

13. In the simplest form, -11 - (-2) is

    A. 7 B. 9 C. -11 D. -9

14. Find the average of 6.46, 5.89, 3.42, .65, 7.09.

    A. 5.812 B. 4.704 C. 3.920 D. 4.705

15. $\dfrac{456.3}{0.89}$ equals

    A. 513.89 13/89   B. 512.69 59/89
    C. 513.89 59/89   D. 512.89 59/89

16. Add 5 hrs. 13 min., 3 hrs. 49 min., and 14 min. The sum is _____ hrs. _____ mins.

    A. 9; 16 B. 8; 16 C. 9; 76 D. 8; 6

17. Suits sold at $65 each. The suits cost $50 each.
    The percentage of increase of the selling price over the cost is

    A. 40% B. 33 1/3% C. 33 1/2% D. 30%

18. Change 0.03125 to a common fraction.

    A. 3/64 B. 1/6 C. 1/64 D. 1/32

19. Divide 7/8 by 7/8.

    A. 1 B. 0 C. 7/8 D. 49/64

20. A worked 5 days on overhauling an old car. B worked 4 days more to finish the job. After the sale of the car, the net profit was $243. They wanted to divide the profit on the basis of the time spent by each.
    A's share of the profit was

    A. $108   B. $135   C. $127   D. $143

21. If A takes 6 days to do a task and B takes 3 days to do the same task, working together they should do the same task in _____ days.

    A. 2 2/3   B. 2   C. 2 1/3   D. 2 1/2

22. In the series 5, 8, 13, 20, the NEXT number should be

    A. 23   B. 26   C. 29   D. 32

23. The interest on $300 at 6% for 10 days is (use 6% method)

    A. $.50   B. $1.50   C. $2.50   D. $5.50

24. If the scale on a map indicates that 1 1/2 inches equals 500 miles, then 5 inches on that map will represent APPROXIMATELY _____ males.

    A. 1800   B. 1600   C. 1300   D. 700

25. 1/2% equals

    A. .002   B. .020   C. .005   D. .050

26. If an employee drew $260 which was 20% of his bonus, his entire bonus was

    A. $2300   B. $2600   C. $1600   D. $1300

27. If a kilogram equals about 35 ounces, the number of grams in one ounce is about

    A. 29   B. 30   C. 31   D. 32

28. The area of a mirror 40 inches long and 20 inches wide is APPROXIMATELY _____ square feet.

    A. 8.5   B. 5.5   C. 8.0   D. 5.0

29. The price per gross of items which sell at the rate of 20 for 30¢ is

    A. $2.16   B. $1.80   C. $3.60   D. $2.40

30. If sound travels at the rate of 1100 ft. per second, in one half minute it will travel about _____ miles.

    A. 6   B. 8   C. 10   D. 3

31. If a kilometer is about 5/8 of a mile, 2 miles are about _____ kilometers.

    A. 1.6   B. 3.2   C. 2.4   D. 75

32. A lecture hall which is 25 ft. wide and 75 ft. long has a perimeter equal to _____ feet(yards).

    A. 1750   B. 200   C. 66 2/3   D. 1875

33. After deducting a discount of 16 2/3%, the price of a coat was $35.00. The list price was

    A. $37.50 B. $38.00 C. $41.75 D. $42.00

34. The number which increased by 1/6 of itself results in 182 is

    A. 156 B. 176 C. 148 D. 160

35. 26,932.43 minus 18,345.86 is

    A. 8,568.75 B. 8,865.57 C. 8,856.75 D. 8,586.57

36. 19 2/3 diminished by 7 1/4 is

    A. 12 1/3 B. 12 3/4 C. 12 5/12 D. 12 1/4

37. 2/3 plus 7/8 plus 1/4 minus 5/9 equals

    A. 37/72 B. 89/72 C. 43/72 D. 55/72

38. The number of years between Caesar's death in 55 B.C. and the fall of Rome in 476 is

    A. 411 B. 531 C. 421 D. 481

39. 1/6 of 9 yards is _____ yards(feet).

    A. 1 2/3 B. 4 2/3 C. 4 1/2 D. 4 1/3

40. 33 1/3% is APPROXIMATELY

    A. 333.3 B. 33.33 C. 3.333 D. .3333

41. On a list price of $200, the difference between a single discount of 25% and successive discounts of 20% and 5% is

    A. $50 B. $48 C. $2 D. $0

42. If a man has only quarters and dimes totaling $2.00, the number of quarters CANNOT be

    A. 2 B. 4 C. 6 D. 3

43. The standing of a baseball team of the 7th grade which won ten games and lost five games is

    A. .667 B. .500 C. .333 D. .200

44. The number of cubic feet of soil needed for a flower box 3 ft. long, 8 in. wide, and 1 ft. deep is

    A. 24 B. 12 C. 4 2/3 D. 2

45. At $1250 per hundred, 288 watches will cost

    A. $3,600 B. $36,000 C. $2,880 D. $360

46. On February 12, 2014, the age of a boy who was born on March 15, 1994 will be _____ years, _____ months, _____ days.

    A. 20; 10; 3 B. 19; 9; 27 C. 20; 1; 3 D. 19; 10; 27

47. On February 12, 2019, the age of a teacher who was born on December 26, 1949 will be _____ years, _____ months, _____ days.   47._____

   A. 70; 2; 26
   B. 69; 1; 16
   C. 69; 10; 26
   D. 70; 2; 16

48. At a simple interest rate of 5% a year, the principal that will give $12.50 interest in 6 months is   48._____

   A. $250
   B. $500
   C. $625
   D. $650

49. If John must have a mark of 80% to pass a test of 35 items, the number of items he may miss and still pass the test is   49._____

   A. 7
   B. 8
   C. 11
   D. 28

50.   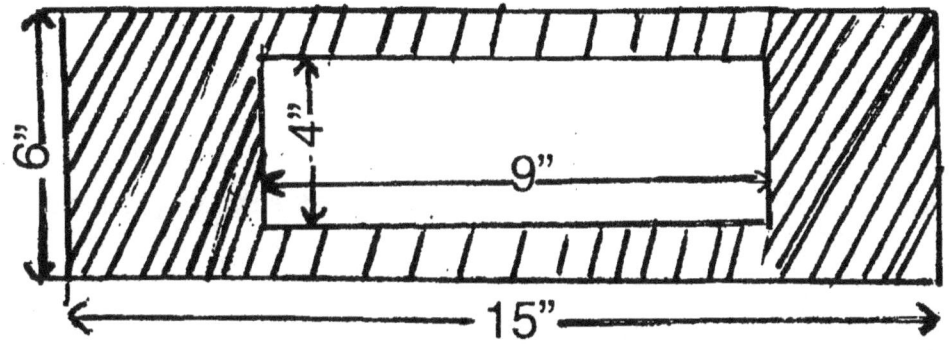   50._____

   The area of the shaded portion of the above rectangle is _____ square inches.

   A. 54
   B. 90
   C. 45
   D. 36

KEY (CORRECT ANSWERS)

1. D	11. A	21. B	31. B	41. C
2. D	12. C	22. C	32. C	42. D
3. B	13. D	23. A	33. D	43. A
4. C	14. B	24. B	34. A	44. D
5. B	15. B	25. C	35. D	45. A
6. B	16. A	26. D	36. C	46. D
7. A	17. D	27. A	37. B	47. B
8. C	18. D	28. B	38. B	48. B
9. C	19. A	29. A	39. C	49. A
10. B	20. B	30. A	40. D	50. A

SOLUTIONS TO PROBLEMS

1. **CORRECT ANSWER: D**
   $.54 x 4 = $2.16
   (lb.rate) = 2.00
   Increase .16

   $$\frac{.16}{200} = \frac{8}{100} = 8\%$$

2. **CORRECT ANSWER: D**
   16 inches x 4 inches = 64 square inches
   Perimeter of the oblong is:
   16 inches x 2 inches = 32 inches
   4 inches x 2 inches = 8 inches
   40 inches
   Perimeter of the square is: 8 inches x 4 = 32 inches
   Perimeter of the oblong (40 inches) exceeds perimeter of the square (32 inches) by 8 inches.

3. **CORRECT ANSWER: B**
   150 miles in 15 minutes = 600 miles in 60 minutes (1 hour)
   700 - 600 = 100 mph excess of speed of sound over plane.

4. **CORRECT ANSWER: C**
   5 inches is 3 1/3 times as great as 1 1/2 inches.
   (3/2 is to 10/2) 500 x 3 1/3 = 1666 2/3 miles or 1650 approximately (closest)

5. **CORRECT ANSWER: B**
   The longer the period used to calculate compound interest, the smaller the interest amount. Answer must be over 17 1/2 years.

6. **CORRECT ANSWER: B**
   1 inch = 2.54 centimeters

   39.37 inches = 1 meter
   −36. inches = 1 yard
   3.37 inches = excess of one meter over one yard

   3.37 x 2.54 = 8.5598 centimeters
   Nearest answer is 10 centimeters.

7. **CORRECT ANSWER: A**
   The team has won 10 out of 15 or 10/15 = .667

8. CORRECT ANSWER: C
   $a^2 + b^2 = c^2$
   $60^2 + 80^2 = c^2$
   $3600 + 6400 = c^2$
   $10,000 = c^2$
   $c = \sqrt{10,000}$ or 100

9. CORRECT ANSWER: C
   1600 x .00375 = 6 or (1600 x 3/8) ÷ 100 = 6

10. CORRECT ANSWER: B
    18 ÷ 1/3 = 54
    16 x 1/3 = 5 1/3 (NOT 5 2/3)
    4 - 3 2/3 = 1/3
    1/3 ÷ 2/3 = 1/2

11. CORRECT ANSWER: A
    1728 cubic inches = 1 cubic foot
    1728:60 = 60:x
    1728 x = 3600
    $x = \dfrac{3600}{1728} = 2 +$ lbs.

12. CORRECT ANSWER: C
    144 ÷ 3 = 48 x .25 = $12.00 Selling Price
                          4.00 Cost
                        $ 8.00 Profit

    $\dfrac{8.00}{4.00} = \dfrac{2}{1} = 200\%$

13. CORRECT ANSWER: D
    -11 - (-2) = 11 + 2 = -9

14. CORRECT ANSWER: B
    6.47
    5.89
    3.42
     .65
    7.09   4.704
    ─────   5)23.520
    23.520

15. **CORRECT ANSWER: B**

```
            5 12. 69
    0.89. )456.30.00
         →       →→
          445
          ―――
          11 3
           8 9
          ―――
           2 40
           1 78
          ―――
             620
             534
            ―――
              860
              801
             ―――
               59
```

16. **CORRECT ANSWER: A**

```
   5'  13"
   3'  49"
       14"
  ―――――――
   9'  16"
```

17. **CORRECT ANSWER: D**

Increase of the selling price over the cost = $15 ($65 - $50)

$\therefore \dfrac{\$15}{\$30} = 30\%$ (percentage of increase of the selling price over the cost)

18. **CORRECT ANSWER: D**

$0.03125 = \dfrac{03125}{100000} = \dfrac{1}{32}$

19. **CORRECT ANSWER: A**

$\dfrac{\frac{7}{8}}{\frac{7}{8}} = \dfrac{7}{8} \times \dfrac{8}{7} = 1$

20. **CORRECT ANSWER: B**

A = 5/9 of the work
B = 4/9 of the work
5/9 x 243 = 5 x 27 = $135

21. **CORRECT ANSWER: B**

A does 1/6 of the task in one day
B does 1/3 of the task in one day
(adding) 1/6 + 1/3 = 3/6 = 1/2 of task in one day

∴ It takes 2 days for A and B working together to do the same task.

22. **CORRECT ANSWER: C**
 5, 8, 13, 20 .... This series progresses by adding 3, 5, 7, respectively, to each of the first three numbers above. Therefore, 9 should be added to the fourth number (20), making the next number in the series 29.

23. **CORRECT ANSWER: A**
 $300 x .06 = $18.00
 ∴ $18.00 ÷ 1/36 (10 days = 1/36 of 360 days) = $.50

24. **CORRECT ANSWER: B**
 $$\frac{5}{1\frac{1}{2}} = \frac{5}{\frac{3}{2}} = 5 \times \frac{2}{3} = \frac{10}{3} = 3\ 1/3$$
 ∴ 500 x 3 1/3 = 500 x 10/3 = 5000/3 = 1666 2/3

25. **CORRECT ANSWER: C**
 1/2% = .005 (by inspection)

26. **CORRECT ANSWER: D**
 If $260 = 1/5 (20%) of his bonus, then $260 x 5 = $1300 (his entire bonus)

27. **CORRECT ANSWER: A**
 A kilogram = 1000 grams (by definition)
 ∴ $\frac{1000}{35}$ = 28.57$^+$ (the number of grams in one ounce)

 Work   28.57
     35)1000.00
        70

        300
        280

        200
        175

        250
        245

28. **CORRECT ANSWER: B**
 40" x 20" = 800 sq. in.
 ∴ 800 144 (there are 144 sq. in. in 1 sq. ft.)= 5.5$^+$ sq. ft.

 Work   5.5
     144)800.0
         720
         ---
         80 0
         72 0

29. **CORRECT ANSWER: A**
 30¢ ÷ 20 =1 1/2¢ (price per 1 item)
 ∴ 144 x 1 1/2¢ = $2.16 (price per gross)

10 (#1)

30. **CORRECT ANSWER: A**
1100 ft. per second = 33,000 ft. in 1/2 minute (30 x 1100) There are 5280 ft. in a mile.
∴ 33,000 ÷ 5280 = 6⁺ miles

31. **CORRECT ANSWER: B**
$$\frac{\frac{2}{5}}{\frac{5}{8}} = 2 \times \frac{8}{5} = \frac{16}{5} = \frac{31}{5} = 3.2$$

32. **CORRECT ANSWER: C**
Perimeter = the sum of the four sides
= 25+25+75+75
= 200 feet
= 66 2/3 yards

33. **CORRECT ANSWER: D**
16 2/3% = 1/6
$35.00 = 5/6 of the list price
$$\therefore \frac{35}{\frac{5}{6}} = 35 \times \frac{6}{5} = \$42.00$$

34. **CORRECT ANSWER: A**
Let x = the number
∴ 7/6x = 182
$$x = \frac{182}{\frac{7}{6}} = 182 \times 6/7 = 156$$

35. **CORRECT ANSWER: D**
26,932.43
-18,345.86
―――――
8,586.57

36. **CORRECT ANSWER: C**

$$19\frac{2}{3} \quad \frac{12}{8}$$

$$7\frac{1}{4} \quad 3$$

$$1\,2 \quad \frac{5}{12}$$

37. **CORRECT ANSWER: B**

$\frac{2}{3}$	24 → 16
$\frac{7}{8}$	21
$\frac{1}{4}$	6
	$\frac{43}{24}$

(2) $\frac{43}{24} - \frac{5}{9} =$

$\frac{129}{72} - \frac{40}{72} =$ (changing fractions to multiples of 72)

$\frac{89}{72}$

38. **CORRECT ANSWER: B**
   55
   +476
   531

   38._____

39. **CORRECT ANSWER: C**
   9 yards = 27 feet
   We then simply take 1/6 of 27, viz.: 1/6 x 27 = 4 1/2 feet

   39._____

40. **CORRECT ANSWER: D**
   33 1/3% = .3333 (by inspection)

   40._____

41. **CORRECT ANSWER: C**
   Single discount of 25% - $200 x .25 = .$50
                                         200 - $50 = $150
   Successive discounts of 20% and 5%
   $200 x .20 = $40; $200 - $40 = $160
   $160 x .05 = $8; $160 - $8 = $152
   ∴ The difference is $2 ($152 - $150)

   41._____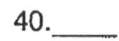

42. **CORRECT ANSWER: D**
   $.25 x 3 = $.75. This would make it impossible to fill out the remainder of the $2.00 ($1.25) by dimes.

   42._____

43. **CORRECT ANSWER: A**
   $\frac{10}{15} = \frac{2}{3} = .667$

   43._____

44. **CORRECT ANSWER: D**
   3 ft. x 2/3 ft. (8 in.) x 1 ft. = 2 cu. ft.

   44._____

45. **CORRECT ANSWER: A**
   288 = 2.88 hundreds
   ∴ $1250 2.88 = $3,600   Work 1250
                                                         2.88
                                                        10000
                                                        10000
                                                        2500
                                                        3600.00

   45._____

46. **CORRECT ANSWER: D**

Given	Years	Months	Days
	2014	2	12
	- 1994	3	15
Change to	2013	13	42
	- 1994	3	15
	19	10	27

47. **CORRECT ANSWER: B**

Given	Years	Months	Days
	2019	2	12
	- 1949	12	26
Change to	2018	13	42
	- 1949	12	26
	69	1	16

48. **CORRECT ANSWER: B**
Given: $12.50 interest in 6 months at interest rate of 5% a year.
This = $25.00 interest in one year
$\therefore \$25.00 \div .05 =$

$$\frac{\$25.00}{\frac{5}{100}} = \$25.00 \times \frac{100}{5} = \frac{\$25.00}{5} = \$500$$

49. **CORRECT ANSWER: A**
4/5 (80%) x 35 = 28 (the number of items he must answer correctly)
$\therefore$ 35 - 28 = 7 (the number of items he may miss)

50. **CORRECT ANSWER: A**
Area of the entire rectangle - 15" x 16" = 90 sq. in.
Area of the inner rectangle - 9" x 4" = 36 sq. in.
$\therefore$ 90 sq. in. - 36 sq. in. = 54 sq. in. (area of the shaded portion of the rectangle)

ARITHMETICAL REASONING
EXAMINATION SECTION
TEST 1

DIRECTIONS: Each question or incomplete statement is followed by several suggested answers or completions. Select the one that BEST answers the question or completes the statement. *PRINT THE LETTER OF THE CORRECT ANSWER IN THE SPACE AT THE RIGHT.*

1. Pipe A can fill a tank in 3 minutes, whereas Pipe B can fill a tank in 4 minutes. How many minutes would it take both pipes, working together, to fill it?

    A. 1 5/7   B. 2 2/7   C. 2 1/4   D. 2 2/3

    1._____

2. Four men can do a job in 48 days.
   How many days will it take 3 men to finish the same job?

    A. 52   B. 58   C. 64   D. 68

    2._____

3. 2/5 of a cargo goes 10 miles. 3/5 of a cargo goes 50 miles.
   What is the average mile haul?

    A. 26   B. 34   C. 38   D. 42

    3._____

4. What is the single discount equivalent to the discount series 20%, 25%, and 10%?

    A. 34%   B. 38%   C. 42%   D. 46%

    4._____

5. The weight of water is 62.4 pounds per cubic foot. How many pounds of water fills a rectangular container 6 inches by 6 inches by 1 foot?

    A. 20   B. 25   C. 30   D. 40

    5._____

6. A 50' ladder reaches a window 40' from the ground. What is the distance, in feet, from the base of the building to the base of the ladder?

    A. 20   B. 25   C. 30   D. 40

    6._____

7. An apple is 3 1/2 inches in diameter. The apple peel is cut off as a strip 1/2 inch in width. How long is the entire peel (in inches)?

    A. 77   B. 79   C. 81   D. 86

    7._____

8. A roller 2" diameter moves 10'. Attached to a frame on the roller is an object moving around the diameter of the frame at the same time as the roller does.
   How far does the object move?

    A. 62.416'   B. 62.832'   C. 63.832'   D. 63.844'

    8._____

9. Sam and Joe are on opposite sides of a circular lake which is 1260' in circumference. They walk around it starting at the same time and in the same direction. Sam walks at the rate of 50 yards a minute and Joe walks at the rate of 60 yards a minute. In how many minutes will Joe overtake Sam?

    A. 21   B. 25   C. 30   D. 32

    9._____

333

10. A tree is struck by lightning. It breaks off 21' from the ground. The broken trunk rests on the stump and reaches the ground at a distance of 28' from the base of the stump. What was the height, in feet, of the tree originally? 10.____

   A. 35 B. 38 C. 42 D. 56

11. Of the following, the POOREST explanation of 47 x 5 is 11.____

   A. 5 x 7 and 5 x 4
   B. 5 x 40 and 5 x 7
   C. 5 x 7 and 5 x 40
   D. 47 + 47 + 47 + 47 + 47

12. Among the following: $3; May 5; page 7; 14 books - the cardinal numbers are 12.____

   A. $3; 14 books
   B. $3; May 5
   C. page 7; 14 books
   D. $3; page 7

13. Of the following, the one which represents an illustration of the commutative law is 13.____

   A. If 4 x 3 = 12, 12 ÷ 4 = 3
   B. If 4 x 3 = 12, 3 x 4 = 12
   C. If 9 - 3 = 6, 9 - 6 = 3
   D. If 8 + 5 = 13, 13 - 8 = 5

14. The LARGEST number of pieces of wire, each 7/8" long, that can be cut from a 1 1/2' length is 14.____

   A. 15 B. 16 C. 20 D. 21

15. Expressions such as 3 x 10^4 are often used in science. 3 x 10^4 means 15.____

   A. 3 x 10 x 4
   B. 30 x 4
   C. 30,000
   D. 3,000

16. How many 3 1/2" labels can be cut from a strip of paper 29" long? Joe solved the problem as follows: 16.____

   29 ÷ 7/2 = 29 x 2/7 = 58/7 = 8 2/7.

   The 2/7 in his answer does NOT represent

   A. 2/7 of a label
   B. 2/7 of an inch
   C. 2/7 of 3 1/2"
   D. 1"

17. The fraction of a number that must be added to 2/3 of a number to produce 3/4 of the number is 17.____

   A. 1/12 B. 1/4 C. 1/3 D. 1/2

18. If the sides of a square are doubled, the area of the resulting square will be 18.____

   A. twice as great
   B. increased by 8
   C. four times as great
   D. increased by 100%

19. Of the following, a pair of equivalent fractions is 19.____

   A. 15/20, 27/35
   B. 15/25, 21/35
   C. 24/36, 9/12
   D. 18/45, 14/42

20. The difference between MDCCCLXXVIII and MDCCLV is 20.____

   A. 123 B. 1023 C. 1203 D. 1230

3 (#1)

21. Class 3-1 has a register of 32 children. During a regular five-day school week, a total of 8 children were absent.
The percentage of attendance for the week was

    A. 3/4%   B. 75%   C. 80%   D. 95%

21._____

22. A purchaser, wishing to buy 1 yard of lace priced at $1.36 per yard, is offered all the lace left on the roll (i.e., 1 yard and 9 inches) at $1.20 per yard and finds that the extra cost to him of purchasing the additional 9 inches of lace will be

    A. $.14   B. $.34   C. $.50   D. $1.50

22._____

23. If each of the monthly payments on a $6500 mortgage consists of $50 principal and monthly interest on the unpaid balance at 6% per annum, the second monthly payment is

    A. $32.25   B. $82.25   C. $82.35   D. $82.50

23._____

24. A pair of numbers in which the second number is the result of correctly rounding off the first number to the nearest hundred is

    A. 4,848; 4,900   B. 6,894; 6,800
    C. 24,834; 24,800   D. 35,706; 35,710

24._____

25. A subway ride used to cost 5 cents. Now it costs 15 cents.
The percentage of increase is _____ %.

    A. 33 1/3   B. 66 2/3   C. 200   D. 300

25._____

26. The total cost of 3 1/2 pounds of meat at $1.10 a pound and 20 oranges at $.60 a dozen will be

    A. $4.65   B. $4.85
    C. $5.05   D. none of the above

26._____

27. 8 divided by zero is equivalent to

    A. $8\overline{)0}$ B. 0
    C. 8   D. none of the above

27._____

28. Decimals are fractions with denominators of _____ of 10.

    A. multiples
    B. powers
    C. reciprocals of multiples
    D. reciprocals of powers

28._____

29. If the base of a parallelogram is doubled, but the altitude is kept constant, the area will be _____ as large.

    A. one-half   B. twice
    C. one-fourth   D. four times

29._____

30. A car is run until the gas tank is 1/8 full. The tank is then filled to capacity by putting in 14 gallons.
Of the following, the number that gives the capacity of the gas tank of the car is _____ gallons.

    A. 14   B. 15   C. 16   D. 17

30._____

31. One cube has an edge that is 6 inches long, and another has an edge 2 inches long. How many of the 2 inch cubes will be needed to equal the volume of one 6 inch cube?

    A. 3   B. 9   C. 18   D. 27

32. Successive discounts of 40% and 20% are equal to a single discount of

    A. 20%   B. 30%   C. 52%   D. 1/3%

33. The radius of a circle is 6".
    The ratio of the number of square inches in its area to the number of inches in its circumference is

    A. 1:1   B. 2:1   C. 3:1   D. 6:1

34. An automobile travels m miles in h hours.
    At this rate, how far will it travel in x hours?

    A. m/x   B. mx/h   C. x = m/h   D. mh/x

35. In a 3-hour examination of 350 questions, there are 50 mathematics problems. If twice as much time should be allowed for each problem as for each of the other questions, how many minutes should be spent on the mathematical problems?
    _____ minutes.

    A. 45   B. 52   C. 60   D. 72

36. A rectangular picture measures 4 1/2" x 6 3/4".
    If the picture is proportionally enlarged so that the shorter side is 7 1/2", what will be the length of the longer side?

    A. 9 3/4"   B. 11 1/4"   C. 13 1/2"   D. 20 1/4"

37. A typewriter was listed at $120.00 and was bought for $96.00.
    What was the rate of discount?

    A. 16 2/3%   B. 20%   C. 24%   D. 25%

38. An individual intelligence test is administered to John A when he is 10 years 8 months old. His recorded M.A. is 160 months.
    What IQ should be recorded?

    A. 80   B. 125   C. 128   D. 160

39. John read a 900 word article in 3 minutes 45 seconds. His reading rate, in words per minute, was

    A. 240   B. 280   C. 290   D. 345

40. Of the following examples in subtraction, the one which cannot be done without *exchange* is

    A. 7 3/4 − 5 1/2   B. 9 13/16 − 2 5/8   C. 4 2/3 − 3/4   D. 9 2/3 − 3

41. You have been allowed 3 hours, 15 minutes to answer these 300 short-answer questions. On the average, therefore, the number of seconds you have in which to answer each question is

    A. 36   B. 39   C. 63   D. 9

42. If a youngster who is 7 years and 7 months old achieves a score on an intelligence test which indicates a mental age of 8 years and 2 months, his IQ computed on that basis, of the following, is CLOSEST to

    A. 93   B. 94   C. 106   D. 108

43. Assuming that cities A and B have the same proportion of *delinquents* within their school populations and that city A has 902 *delinquents* in a total school population of 950,000, then, if city B has a school population of 10,500, its number of delinquents is, of the following, CLOSEST to

    A. 10   B. 100   C. 50   D. 200

44. As the denominator of a fraction with a given numerator is increased, the value of the fraction

    A. decreases
    B. remains the same
    C. increases
    D. doubles its original value

45. Of the following, the ratio between diameter and circumference of the same circle is CLOSEST to

    A. 3 1/6   B. 3.1416   C. 3 1/7   D. 3.1428

46. The retailer paid $24 for a clock radio, to which he added 15% for overhead expense. To secure a profit of 20% on the selling price, he must sell the radio for

    A. $32.40   B. $33.12   C. $33.27   D. $34.50

47. If we subtract 5 gallons and 2 1/4 quarts from 9 gallons and 1 3/4 quarts, we get the answer

    A. 3 gallons   B. 3 gallons 3 1/2 quarts
    C. 4 gallons 1 1/2 quarts   D. 4 gallons 3 quarts

48. The Statue of Liberty, consisting of a steel frame covered with copper, weighs 450,000 lbs. The copper alone weighs 90 tons.
    Therefore, the percent of the total weight represented by the steel frame is _____ %.

    A. 40   B. 45   C. 60   D. 65

49. Miss Smith's class decided to cultivate a garden. The principal gave them a piece of ground 40 feet long and 30 feet wide. There are 18 boys and 12 girls in the class. The class voted that each pupil should be allowed an equal amount of the space in the garden. The number of square feet which was set aside for the exclusive use of the boys was

    A. 30   B. 40   C. 480   D. 720

50. The chef allowed 20 minutes cooking time per pound for a roast weighing 6 lbs. 12 ozs. 50.____
If the roast was placed in the oven at 4:20 P.M., it should be done by _____ P.M.

   A. 6:00   B. 6:32   C. 6:35   D. 7:12

KEY (CORRECT ANSWERS)

1. A	11. A	21. B	31. D	41. B
2. C	12. A	22. A	32. C	42. D
3. B	13. B	23. B	33. C	43. A
4. D	14. C	24. C	34. B	44. A
5. A	15. C	25. C	35. A	45. B
6. C	16. B	26. B	36. B	46. D
7. A	17. A	27. D	37. B	47. B
8. B	18. C	28. B	38. B	48. C
9. A	19. B	29. B	39. A	49. D
10. D	20. A	30. C	40. C	50. C

SOLUTIONS TO PROBLEMS

1. Pipe A can fill a tank in 3 minutes; therefore, it can fill 1/3 of the tank in one minute. Pipe B can fill a tank in 4 minutes; therefore, it can fill 1/4 of the tank in one minute.
   1/3 + 1/4 is 7/12
   Pipe A and Pipe B can fill 7/12 of the tank in one minute; therefore, they can fill the tank in 12/7 or 1 5/7 minutes.

2. One man can do the job in 48 x 4 or 192 days. Three men can do the job in 192 divided by 3, or 64 days.

3. $\dfrac{(2 \times 10)+(3 \times 50)}{5} = 34$ (average mile haul)

4. 20% + 25% = 45% or .45
   20% x 25% = .0500; .45 - .05 = .40
   .40 + .10 = .50
   .40 x .10 = .0400; .50 - .04 = .46 or 46%

5. 1/2 x 1/2 x 1 = 1/4
   1/4 x 62.4 = 15.6 pounds

6. 50 squared = 40 squared + x squared or $50^2 = 40^2 + x^2$; $x^2 = 2500 - 1600$; $x^2 = 900$; x = 30

7. $4\pi r^2$ = area of sphere
   Therefore, 2(4 x 3 1/7 x 7/4 squared) = the length (in inches) or 77 inches.

8. 2 x 3.1416 x 10 = 62.832'

9. 30' is the difference in the rate between the two
   30' x 2 (men) = 60' (rate)
   1260 ÷ 60 = 21 minutes

10. $x^2 = 21^2 + 28^2$; $x^2 = 1225$; x = 35   35' + 21' = 56'
    (original height)

11. By inspection, (5 x 7 = 35; 5 x 4= 20; 35 + 20 = 55) not 235(47 x 5))

12. By inspection (A cardinal number is any of the numbers one, two, etc. – in distinction from first, second, etc.)

13. By definition. The order in which two numbers are added or multiplied does not affect the sum.

14. 1 1/2' = 18"; 18/1 / 7/8 = 18/1 x 8/7 = 144/7 = 20 4/7

8 (#1)

15. By definition and exposition.
$10^4 = 10 \times 10 \times 10 \times 10 = 10,000$
$3 \times 10,000 = 30,000$

15._____

16. The 2/7 represents that part of a 3 1/2" label, NOT 2/7 of an inch.

16._____

17. Let x = the fraction added to 2/3
$2/3 + x = 3/4$; $x = 9/12 - 8/12$
$x = 3/4 - 2/3$; $x = 1/12$

17._____

18. Area of a square = length x width
Let x = side of square; therefore, area = x^2
Let 2x = side of square; therefore, area = $4x^2$ (four times as great)

18._____

19. 15/25, 21/35 = 3/5, 3/5

19._____

20.
```
 1000      1500      1878
  500       200     -1755
  300        55      123
   70      ----
    8      1755
 ----
 1878
```

20._____

21. 24/32 = 3/4 = 75%

21._____

22. 9" = 9/36 = 1/4 yd.

```
$1.20        $1.50
+ .30        -1.36
-----        -----
$1.50        $ .14
```

22._____

23.
```
$6500
-  50
-----
$6450
x .0005    (1/2% a month)
-----
$32.25
 50.00
-----
```

23._____

24. By inspection.

24._____

25. Present cost = 15¢
Increase is 10¢
Original cost is 5¢
10/5 = 2 or 200%

25._____

26. $1.10 x 3 1/2 = $3.85
5¢ x 20 = 1.00
$3.85 + $1.00 = $4.85

26._____

27. 8/4 8/2 8/1 8/1/2 8/0 = infinity

27._____

28. .2 = 2/10 .02 = 2/100 .002 = 2/1000

28._____

29. Area of a parallelogram = bxh
    Let b = 6, h = 4; therefore, area = 24
    Let b = 12, h = 4; therefore, area = 48 (twice as large)

30. Tank holds 8/8; in tank 1/8; added gas 7/8;
    x = capacity of the gas tank
    7/8x = 14; x = 14 ÷ 7/8; x = 14 x 8/7; x = 2 x 8 = 16 gallons

31. $V1 = 6^3 = \cancel{6} \times \cancel{6} \times \cancel{6} \,\, \overset{3}{} \,\, \overset{3}{} \,\, \overset{3}{} = 27$

    $V2 = 2^3 \,\, \dfrac{1}{\cancel{x}} \times \dfrac{1}{\cancel{x}} \times \dfrac{1}{\cancel{x}}$

32. $100 Price list $60   1st selling price
    × .40   .20
    ─────   ──────
    $ 40 1st discount $12.00 2nd discount

    $60.00 $100.00   List price
     12.00   48.00   selling price
    ──────   ───────
    $48.00 2st selling price $ 52.00 Total price

    $\dfrac{\$52}{\$100} = 52\%$

33. $\dfrac{A}{C} = \dfrac{\pi R^2}{2\pi R} = \dfrac{R}{2} = \dfrac{6}{2} = \dfrac{3}{1}$ Proportion

    OR

    $A = \pi R^2 \quad C = 2\pi R \quad \dfrac{36\pi}{12\pi} = \dfrac{3}{1} = \pi 36 = \pi 12$

34. D = R x T
    Let y = distance traveled in x hours
    m = m/h x h (substituting)
    y = m/h x x = mx/h

35. GIVEN
    1 mathematics problem equivalent to 2 other questions in time
    to be spent
    50 mathematics problems equivalent to 100 regular questions
    in time to be spent
    350 questions (including mathematics problems) equivalent to
    400 regular questions in time to be spent
    3 hours for 400 (regular) questions

    SOLVING
    100 of the 400 is mathematics (2 x 50)

    100/400 = time devoted to 50 mathematics problems 1/4 of 3 hours = 45 minutes

36.

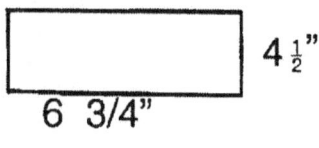 

4 1/2 /7 1/2 = 6 3/4 /x Proportion
SOLVING

$4\frac{1}{2} x = 6\, 3/4 \times 7\frac{1}{2}$; $\frac{9x}{2} = \frac{27}{4} \times \frac{15}{2}$; $x = \frac{\frac{27}{4} \times \frac{15}{2}}{\frac{9}{2}}$

$x = \frac{27}{4} \times \frac{15}{2} \times \frac{2}{9} = \frac{45}{4} = 11\frac{1}{4}$"

37. C = $96, L.P. = $120, Disc. = $24

$\frac{24}{120} = \frac{2}{10} = 20\%$

38. 10 years, 8 months = 128 months FORMULA:

$\frac{160\,(MA)}{128\,(CA)} = \frac{5}{4} = 1\frac{1}{4} = 125$ $\frac{MA}{CA} \times 100$

39. 3 minutes, 45 seconds = 3 3/4 minutes = 15/4 minutes

$\frac{900}{1} \div \frac{15}{4} = 240$ words

40. By inspection: 3/4 is greater than 2/3.

41. 3 hours, 15 minutes = 198 minutes = 11,880 seconds 300 ÷ 11,880 = 39 seconds

42. Chronological age - 7 years, 7 months = 91 months MA = 8 years, 2 months = 98 months
91 v 98 = 108 IQ

11 (#1)

43. $\dfrac{\text{Population A}}{\text{Population B}} = \dfrac{\text{Delinquents A}}{\text{Deliquents B}}$

                                        Rounding out   (proportion)

    $\dfrac{950{,}000}{10{,}500} = \dfrac{902}{x}$ $\dfrac{1{,}000{,}000}{10{,}000} = \dfrac{100}{x}$

    $1000x = 1000$

         $x = 10$

44. 1/2, 1/3, 1/4, 1/5 ... By inspection.

45. $C = \pi D,\ \pi = \dfrac{22}{7} = 3.1416$

46. Cost = $24.00
Overhead = 3.60 (24 x .15 = 3.60)
Cost +
Overhead = $27.60
Let x = selling price; Profit = .20x
x = $27.60 + .2x
10x = $276 + 2x
8x = $276
x = $34.50

47.   8   5
  ~~9~~ gal.   ~~1~~ 3/4 quarts
  5 gal.   2 1/4 quarts
  ―――――――――――
  3 gal.   3 1/2 quarts

48. Total weight   450,000 lbs.
    copper   180,000 lbs.
    ――――――――――――――
    steel frame   270,000

    $\dfrac{270{,}000}{450{,}000} = \dfrac{3}{5} = 60\%$

49.
```
         40 feet
   ┌─────────────────┐
   │                 │
   │ 1200 square feet│  30 feet
   │                 │
   └─────────────────┘
```

                                            $\dfrac{40}{30\overline{)1200}}$

                                  18 (boys) x 40 = 720 sq.ft.

12 (#1)

50. 20 minutes for 1 lb. $\therefore \dfrac{12\,oz.}{16\,oz.} = \dfrac{3}{4} lb$ 50._____

    3/4 x 20 = 15 minutes; 20 x 6 = 120 minutes

```
   120
  + 15
  ─────
   135 minutes
  -120 minutes (2 hours)
  ─────
    15 minutes
```

```
 4:20 P.M.
+2:15 (2hrs. 15min.)
─────
 6:35  P.M.
```